THE FIGHTING EDGE

Using Your Martial Arts to Fight Better

James LaFond

Paladin Press · Boulder, Colorado

Also by James LaFond:
Logic of Steel: A Fighter's View of Blade and Shank Encounters

To my coaches, teammates, training partners, students, and
antagonists. You have all taught me, knowingly or not,
regardless of how willing I was to learn.

The Fighting Edge: Using Your Martial Arts to Fight Better
by James LaFond

Copyright © 2000 by James LaFond
ISBN 10: 1-58160-063-1
ISBN 13: 978-1-58160-063-6
Printed in the United States of America

Published by Paladin Press, a division of
Paladin Enterprises, Inc.
Gunbarrel Tech Center
7077 Winchester Circle
Boulder, Colorado 80301 USA
+1.303.443.7250

Direct inquiries and/or orders to the above address.

PALADIN, PALADIN PRESS, and the "horse head" design
are trademarks belonging to Paladin Enterprises and
registered in United States Patent and Trademark Office.

Visit our Web site at www.paladin-press.com

TABLE OF

Contents

Acknowledgments

Thanks to the following people:

Ted and Betty, for this nifty body, that still works when you give it a good whack.

"Reds" Foley, for not letting me fight that middleweight in Charleroi.

"Irish" Johnny Coiley, for teaching me how *not* to eat leather.

Cindy, for this word processor.

Doreen Rockel, CMT, for teaching me how to walk again.

Ralph Gervasio, Jr., for being a great writing coach.

Joseph Estwanik, M.D., for answering my medical questions.

Paul Behrendt, for planting this big idea in my fertile brain.

Steve Sechi, for convincing me to try nonfiction.

Rick Sensky, for his encouragement and assistance.

Master Joe Nawrozki, for providing valuable insights and commentary.

Warning

This manual is not intended as a substitute for instruction and training in the martial arts or self-defense. Neither the author nor the publisher is responsible for the use or misuse of information contained herein. It is intended for *academic study only*.

Introduction

Paul, a fit, educated young man, was seated to my right as I discussed a recent altercation with some punks. (He was about to find out what kind of people belonged to his gaming group.) As I finished and the approving grunts faded, Paul mentioned that he was interested in developing the ability to defend himself and that he might cancel his spa membership in favor of boxing lessons.

The advice flowed freely. I recommended that he continue his strength training because he could expect to be grabbed if attacked. The sensei to my left suggested that Paul enroll in his karate class. Walt, a truck driver, lowered a skin magazine long enough to promote gun ownership as the last best hope for the preservation of Western civilization. The kick-boxer across the table suggested aikido lessons and then demonstrated how to kill with the elbow. . . .

On our way home Paul asked some hard questions that would have brought glares of disapproval from many a martial artist. "What is it like to be in a *real* fight?" "How does it feel to be punched in the head?" "What about these various martial arts methods and their claims—are they valid?" Being quizzed about something I often did, but rarely thought of, was unsettling enough to inspire this project. This book is an exploration of the practical value, study, and application of the martial arts in relation to real violence. It began as a simple effort to make sense of a life defined by violent misadventure. As it grew into a serious study I found it necessary to embrace a broad definition of the martial arts and a critical examination of their nature. Since childhood I have sought to understand how fighters—primarily soldiers and prize-fighters—have prevailed in the face of real adversity. I suppose this look into the modern martial arts phenomena and the realities of ordinary violence is the logical extension of that desire to understand combat. I hope you find it useful.

—James LaFond, January 2000

CHAPTER
1

Reality

"All I saw was boots, lots of boots. Man, long hair sucks!"

—MARK

SETUP: I was at work, pushing a loaded dolly, still cooling down after an argument with my supervisor and his assistant. Pumped up on whiskey and PCP, they had come to work in a racist frenzy. I'd told them that if they attacked my partner (a black guy) they'd have to deal with me. I could fight, and they knew it. I was young and didn't realize that their fear of me was to my disadvantage. I kept moving, considering my options. They were two aisles over when I heard the super yell, "All you niggers and hippies are gonna die!"

They'd hit me after work on the parking lot, I had reasoned—they wouldn't risk losing a union-wage job. I knew that the super kept a baseball bat in his car, so I made a mental note to leave with a mop handle. For now I had freight to spot. I turned into the detergent aisle, as the part-time kid to my right headed to the back room at a run. Was he sick? Or did he hear the phone?

IMPACT: The super shouted, "Get 'im!" I stopped as I heard a single slapping footstep behind me. I began to look back just as a heavy, grunting body slammed onto my shoulders and a hairy, muscular left arm wrapped around my neck. It was Geno, the assistant. At 5 foot 8 inches and 147 pounds, I was balancing seven bales of dog food on two wheels, with 170 pounds of mean Italian on my back—trying to rip my head off! For a second I tried to stand. As I went down I pushed the dolly handle to the right. As it crashed the steel blade flipped up to the left in time to catch me in the chest as I fell forward to the left. Geno landed on his feet as the super tried to push past him, yelling, "Don't let 'im up!"

THE FLOOR: I rolled back off the blade as Geno trapped my right shoulder with his left hand, pushing me back against the shelving, firing short rights into my face. After eating a few, I pushed off the floor with my left hand, scooted into a semi-sitting position, tucked my chin, and raised my right to the cross-arm guard.

THE BEATING: Geno stepped back and growled, "Get up!" I refused, and he hit me with a right cross over the left lip. I tucked my chin and gritted my teeth as the maniac whacked away with what turned out to be his standard combo—left, right; left, right, right—all hitting my forehead with a dull, wooden thud. He was punching down out of a bent squat, and that double right would pull him off balance. He pushed off the shelving to my back to right himself and launched another combo. His punching was ineffective, and there was a stack of freight between the super and me. I sat tight.

CHAOS: Geno was getting frustrated. He wasn't attacking me out of hatred, which was the super's motivation. This was a dominance thing for him. He had to be the toughest guy on the crew. He stood back and yelled, "Get up and fight!" The super stepped in and kicked my right leg behind the knee. Geno shot him an angry glare and leaned in with another combo. At this point Geno still wanted to beat me in a fight. The super wanted to drop a case of Ajax on my head and end it.

COMEDY: Again, Geno stepped back and said, "Get up and fight!" And, again, the super stepped in—but Geno pushed him back and growled, "He's mine!" I had to grin. I was getting worked over by Abbot and Costello!

THE KILL: Geno wiped the smirk off my face with a big combo. He actually got his weight into those last five punches. I didn't feel anything, but my head moved. This time when he lost balance, he grabbed my head in both hands and started slamming it against the metal shelving behind me. He caught me with the corner of the Ivory soap shelf. I felt a sharp pinch at the back of my skull every time it hit. My head would bounce back as the tinny rattle of the shelving rang in my ears—my clearest memory of this incident. That sound still gives me chills when I hear it.

After a point—I had lost any sense of timing and repetition—I noticed that every time he pulled my head toward his chest blood would arc over his shoulder. It was mine. I discarded the pacifist attitude.

SURVIVAL: I didn't want to lose consciousness around these two. Besides, I had never been knocked out and wouldn't give that fat pig the pleasure of being the first to do it. I grabbed him by the throat, pushing my thumbs into his windpipe. I was surprised that his neck was so small. He let go of my head and grabbed my forearms. He began to get weak and stepped back. The super stepped in and helped pry my hands off his throat. Geno didn't complain.

THE BREAK: Geno stepped back as the super stepped right. Jomo, a big West Indian black, walked up behind the super. I was bleeding, Geno was heaving, and the super was sweating a river of whiskey. The super took one look at Jomo standing there with crossed arms and yelled, "I'm not in it!" (The supervisor and Geno never "talked." Everything was yelled, growled, or grunted.)

THE GRAPPLE: I was ready to even things up. I had a

vague notion of knifing the super (I was armed, but the knife was in my pocket) after I finished Geno. That thought evaporated when I tried to stand. I grabbed the shelving with my left hand and got my left foot under me. Geno jumped on me while my right knee and hand were still on the floor. He put me in a side headlock as he kicked the dolly under me with his right foot. As he held my throat over the blade's edge, he growled, "I'm gonna break your fuckin' neck!"

I said, "I know," reached around his back with my right hand, and gouged his right eye with my middle finger. He shifted enough to turn his face, which allowed me to get my right foot under me. He didn't have enough left to take me down from this position. On the other hand, I had forgotten how to break a headlock and couldn't find his eye. The aisle was suddenly full of people. The super was calling the boss' daughter a slut. The boss (a little old lady) was beating on Geno's big biceps with her little fist. This was pissing him off, so he started to crank the hold.

CONCLUSION: I grabbed for Geno's balls, but his jeans were so tight I couldn't get a grip. He was becoming indecisive, no longer trying to take me down. The boss must have hit his arm 20 times. I jammed my hand down the back of his pants, snaking it into his underwear. He broke the hold and snarled, "I'm out of here."

The super yelled, "I quit," and hurried away. Geno snorted, "Me too" and walked after him. The boss pointed her finger at me and said, "You are fired for fighting!"

AFTERMATH: I had lost a lot of blood and wouldn't leave the store because I knew that Geno and the super were waiting for me in the parking lot with a bat and a station wagon. None of the blacks on the crew would take me to the hospital. The part-time kid had found and removed a steel pipe earlier that evening, not far from where I had been jumped. I remembered seeing the super with it the night before. A real nice guy.

A cop came to make me leave. When he saw the scalp peeling off the back of my head, he suggested I arrange for a ride to the hospital. While he was taking my name and address the boss' daughter called a friend to pick me up. The cop informed me that Geno was pressing charges; the super claimed he had seen me jump Geno from behind. The cop suggested I get a lawyer, as he asked for my name and address to complete the form he was required to fill out. Now the supervisor and Geno would know where I lived! Months of legal hassles followed.

My injuries included a scalp laceration (which was closed with staples), a concussion, bruised ribs, and three damaged teeth that required root canals.

PERSPECTIVE: My "partner" thanked me for offering to defend him. He explained, however, that the threats against him had been a ruse to set me up. The supervisor and Geno knew of his gang affiliation and that he carried a .38 special. (That was news to me.) Besides, he pointed out, he was just a "nigger"; I was a "nigger lover." I rated higher on the hate scale with the supervisor and Geno.

Afterwards, I realized that I had some hard questions to answer.

How well had I handled the situation?

I had expected to do better. On the other hand, things could have been worse. I had survived. They had counted on an easy maiming, with Geno holding me as the super broke my legs with the pipe. Things hadn't gone the way they'd planned. Geno hit me short of the ambush point, and this aisle was too crowded for the super to get to the stashed pipe, which was gone in any case—thanks to the part-time kid. The super panicked without his weapon. Geno, to his credit, did try to salvage the situation by turning it into a stand-up fight. Frustrated by his ineffectiveness, he then tried to kill me and failed again.

I got hurt but got my job back, a bonus, and a vacation. I had accepted danger as a job condition—otherwise I would have quit two weeks earlier when Geno and the super threatened to break my legs. They lost their jobs, which they had obviously been willing to do. I suppose that's what you call a draw.

Was it really a "fight"?
At first I didn't think so. It wasn't the kind of violence I had trained for. I went into denial. The epic "street fight" I had cultivated in my head had never come to pass. I had missed that chance when I turned down their earlier challenges. The false confidence I had built facing them down and then walking away had crippled my awareness and convinced them of the need for, and likely success of, an ambush. However, it certainly was a fight, a fight for my life.

Did my years of training help—were they even a factor?
Overall, my training had taught me to expect and counter adversity. My knack for lasting against better athletes had prepared me well. Specifically:

- Two years as a third-string rubber dummy on a school wrestling team had taught me to relax in the grapple, which enabled me to gain strength in the clinch while Geno strained.
- Four years of boxing and kick-boxing had taught me how to take a punch. I don't have thick bones or a muscular neck. Had I not been trained to "tuck and roll," the natural human reaction to pull the face away from an attacker could have resulted in some horrible facial injuries, of the kind often sustained by severely battered women.
- Honestly, two years of dueling with wooden swords and medieval weapons paid no dividends on the floor. However, the few "pitched field battles" I had participated in went a long way toward making sure I stayed cool during the confusion.

Had my real fighting experience—mostly in stand-up brawls with high school athletes—helped in this encounter?
Yes. I knew what it was like to be hated by people who were sweating and breathing on me. I knew that they would have to kill me: I also knew that they could; that they would; and that they'd have to work dammed hard to do it. The question mark was on them.

What went wrong?
I was lacking in awareness and technical versatility. This inspired my exploration of the Asian martial arts.

My "partner" said that at least two minutes had elapsed between the time he heard the dolly crash and the time he got the boss into the aisle. According to the clock, it couldn't have gone five minutes. Sounds like two to three minutes.

Of a dozen fights, this was my longest. Perhaps two others went a minute. Few, however, lasted more than 10 seconds. According to the many bar fighters, punks, bouncers, and criminals I have interviewed, this is beyond the norm. Two to five seconds is the average. My fights have gone long because I lack size and my larger opponents have lacked skill. All fights do not go down a certain way. There are tendencies and constants, but you are unique, as may be your experiences. Also, most violence cannot easily be labeled as "a fight." "Stand-up fights"—legally mutual combats—occupy only a narrow band of a broad range of personal violence, ranging from push-downs to savage brawls, all subject to chance and escalation.

PARAMETERS: Some points to keep in mind when considering real violence:

- Cops are law officers charged with enforcing the law. If you operate a business, are wealthy, or are a woman, those laws may offer protection. If you are a regular guy, the law generally inhibits your ability to protect yourself effectively.
- Cars and houses do not cast an invisible force field. These assets are targets of criminal activity. Many people feel safe sitting behind a light glass panel. Two nights ago I was crossing a street in a high-crime district. A woman in a luxury sedan was attempting an illegal U-turn. I stepped in her way. She threatened me. I was close enough to pull her from the car. Three weeks ago a female cop was pistol-whipped while behind the wheel of her squad car, less than five blocks from where this rich woman threatened a poorly dressed, athletic male with something in his hand. That dri-

ver is not alone—many Americans feel safe sitting within reach of potential assailants.

To appreciate how the violent experiences of others may relate to your experience and training, consider all personal violence from the following first-person perspectives:

Class 1. *Subject of physical threat or assault.* Whether it's a robbery or an arrest, your options are limited.
Class 2. *Willing participant in a fight or mutual combat, such as a barroom brawl, challenge match, or prize fight.* Most available anecdotal evidence falls into this category.
Class 3. *Aggressor.* Predators, avengers, and gangbangers, who initiate violence are, in terms of situation dynamics, no different from bouncers or cops initiating lawful force.

A bouncer about to blind-side a drunk who is beating his date has the same functional relationship with his target as a rapist stalking an intoxicated woman fumbling with her car keys. Conversely, the woman has about as much chance against Jack the Ripper as the jerk does against BoBo the Bouncer.

My experience with Geno and the super was Class 1 violence. Sport combat and adolescent stupidity provided me with plenty of Class 2 violence. Defending family members has provided me with experience dispensing Class 3 violence.

We experience violence as the subject, a willing participant, or the aggressor. The value of defining violence in these terms will become clear by answering the following questions.

Should a woman in need of a self-defense instructor seek out an undefeated "reality combat" champion who has never dealt with simple intimidation let alone rape? Or would she be better served studying under a karate instructor who couldn't last 20 seconds with the "ultimate fighter" but is a cop with knowledge of a woman's risks and of the methods used by rapists, and also has experience subduing boys about her size?

Unfortunately, most aspiring martial artists would choose the superior fighter lacking in empathy and relative practical knowledge. On the other hand, a beefy construction worker looking to sharpen his barfighting skills would be best served studying under the prizefighter.

I am writing this book under the assumption that the reader will be more concerned with defending against an assault than prevailing in bar fights or doing vigilante work. These are very different skills.

My research has resulted in the not-so-startling discovery that prize-fighters score devastating victories in virtually all of the bar fights in which they engage. However, I have a friend who was a nationally ranked heavyweight kick-boxer and seasoned bouncer, with more than 100 victories in barroom brawls. At 27 he was successfully mugged by an unarmed 40-year-old slob! It was the situation. If they ever meet in a bar. . . . Also, Simon Brown, one of the most dangerous boxers of his day, was mugged by some vagrant while the boxer was in his prime!

Personal violence just isn't as simple as the "experts" would have us believe.

A serious criminal attack is not likely to occur on a mat, in a boxing ring, or on the meticulously maintained floor of a traditional dojo. Likewise, you can expect to be wearing shoes and (real) clothes in real situations. Most martial artists do not realize how dependent their art is on specialized surfacing and attire.

If you are a martial artist you may have a problem with two of the basic tenets of this book: (1) that combat sports are martial arts and (2) that "little things, such as your attire, are a big deal. The following real-life event makes these points better than any theoretical argument.

It was a wet autumn day. A very large and dangerous man (my roommate) was preparing to lead his pickup football team to the slaughter against a larger, more dangerous collection of minor league and college players. These affairs typically resulted in serious injuries. The men, most wearing sweats and sneakers, exchanged threats and drank beer.

When "Rugby," at 5 feet 6 inches, walked onto the field to join the "losing" team he was jeered and threatened by the "big boys" from across the field. Like most effective face-to-face fighters Rugby exhibited the age-old characteristics of the true warrior: the body of an athlete; an inner peace that made drug use obsolete; kindness, which paradoxically permitted him to focus aggression when and where necessary; and the practical intelligence to equip himself appropriately with cleats, shorts, and mouthpiece only.

Rugby took the ball up the middle on the first play. As two linemen closed in, he knocked out the leader with a stiff arm. As the second man attempted to grab his naked torso, he broke the man's left ankle with his right cleat and fractured some ribs with a right elbow. He followed up by spearing the middle linebacker in the chin, breaking the man's jaw as he bit down safely on his own mouthpiece. End of game.

Rugby turned their attempted pile-on into orthopedic artistry because he had traction and, with nothing to grab, they had no immediate take-down hold. The gridiron is as much a battlefield as a bar, boxing ring, or karate dojo.

Streetfighting is a term that distorts the entire question of serious violence. "The street" is a broad modern concept of mythological significance that has little bearing on the subject of survival fighting. Road surfaces are not commonly used as fighting platforms by barroom brawlers or muggers. The most dangerous thing on the road is your grandma cruising to the pharmacy in her Buick.

Self-defense is an unfortunate term. This hyphenated mantra implies selfishness and timidity, characteristics that inhibit the development of combat effectiveness. Your concern is personal security: preserving your life, ensuring your own physical autonomy, and, ultimately, protecting those less able. These goals necessitate sacrifice in training and aggressiveness in application.

The style you study is not as important as its practical application.

Reality is circumstantial and subjective. A lifeguard working a beach and a newspaper vendor working a street corner have vastly different—possibly opposite—goals regarding practical martial arts study. Consider the differing body types, likely survival situations, probable attire, and possible fighting surfaces applicable to these occupations.

Which man should train in kali (stick/knife/rolled newspaper fighting)?

Which man should study Brazilian jiu-jitsu (a form of submission wrestling suited for soft surfaces and promoted by combat athletes who are usually built like swimmers)?

"Winning" streetfights should never be your goal. Attempts to "win" in a real confrontation will increase your chances of winning—and also of losing. In either case, the risk of serious injury to you or to your antagonist will increase. In most cases "winners" go to jail and "losers" go to the hospital. In some cases the "winner" goes to prison because the loser—who at this point really is a loser—went to the morgue. Real fighting is about survival, not ego gratification. For many reasons, your best bet will often be a draw. This isn't ESPN!

Here is a summary of the above points.

- Real assaults are ugly.
- Streetfighting is for bad musicals.
- Self-defense is a form of voluntary delusion.
- Style is for artists.
- Reality really does make sense.
- Winning is a perception.

ATTACKER PROFILE

- Is an adolescent or adult male
- Has physical, numerical, or weapon advantage
- Has the initiative, possibly the benefit of surprise
- Is an experienced aggressor
- Is a fast runner because of his probable youth
- Has one, two, or three effective attacks
- Feels justified in attacking you
- Lacks will
- Lacks wind
- Lacks skill (his lack of balanced mobility and *defensive* skills will likely be absolute)
- Needs to do *you now*, not two minutes from now

- Will trigger some very strange feelings within you
- Is aware of the above points
- Expects to be successful
- Will not respect you in the morning

COMMON MISCONCEPTIONS

- Your reputation or belt rank will deter attack.
- You will have time to "get set" in your stance.
- Fights are "ready, set, go!" affairs.
- Fights are "won" on the ground.
- There will be a clear "winner" and "loser."
- Pain will be a major factor.

REASONABLE EXPECTATIONS

- Expect to face a serious threat.
- Expect fear to be the major factor.
- Expect to be grabbed.
- Expect to be punched in the head.
- Expect size to matter, a lot.
- Expect your stamina to be reduced tenfold as your blood thickens to the consistency of pancake syrup.
- Expect your opponent to attempt to beat you to the ground. If he can't, or fears he can't, he will try to take you down and beat you there. He will prefer to finish on his feet and, if successful, with his feet—using the shoe or boot as a weapon.
- Do not expect to take him out with one strike.

SOME HARD REALITIES

- Minor injuries are common.
- Most maiming happens on the floor or sidewalk.
- Nonweapon deaths occur primarily from heart failure among middle-aged men, knockdowns that drive the head into the pavement, and kicks to the head of a prone defender.
- You must manage your fear to manage your enemy.

- When facing a truly dangerous adversary motivated by bad intentions, do not expect perfect results. The resolution—satisfactory to you or not—may well be unsatisfactory to others. Expect plenty of Monday morning quarterbacking. If you are a man, those who say "I would have done this or that" may well outnumber those who say "I wish I was there with you."
- Preparation for weak opposition is preparation for failure.
- Action beats reaction.
- Martial beats art.
- Tricks are not reliable; habits are.
- Serious violence results in serious consequences.

Refer to these lists as you read on. I recommend reading the book in order, dog-earing pages of particular interest, and highlighting specific points with a marker.

CHAPTER 2

Motivation

"The martial artist is looking for an edge. This guy likes to fight!"

—SENSEI ED

You may or may not be a martial artist. You are, however, looking for an edge. (If you were just some moron who liked to fight, you wouldn't be reading this book.) That edge is the practical ability to handle yourself in a fight or survival situation. You want fighting ability. You are specifically interested in the following points:

1. Can martial arts training develop that edge?
2. How can you maximize training?
3. How can you minimize related costs and hassles?
4. What is it like to deal with real violence?

The answer to one is yes. The other points will be answered in detail from a variety of perspectives throughout the book.

People practice the martial arts for many reasons. However, the promise of fighting ability is unique to the martial arts and provides a common thread. If you are new to the martial arts, proceed with skepticism. Despite claims, most martial arts training does not prepare one to deal effectively with physical aggression. No fighting system is perfect, and most are seriously flawed. Many black belts possess no practical fighting ability. Some training methods are worse than useless and may actually erode your natural defense mechanisms.

The concept of self-defense relating to the martial arts is hype. People who do not understand the nature of illness often fall prey to scam artists offering secret cures. Likewise, those who do not understand violence often fall prey to martial artists offering secret skills. Invincibility based on the exclusive possession of lethal knowledge is the core lie—and key dynamic—that drives the martial arts industry.

Now, having exposed the lie that drew your inquiry, let's uncover the truth that will inspire your study.

You want to be free of domination: handing over your lunch to an upperclassman, your wallet to a punk, your parking space to a fat co-worker, your mother's jewelry to your cokehead boyfriend. Under threat of force, all these actions tend to dull life's luster. Maintaining your personal freedom can get real physical. Lives are more often limited by threat than ended by force. You've had it with the threat and want to be able to deal with the force.

In considering the martial arts you must develop a deep understanding and clear goals to sort through this veritable flea market of combat theories and practices. You should also come to grips with your desire to develop fighting ability. Clearly and objectively, confronting your underlying motivations will develop a valuable pool of self-knowledge. Self-knowledge is valuable in developing appropriate training methods. It is also the basis for self-control, and self-control is essential to consistent, effective fighting ability. If you are not in control of yourself, someone else is.

A good hard look within, as well as a look back, will help identify those personal traits that may well up and seize control when you come under extreme pressure. No, I'm not about to

descend into the abyss of pop psychology. Let me put it this way
. . . do you have a problem?

- What is the single most important factor driving your desire for fighting ability?
- Are you afraid of pain or injury?
- Do you dread confrontations?
- Are you timid?
- Would you fight to defend a stranger?
- Can you visualize yourself fighting for survival?
- Do you lack self-control?
- Do you like the idea of hurting someone?
- Do you have emotional buttons that are easily pressed?
- Do you fantasize about beating up bad guys?
- If possible, would you decline to fight even if you were certain to win?
- Do you just want to kick some ass?
- Are you pleased with your answers?

If you were a real head case you would be the last to know. Since you are contemplative enough to read a book on a subject that most people consider a no-brainer, you probably have your head on straight. However, if you are getting into this for the same reasons I did, it's safe to assume that you have a few screws loose.

I'll offer myself as an example. When I realized that this self-evaluation would be necessary, I considered giving up the book project. It took two weeks to sort out the mess in my head. I've got some pretty touchy buttons hard-wired into what's left of my brain, in relation to events early in life.

I started by asking the obvious question: Why must I be able to fight—why do I not feel whole unless I am able to fight effectively?

Over the past four years I have been physically disabled for 10 months from back injuries. What bothered me the most? Not being able to support my family? Not playing ball with my son? Not having sex with my wife? None of the above.

Sure, it was an all-round raw deal. But what really killed me was knowing I wouldn't be able to fight my way out of an accountant's convention! Hell, I was as helpless on that traction table as I was at age 6 when my mother dropped me off for my first day of school into the arms of three older kids. They bounced me off a roll of wire fencing until a kid named Chris ran them off. I just figured that's the way it was. Guys like Chris could fight; little fat kids like me couldn't.

What followed were years of schoolyard beatings and biannual torture at the hands of a sadistic uncle and his son. Most holidays would be punctuated by a test of pain tolerance administered by Unk. He would also, on occasion, confiscate my toys and direct Cuz to instruct me in the manly arts of carpet eating and pretzel imitating. Cuz was a wrestler ever in need of fresh practice material. I can still remember the excruciating low back and joint pain, rug burns, and oxygen deprivation. I always struggled silently, afraid to alert Unk—the master tormentor—to my helpless state. Worst of all were the helplessness and embarrassment of not being able to defend myself.

I hate to admit that these two had a role in forming the man who's sitting at this desk writing these words, but that is the case. To this day I have a chip on my shoulder concerning bullies and big jocks. This defiant attitude has accounted for most of my fights. I can't back down from their kind—not with that little fat kid inside of me screaming for vengeance!

At the age of 8 I was approached by two Hispanic kids and their dog on a deserted basketball court. The dog growled, and I stepped back. It attacked and dragged me across the asphalt while the kids kicked me.

Talk about a hot-button! Any large dog that growls at me and isn't safe behind a fence gets punched, kicked, thrown, stomped, and stoned! Last month I beat a golden retriever and tried to corner a rottweiler. Is this a strength or a weakness? I could care less.

My childhood association with Cuz culminated in a sadistic swimming lesson. I was a poor swimmer. The surf was high, and the undertow was powerful. As our families lounged on the beach Cuz threw me into the surf. Crawling and clawing my way through the swirling sand and saltwater left me breathless at his feet. He picked me up and tossed me over the next wave time and time again. I thought I was going to die. I tried yelling for help, but I couldn't. I sucked in air while he threw me back. He was the only person in my world. One of the waves broke over my back, knocking the wind out of me. I still managed to claw my way back to his feet, only to be tossed farther out. I crawled to shore under the surf, swallowing sand and water. It seemed like forever, but I made it. He was gone. I suppose he got tired, like that dog on the ball court. I had discovered my secret weapon: tenacity. The ability to endure brought a weird sense of confidence. It was time to fight back, and it wouldn't be long before I saw what a trained fighter could do. . . .

The lightweight champion of the world was being interviewed on TV, while preparing for a title defense. He trained furiously and attributed his incredible stamina to swimming daily across a broad body of water to get food. Once he ate so much he nearly drowned swimming back. He had my attention.

His fight ended quickly with the total destruction of his opponent—taken out on a stretcher. My mother recoiled from the televised slaughter, but I was inspired. Having seen in graphic detail how a fighter trained and what he could do, I announced my intention to box. Not bothering to comfort my horrified mother, I went to the basement to begin my training. My little sister had a jump rope, and I had a shadow—and a bathrobe. It wasn't much, but it was a start. I joined the school wrestling team. One day Dad came home with a speed bag. A week later it was a heavy bag. Then came the weights. . . .

The family doctor talked about brain damage. Unk said that boxing was stupid. My friends said whites couldn't fight. None of that mattered. I had lived my last days as a wimp. My body would no longer be a cage in which I was tortured, but a weapon. This wasn't about "self-defense." I was tasting freedom! Besides, nobody would ever take away Roberto Duran's Matchbox cars—not even Unk!

More than 20 years later, I finally understand how my character defines me as a martial artist. Ignoring your true character offers no advantage.

I'm not a martial arts expert, I haven't won dozens of street fights, I am not an accomplished athlete, and I probably can't even kick your ass. But this book is not a combat manual. It is a guidebook. In evolving from clumsy wimp to savage fighter to savvy survivor, I've experienced the pitfalls, dead-ends, rip-offs, hype, and raw deals that await the martial artist. In that sense, I am qualified to serve as your guide. You just need to know where you are coming from and where you're headed.

CHAPTER 3

Understanding the Martial Arts

"Fighting was an act of self-expression by which a man displayed not only his courage but also his individuality."

—JOHN KEEGAN, *A History of Warfare*

There are four basic points necessary to understanding the modern phenomenon of the martial arts.

1. Most popularly practiced martial arts are of recent origin, being younger than the Industrial Revolution. Few arts can be reliably traced by trained historians to origins predating the Modern Age (1450–1500 A.D.) However, this does not prevent martial arts enthusiasts from contriving elaborate "histories" that trace their style's pedigree into the mists of prehistory.

2. A martial art is a medium for developing the characteristics befitting a warrior. Hence, the practical pursuit of a martial art is the pursuit of fighting skill. Every martial art reflects this quest to preserve the warrior tradition.

3. The central promise of martial arts study is the acquisition of fighting skill sufficient to nullify the physical advantages of an attacker. The belief that skill trumps size is held sacred by legions of students, who—lacking experience with real vio-

lence—do not understand that technical skill and physical advantage are but two of many variables affecting combat.

4. The martial arts are currently defined by the politics of exclusion. As is often the case in political matters, the terms of debate are corrupted by greed, fear, ignorance, and elitism.

Greed results in disputes over teaching fees between master and assistant, fueling the division and multiplication of commercial arts, whose purveyors squabble over, rather than compete for, the status of "ultimate art."

Fear of athletes—particularly black athletes—breeds resentment among many martial artists, who soothe their threatened egos by dismissing such arts as boxing and wrestling as mere sports. The real problem people have with boxing and wrestling is that these arts are so physical few martial artists could expect to survive participation with their brittle egos intact. In other words, these arts are too martial!

Ignorance leads men who use their art for ego projection to dismiss gentle arts such as t'ai chi and aikido as not martial enough. Yes, these are often the same men who characterize the prizefighter as a dimwitted ape, unsuited for "real combat."

Elitism is the most common form of bigotry afflicting the martial arts. All arts produce blind adherents. The dismissal of other arts as false, inferior, or fraudulent is similar to religious zeal and political ideology—which points to the cult-like appeal of the martial arts. Those "characteristics befitting a warrior" are an intoxicating lure to the conflicted modern mind.

In fact, face-to-face fighting ability and elitism have been synonymous for a long, long time.

STICKS AND STONES

"Weapons have always been the first choice."
—PEYTON QUINN, *A Bouncer's Guide to Barroom Brawling*

The notion of arming ourselves is instinctive. For example, my wife and I had agreed not to expose our son to violence of any kind—TV, martial arts, toy guns, etc. I was astonished one day to see him, at the age of 2, begin to impose himself upon the pets, wild animals, and, eventually, adults of his little world. During the course of his second summer he developed a spear, dagger, club, and cache of throwing rocks—the entire arsenal of the prehistoric warrior! He was soon lord of the back and front yards—until Mom adopted a rigorous arms-control policy.

In the beginning, to be a man was to be a killer, to struggle for survival with hand weapons. Among primitives, virtually all adult males could be relied on to hunt and kill dangerous animals. However, there was a price to pay. That price was guilt. Few modern men have the stomach to kill their own food, even though they have no affinity for such animals—which come to us neatly portioned in plastic trays. For the primitive, the dilemma is double. His life is so closely linked with the animal world that his empathy for these creatures surpasses modern man's relationship with his household pet. Guilt associated with the hunt is central to primitive religion.[1]

The hunter was the warrior prototype. Hunting was a ritual sacred to the warrior class. Hunting and herding peoples—nomads—were the military scourge of the ancient world. Such societies consistently produced superior fighting men. This has proven true into modern times. The worst disasters suffered by modern armies fighting primitive peoples were inflicted by warriors defending hunting and herding economies at the battles of Little Bighorn and Isandlwana. If you doubt the effects of ancient hunting traditions on modern societies, try to identify a sport that does not involve one of the two crucial elements of the hunt: aiming or chasing.

What happened when men were first called upon to hunt other men? Not much. Small groups would usually skirmish until someone got killed—and you can bet that it was a select few who actually did the killing while the rest postured and threatened. Then everybody went home. Few men were suited for the task.

The majority of soldiers have never had the nerve to fight face-to-face. This has long been the distinction of the champion, his role now preserved in our sport traditions. Only three in ten U.S. soldiers admitted to firing at an enemy in a study conducted after World War II. Not coincidentally, combat units sustaining losses of 30 percent or more are usually rendered "ineffective." In the age of muscle-powered warfare most battles were won by tiny bands of elite fighters. The majority hung back or crowded in waiting for the cue to flee or pursue. Is it any wonder that the qualities that awed and cowed the common soldier of the past—wetting himself as he stood among his companions—offers such a powerful lure to the modern mind?

The martial artist seeks the qualities revered and sought by elite fighters throughout the ages: the warrior ethic personified by the file leaders, standard bearers, champions, and heroes of the ancient battlefield. The mental and emotional ability to fight in such a manner has always been rare. Only 10 to 30 percent of men are psychologically suited for hand-to-hand combat. So how, when men waged war at arm's length, did people such as the Spartans, Romans, or Samurai dominate vast populations?

Face-to-face battles were won by the force with a higher percentage of men willing to go belly to belly with a blade. To accomplish this with any consistency required a powerful combat ethic. Gladiatorial combats were one way to administer this bitter social medicine. The usual solution was the development of warrior cults, probably based on the ancient hunting societies. The Knights Templar of Europe and the Shaolin monks of China are two examples. Members of such organizations may have been the first to explore empty-hand striking methods. They were to the common soldier of the day what a U.S. Navy SEAL is to a National Guardsman. These warrior societies, the fighters they produced, and the myths they inspired were reborn with the modern martial arts movement. Whether the fighter in question is Samson or Mike Tyson, elitism is the whole idea.

If this all seems a bit esoteric, remember that, regardless of your art, the means to defend yourself effectively against a serious assault has everything to do with the realities of the ancient battlefield and the modern prizefighting arena and nothing to do with the antics of martial arts movie stars. This is an important point, because the popular attraction to martial arts training is based more on modern theatrics than on ancient realities.

EMPTY HANDS

"I nomally uses a tableg—dough I's damagin widoutit. Aks da boyz."

—MUMBLEJACK

The development of unarmed combat methods reflect three ancient dilemmas:

1. The hunter's need for dominance rituals (wrestling)
2. The warrior's need for combat rituals (boxing)
3. The unarmed man's desire to defend himself (largely a modern phenomenon). In fact, in premodern times "unarmed man" was a contradictory statement. To be a man was to be armed. Women, children, slaves, and perhaps holy men went unarmed. But even the despised peasants, artisans, and merchants wielded a deadly array of sticks, knives, and trade tools.

Mythical origins of the unarmed fighting arts include Okinawan peasants punching out armored samurai, Korean infantrymen unhorsing invading samurai with flying side kicks, jujutsu masters hip-throwing samurai swordsmen, and Chinese nuns applying the "righteous fist" to Manchu soldiers. Do you notice a pattern here? (If these claims make perfect sense to you, please mail me a check for $300, and you will receive my photo, which, if worn over your heart, will protect you from harm.)

Empty-hand fighting arts did not proliferate in Asia or Europe until the sword was banned or the sword-bearing nobility was disenfranchised. The demise of the warrior class, not the timeless oppression of the peasant class, was the catalyst for the proliferation of empty-hand arts. For the malnourished peasant armed with lethal farming implements, laboring dusk to dawn, and—in Asia—debilitated by the blood and intestinal parasites endemic to primitive rice-paddy cultivation, nothing could make less sense than adopting a rigorous boxing routine. Keeping a keen edge on that trusty pitchfork would be more practical.

Stick, knife, improvised weapon (such as oar and sai), and empty-hand fighting arts are by-products of social conditions, not the catalysts for liberation imagined by the modern martial arts enthusiast. The individual fighter has been obscured by events throughout history. In the West the way of the warrior was obscured, submerged, and eventually eclipsed by the world-shaping pace of military technology. In the East, the same age-old quest for fighting prowess has been shrouded, stifled, and ultimately corrupted by the heavy weight of tradition, philosophy, and religion.

In the West the desire of the face-to-face fighting man to retain a sense of relevance despite the increasingly impersonal nature of battle resulted in a proliferation of combat sports. In 19th century Western Europe, the popularity of boxing, savate, fencing, and the carrying of a cane was in response to anti sword laws and sentiments. The idea was to preserve the tradition of individual combat.

In the East the same period saw the forced introduction of Western ways and a similar effort to extinguish the warrior class. The Asian response to modernization had to do more than provide a combat forum. The wholesale adoption of alien military and political systems threatened to extinguish the individual fighter and his world. Consequently, much of the Asian warrior tradition was preserved in isolation or in secret, along with lifestyle aspects having little or no relation to combat.

Gouging and biting are basic animal fighting skills, quite inadequate for ejecting a cave bear from his lair, but fine for inflicting injury on our own kind. Whether stigmatized as a sports foul, preserved as a useful survival tactic, or enshrined as the "deadly claw" of Hu Ful Yu kung fu, tooth and nail is here to stay.

Wrestling, also known as grappling or throwing, encompasses the manipulative methods of unarmed fighting. Surviving in more than 50 forms, wrestling was the first martial art. Wrestling predates civilization or even settled life. French cave paintings depicting wrestlers date back 20,000 years. There are references to wrestling in the Bible and the Greek Olympiad of 708 B.C. In the Andean city of Cajamarca, the Spanish wrestling champion Alonso Diaz defeated the famed Inca wrestler Tucycuyuche in what was described as a grueling bout in 1531 A.D., not long before the great Inca was murdered. Wrestling proved such a constant that people separated by an ice age and an ocean found it to be one of their few common customs.

The fragile nature of a hunting economy makes mortal combat an unlikely social tool. Naturally, wrestling became the first unarmed fighting form. As a personal display of dominance between hunters, wrestling is ideal. The throw demonstrates control. The submission is symbolic of death—the prey's last gasp. The pin is symbolic of male dominance, with the loser temporarily assuming the female position. The hands are designed for gripping, and gripping is a natural defensive impulse, which wrestling fully accommodates.

Boxing, also known as striking or karate (empty hand), encompasses the percussive methods of unarmed fighting. Primitive Western boxing is the earliest verifiable unarmed striking art. Since unarmed striking is of little value to warriors armed with edged weapons, the practice likely spread through India to Asia, where it was modified.

Boxing refers to the closed or "clubbed" or "boxed" hand. Various gung fu (Cantonese) and kung fu (Mandarin) styles are referred to as Chinese boxing. T'ai chi chuan translates as "grand ultimate boxing." Hsing-i chuan means "mind and will boxing."

Most cultures developed an indigenous wrestling tradition, but boxing is a rare phenomenon. Striking with the body, especially the clenched hand, is an imitation of weapon use, specifically the hand-held rock—not a natural impulse. Although punching probably has primordial roots among sociopaths, boxing traditions only emerged in association with the rise or decline of a dominant military class. Boxing may be preserved as a spectacle, meditation, dance, hobby, or means of unarmed combat. However, boxing probably originated as a surrogate for weapon sparring. Even wooden weapons are deadly.

Boxing's relationship to the warrior has always been more metaphorical than practical. As a means for measuring or enhancing the attributes of the warrior, boxing is superb. However, do not assume that punching or kicking was ever effective as a battlefield tactic. Fist against sword is a statement, not a solution.

At the battle of Isandlwana, the Zulu victors were astonished by the sight of hopelessly outnumbered British soldiers (out of ammo) fighting with fists. It was a statement that cut across, race, language, and culture. The Zulus said of the British, "Like lions they fought." It was, in part, this demonstration of the universal warrior ethic that convinced Cetshwayo, the Zulu king, that his cause was lost.

ECHOES OF BATTLE

"Warfare in the age of edged weapons required yet another vanished military quality . . . empathy with one's adversary . . . which would allow a man to look a stranger in the face and strike to fell him. Prizefighters, of course, possess this quality, whether learned or inherited and by reason of this fact alone have for the common man an intense, almost zoological fascination."

—JOHN KEEGAN, *The Face of Battle*

Style usually refers to the curriculum, doctrine, and traditions of an art or subart. The obsession to find or develop the "ultimate style" is so pervasive that it keeps magazine and book publishers in business. The style-versus-style obsession is an empty one in regard to real violence. It's like comparing an apple to an orange to determine the taste of an avocado. The survival fighter focuses on the undisciplined opportunistic attacker. Learning how to combat trained fighters is a secondary goal. Unfortunately the political, commercial, and egotistical nature of the arts make "style" a big seller.

Orientation (context) of practice is what truly defines martial arts study. A style may be practiced in a theatrical or sport context. In fact, well-run schools may offer the same art in various ways. For example, a tae kwon do academy may offer a traditional class, an aerobic kick-boxing class, and a self-defense class. This same school may also have a kick-boxing team whose members compete on local fight cards and a tournament troupe that does theatrical demonstrations. One style, five ways.

By contrast, a shabby operation may attempt to incorporate all these varied applications of an art—or arts—into one program. You may encounter both, as well as more specialized programs devoted to one training context. Learn to see through the style to discern the practitioner's relationship with the style. The style is the vehicle, not the journey.

There are currently seven major trends in martial arts study. These are not always honestly presented for what they are. Few people study an art along a single clearly defined path. I have listed these seven parallel ways in which people relate to their art in a deliberate order. We will begin with those furthest removed from real violence and progressively move toward those training contexts that bring us closer to understanding and overcoming the realities of personal combat.

Political (Cultural)

"The associations are not unlike large political parties."

—MASTER JOE NAWROZKI

Many martial arts are cultural exports. In proportion to their economy or military, Korea, the Philippines, and Brazil have more influence on the martial arts than in any other field. If you are going to war with Russia, bringing in Brazil on your side is likely to be a low priority. However, if you are headed to Moscow to fight the Russian sambo champion, you better employ a Brazilian grappling coach.

Few folks relate to their art on a purely political basis, yet national and cultural pride still influences our lives. Such nations as Korea and China have made great efforts to have their indigenous combat arts included in the Olympic games.

The politics of the martial arts are important to the extent that they limit and corrupt the curriculum of arts available for your study. Most arts are political to a certain degree. No matter where they teach, boxing coaches bark at their fighters in English, and karate senseis count to 10 in Japanese. This provides the fighter with a sense of continuity with the past. Fighting men have always sought stability in some form of collective identity in order to counteract the chaos of battle. The modern student, fearful of potential muggers, will seek identification with his art in much the same way. Believing in your art really is a prerequisite for success.

This brings us to the most common form of political expression in the arts: a parochial attachment to one's style. This unfortunate mind-set limits your options and spoils valuable cross-training opportunities. As soon as a fighter carves his method "in stone" and says, "Those are the parameters, and these are the answers," he has forfeited the ability to adapt to the chaos of combat. Unfortunately, most teachers fall into this trap, often compelled to do so by the economics of their business.

Commercial (Economic)

"Instructors have to operate their schools using management techniques drawn from Western business practices. Such practices were developed specifically to enable businesses in the West to generate an income—one equal to other professionals, such as doctors, lawyers, architects, etc.—for those who run them."

—JIM MATHER, *Black Belt*, December 1997

Commercialism is the dominant ethos in U.S. martial arts. To operate a lucrative chain of schools one gives a nod to tradition, sport, and real combat. But the theatrical and recreational appeals of the Asian arts will always be the major selling points.

Otherwise known as "ghetto fu," "cartoon karate," "fast fu," or just plain crap, these operations tend to combine the superficial elements of sport and tradition with a noxious overlay of theatrics. The resulting product is suitable for occupying otherwise idle children and generating income for the purveyor. The synthesis of celebrity-driven U.S. pop culture and stifling Asian tradition provides a social microcosm where the corrupt, the deluded, and the petty are free to pursue a powerful self-image.

In a properly run commercial strip mall karate studio, the "master" of the school takes on a business role and delegates instruction duties to 18-to-22-year-old black belts with three to five years of study and little or no real fighting experience.

When competing commercial operations clash they engage in the most advanced U.S. combat art: civil litigation. Two local—legitimate—tae kwon do masters are currently suing each other over student enrollment. These guys can—or could once—fight. Some of the older man's assistants apologetically explained to me that even though they taught at his schools they could indeed fight. Commercialism is the mental illness of martial arts study, an affliction that degrades fighting ability.

Theatrical (Dance)

"What the hell is that?"

— BIG JOHN, on musical forms competition

Any physical art will naturally lend itself to theatrical expression. Theatrics are far more popular than combat. Invite 100 people to a dance and 50 will show. Invite the same 100 to a fight—or just a rugby match—and you might get five. Strictly speaking, theatrical martial arts include Chinese opera, action movie stunt work, swordplay on the Shakespearean stage, and musical forms competition at martial arts tournaments.

This stuff is what draws most new students to the arts. In light of this fact it is ridiculous to assume that most martial arts programs will focus on practical survival fighting. The stress will always be on what "looks good." Paradoxically, what looks good to the untrained eye is precisely what won't work in a fight. Effective fighting has a lot to do with using tactics that are subtle—even if brutal—and are therefore not visually impressive. The performer seeks a strong visual impression. The fighter strives to conceal his intent, and economize his motion, leaving a weak visual impression.

If you do not grasp this last point do the following:

1. Put this book down.
2. Join the karate school that has the biggest ad or most listings in the local yellow pages.
3. Sign a one-year contract and fulfill your obligation.
4. Go to a boxing gym in a poor section of the nearest major metropolitan area. Inform the proprietor that you would like to test your skills in the ring.
5. Finish reading this book while you recuperate.

Theatrics are the metastatic cancer of the martial arts. They corrupt and undermine most traditional, many sport, and some combat arts. Whenever appearances are judged to be equal or superior to effect, the art is degraded. Tournament "point fighting," Olympic boxing, and Olympic tae kwon do are prominent examples of degraded combat arts.

Recreational (Hobby/Fitness)

"If ya wanna look like a fighter, you train like a fighter!"
> —Jake "The Snake" Smith, training a white-collar boxer

This category of training appeals to bored fitness buffs and is generally featured as a sideline by boxing gyms, spas, or karate studios. It includes white-collar boxing programs, aerobic kick-boxing, Boxergenics, etc. This can be a good way to begin training, especially for older folks and is particularly popular among women. How useful the subject matter is depends on the quality of instruction.

Traditional (Meditation)

"If you are going to be successful in your traditional training, you must do two things. First, in order to achieve greatness, you need to believe in your instructor's knowledge and beliefs. If your teacher holds up an apple and says, 'This is a pencil,' you must believe him with all of your heart."

—Dominick Giacobbe, *MA Training*, September 1998

Traditional martial arts study refers to an Asian fighting method intended as a tool for attaining physical, social, and spiritual development, often pursued as a meditation on "the way of the warrior." Practitioners strive to perfect techniques as developed by the original founder of the "school," "way," "style," etc. Strict attention is paid to etiquette, lineage, and philosophical concepts. Practical self-defense is an important though secondary concern. Belonging to the "brotherhood" and being on "the Path" are of central importance. These are first and foremost social organizations.

Those arts placing more emphasis on fighting than on meditation and health are called *external*. Arts primarily concerned with well-being are known as *internal* styles.

Arts that advocate direct power striking and forceful defenses are regarded as *hard* styles. Arts that stress evasion, circular movement patterns, and the doctrine of not opposing force are called *soft* styles.

Pure traditional instruction is rare in the United States. Most schools have been corrupted by commercialism and theatrics to some degree. Pure traditionalism means doing things the way they have always been done in the belief that the human understanding of battle has decreased rather than increased over time. The ancients knew best. We can only hope to follow their well-worn path.

To deal productively with traditionalists one must understand that traditional study is very often a religious undertaking. The second most important point is that the traditional student seeks to prove himself in practice, not in competition or combat. He seeks the good to be had from journeying the "warrior path," without suffering the bad: death, maiming, egotism. This is a noble sentiment, but the downside is that traditional training—because it is a test and protective gear is usually discouraged—often results in much injury. The introduction of sport, commercialism, and theatrics into the study of traditional arts was, in large part, an attempt to replace or retain students lost to chronic and traumatic—though often minor—training injuries.

To put traditional martial art study in perspective, understand that it was the Asian response to military modernization, just as the pursuit of sport and recreational combat was in the West. The last generation of the 19th century saw the popularization of these warrior pastimes even as the hand-to-hand fighting man was finally blown off the battlefield by the rifle, howitzer, and Maxim gun.

The Boxers of China, the Ghost Dancers of the American West, the dervishes at Omdurman, and the Maji-Maji rebels of Tanganyika went to their death against modern armies in the belief that a divine force would protect them from bullets. It seems foolish to us, but these primitive people were attempting to do the same thing on the battlefield that the savateurs of France and the karateka of Okinawa were attempting to do in their practice halls: preserve the traditions of the face-to-face warrior.

In regard to real modern unarmed combat, the strength of the traditional arts is an acceptance of the totality of combat—anything goes, no holds barred. This usually leads to a pretty keen understanding of vital anatomy. Traditional training methods, such as prearranged fighting "forms" and one-hit sparring do not, however, prepare the student for the "feel" of combat. In other words, traditional study is strong on theory and weak on application.

Instructing in a hierarchical group setting is the hallmark of

Korean, Japanese, and Okinawan arts. Other Asian arts tend to be taught in a more patriarchal family-like atmosphere. In any case these methods reflect the Asian reverence for the group over the individual, wisdom over youth, and obedience over accomplishment. A student's character is measured through tests of patience, humility, and discipline before he will be trained to fight effectively. By denying young, aggressive students true fighting ability through the teaching of extraneous art, the instructor maintains the ability to physically discipline and awe his students. Because all students are taught to fight exactly like the instructor—and by extension the style's founder—regardless of their body type or mind-set, senior practitioners hold a disproportionate advantage in sparring. The ultimate purpose is to ensure that the elderly master has technical superiority over his physically superior students. This has the positive result of suppressing bullies.

To be fair, sifus—teachers of Chinese arts—do not like to think of themselves as instructors. "Brotherhood" is a recurrent theme in Chinese arts. By comparison, many of the Northeast Asian arts seem almost paramilitary.

Traditional teaching is usually done by example (monkey see, monkey do). Consequently, the teacher assumes the central role. This factor, combined with Western machismo, continues to debase the Asian arts in America. The Asian reverence for humility is the first casualty in the many battles for the soul of the modern martial artist.

One final point concerning the traditional arts: when questions of liability in regard to martial arts study are raised in a court of law, such arts are invariably deemed to be hobbies, pastimes, or sports.

Sport (Spectacle)

"He knocked me down, and I don't remember getting back up. I woke up in the dressing room and asked my manager, Joe Ponce, what round I had gotten knocked out in. He told me I had won the fight."

—Bobby Chacon

When dynamic physical aspects of a culture become obsolete they are often preserved through sport. In many cases the sport coexists with the root tradition as a preparatory ritual. Sports are either ritual hunts, fights, or wars. Individual combat sports are ritualized duels, demonstrating the combatant's ability to defeat an opponent under restricted circumstances for the benefit (in the modern sense, entertainment) of the greater society.

The modern athlete preserves the role of the primitive champion who fought for those less able. The ancient champion was, in a sense, a link between the people and their ruler. (Note the president of the United States sucking up to the victors after major sports championships, such as the World Series, the Super Bowl, or the NBA Finals.) The champion is a compelling figure. Whether he is avenging the honor of his clan, raping and pillaging with a robber baron, championing the cause of a nation, or making us spill beer on Saturday night, the champion can trace his lineage back to the first man who stepped forward to challenge a lion for a kill.

To thrive, a combat sport must operate under strict rules. This honors the age-old desire to ensure technical symmetry, reflecting the reverence of the elusive warrior spirit over mere technical expertise. Strict rules also limit maiming, which ensures a deeper pool of able and talented athletes.

Sport combat—when unadulterated by theatrical concerns—prepares the martial artist for the intensity of real combat, affording the opportunity to search within for the antidote for defeat. Sport combat cannot prepare the martial artist for the many variables of real combat. Sport training is strong on application and weak on theory.

Coaching and training, rather than instruction and practice, are the bywords of excellence in sports. The coach or trainer is very often a former competitor of average ability who seeks expression through the still-young bodies of his athletes. Unlike the traditional master, the coach is an assistant, even peripheral, figure. The athlete is central. The priority of coaching is "practical immersion." The specific need is to instill the sum of the coach's knowledge and experience in the athlete while he is still young enough for vigorous application. This dynamic results in a relatively simple art, because the athlete can only absorb so much during the brief span of his career. There are also two other long-term results of this method, one negative and one positive.

1. The quest for victory within the necessarily limited contexts of the sports arena results in tactics that permit the fighter to "game the system" to win. Very often these same tactics would be suicidal in an alley and aren't easily generalized to survival situations.
2. The quest for victory and the accumulation and transfer of knowledge from coach to athlete—as opposed to the Asian master withholding his deadliest technique from all but his chosen successor—result in the development of progressively more effective methods for dealing with basic problems. A sport is a giant laboratory where tactics are tested millions of times against determined opposition.

The goal of the combat athlete is to prove himself in competition. Those who have done so often demonstrate a profound peace of mind similar to that demonstrated by traditional Asian masters and those military combat veterans who had the character to accept their experience without being corrupted by it.

Combat sports have recently begun to gain acceptance among martial artists, largely due to the new breed of "reality combat," "no-rules," or "mixed martial arts" competitions, such as the Ultimate Fighting Challenge. These events have been dominated by wrestlers who can box and kick-boxers who can wrestle. Traditional and combat artists are fed into these tournaments like meat into a grinder. Surprisingly, some untrained fighters have done well in such events. Although these venues do not accurately depict typical real-fighting scenarios, they come closer than other sports. Two unmistakable conclusions that one does draw from these extraordinary events that are transferable to more ordinary violence are as follows:

1. Fighting is an athletic act; therefore athletes hold a natural advantage over nonathletes when the two engage in a physical struggle.
2. Size is a *big* deal.

Another reason for the acceptance of combat sports is the age-old truth that real fighters recognize and respect each other more often than not. A real hard-core karateka from rural Okinawa has more in common with a Puerto Rican boxer from an urban U.S. slum than with a white-collar karate student.

The various commentators and partisans railing against the resurgence of sport combat from their ivory towers do not realize how intertwined Western sport and Eastern tradition are at "street level," where those who fight real fights work, train, and socialize.

As an example, last night I attended an amateur boxing benefit with two friends: a wing chun sifu and a former wrestler. Five of the fighters were trained by a muay Thai/san shou fighter with a black belt in tae kwon do. One of the kids had been trained by a former boxer and current bouncer who is a karate black belt. His boy used classic Japanese footwork. Two of the best fighters were trained by a former pro boxer with a black belt in Okinawan karate. The referee was one of my training partners, who was an amateur boxer and kung fu stylist. Seventy percent of the audience consisted of trained fighters. People were being invited to kung fu events, boxing gyms, and go-go bars—where a sizable segment of the crowd were employed as bouncers. This was not just a very bad place to pick a fight, but also proof that the most fertile ground for modern empty-hand combat is where tradition and sport come together through people who simply regard them as two sides of the same coin.

On another level, we can thank a few practical geniuses for combining Eastern tradition and Western sport into a useful context.

Combat (Practical)

"Tactics are the brainwork of fighting."

—BRUCE LEE, *Tao of Jeet Kune Do*

Any traditional or sport art may be modified for real combat and practical survival training. Combat methods fall into three categories:

1. Eclectic arts
2. Military systems
3. Self-defense systems

Eclectic arts pop up every year. When an instructor in one style earns a black belt in a second style, he may take what he prefers from each and synthesize these components into his own "system." The utility of such efforts depends on the real fighting experience and intelligence of the developer. The more advanced eclectic arts, such as jeet kune do and chu fen do, were pioneered and promoted by individuals with deep philosophical insights and a lot of personal assets, such as physique, charisma, and good looks.

Whereas arts promoted on the local level can be expected to die with their originator, the ones that go national or international soon begin to take on the trappings of traditional arts. In my estimation, jeet kune do is better than halfway there. This is an important point. To understand how traditional arts developed simply trace the progress of the modern "combat" arts. You will see them ossify before your eyes.

The eclectic arts offer everything from crap to gold. So long as the teacher remains willing to experiment, this type of art is superior to the other options. The pitfalls that eclectic artists commonly fall into are as follows:

1. An obsession with defeating other arts
2. A tendency to hype the language with terms like blast, shatter, crush, etc.—the first step toward deluded thought
3. The practice of having a student mimic a sport or traditional art in the belief that this constitutes real cross training. "Big Ed" pretending to wrestle you does not constitute facing a wrestler.

Military systems are designed to prepare healthy, aggressive, male soldiers to kill with their bare hands. Such training cannot be a priority for modern military men, so it is necessarily brief. (My brother was in an elite U.S. airborne unit in the 1980s. His entire hand-to-hand combat training consisted of yelling "Kill! Kill!" and charging from a crouch.)

Military-style close combat focuses on maiming and killing with gouges, locks, and strikes, as well as employing and defending against hand weapons. Such systems focus on developing a combat mind-set. The techniques employed are a mix of traditional, sport, and combat-proven methods. Such systems may be named after military units, but most will incorporate combat or survival into the label. Meta Combat, Combato, and Survival are three such systems developed in New York and New Jersey. The innovators that develop these no-nonsense fighting styles are usually military veterans with martial arts and real-fighting experience.

The Israeli combat art of krav maga has been modified to meet civilian needs and may ive up to expectations. If you're outside the Los Angeles or New York areas you can kiss top-rated instruction good-bye. The marketing of combat systems in urban areas is a strong trend that will likely leave the small-town student to cobble together his own combat doctrine from strip-mall karate, scholastic wrestling, and mediocre boxing programs.

Most current military-style maiming or survival systems do not have a direct military lineage. This does not detract from their value. It is the combative kill-or-be-killed attitude that is important. "Technical" virtuosity is the last thing these people care about—just get it done! It is the brutal mind-set that is key and that stands in stark contrast to the "duelist" mentality of the eclectic combat artist, who derives aesthetic pleasure from the practice and application of his fighting ability. The eclectic artist trains for a no-holds-barred, face-to-face fight, while the military type concentrates on dealing with predatory violence, such as the ambush. The eclectic artist has traditional and sport roots. The military-style fighter has more in common with the experienced untrained fighter—a dangerous critter.

Self-defense systems are designed primarily for rape prevention, such as those offered in most major cities or university towns. If you're female or looking at prison time, you should check out these programs or ask for a recommendation at a good local martial arts school.

Another specialized branch of the combat arts is "tactical law enforcement" training, which concentrates on subduing violent criminals in a humane manner so as to avoid excessive-force complaints. This mind-set is the complete opposite of the military one, which is all about the brutal application of extreme force. The law-enforcement stuff is for use by well-armed authority figures, who are usually larger than their opponents, typically have the initiative, and can expect help.

SUMMARY

The incredible variety of modern martial arts represents the sum of the world's face-to-face warrior traditions. These have been preserved or resurrected by enthusiasts who relate to their arts in one or more ways:

1. Politically, as an expression of cultural, national, or parochial pride
2. Commercially, as a business or profession
3. Theatrically, as a performer
4. Recreationally, as a hobbyist
5. Traditionally, as a means of self-improvement
6. As an athlete, who seeks to prevail in sport combat
7. As a combat-oriented student, who fights as a means of pure artistic expression, for the purpose of personal defense, or as a method of applying lawful force in the course of security, police, or military operations

Of these seven study trends, only tradition, sport, and combat offer practical solutions to real violence. Tradition embraces skill as the answer, encouraging the student to acquire a (usually vast) array of technical solutions to specific dilemmas. This comes down to a reliance on tricks to survive combat. Sport encourages the development of habits, because generalized instinctive responses are more reliable in the heat of battle than are consciously selected options. However, training for instinct does sacrifice versatility. Combat arts generally attempt to incorporate the best from tradition and sport, with varying degrees of success.

Your ability to identify and avoid useless study and to incorporate the practical aspects of sport-, tradition-, and combat-oriented arts will help you develop a more effective fighting style.

NOTES

I have undoubtedly failed to address some important aspect of the martial arts. As for the potentially controversial points I have raised, you may wish to consult some of the following references noted in the text:

1. Joseph Campbell, *The Power of Myth* (New York: Doubleday, 1988), pp. 72–74. Campbell's basic contention, made throughout his many works on preagricultural mythologies (of which *The Power of Myth* is the most accessible), is that the prime function of such belief systems is to permit "joyless" participation in the necessary sorrows of life, such as murdering an innocent beast.

    The hunter's need to believe that he is participating in partnership with his prey in a sacred life cycle is akin to the overmatched athlete's need to believe his coach's assertion that he is unbeatable in order for him to enter the contest with the genuine enthusiasm necessary for the life of the sport. Hunter, warrior, and athlete all require a positive belief in the basis for their actions in order to function effectively and consistently in their field.

    To the modern atheistic way of thinking, such "beliefs" amount to *buying into the "Big Lie,"* which logically results in such senselessly brutal acts as religious wars, terrorist attacks, and the return to the ring of a washed-up prizefighter.

2. William H. McNeill, *Plagues and Peoples* (New York: Monticello Editions, 1976), pp. 43–45.

• • •

For those interested in the relationship of warrior cultures, warfare, and technology, I recommend anything by John Keegan and Robert L. O'Connell.

Personal Risks

"Say whiteboy, you goin' to visit yer gramma? . . . Well, I don' feel right leavin' ya off here, not t'night. . . . Good luck."

—BUS DRIVER

The most important fact to keep in mind when considering your risk factors and training methods is that most attackers must perceive a predator-prey relationship with you before acting on their violent impulses. This makes your personal image and social status as important as your actions in regard to potential antagonists. Traditionally, martial artists train to deal with other martial artists and people foolish enough to initiate a stand-up fight with a stranger. But real violence is far more predatory than the experts would have you believe.

The following is a profile of a violent criminal:

The 19-year-old on foot, whom we'll call the creep, spotted a 16-year-old boy pull into a convenience store parking lot on a bicycle. He knocked the kid off the bike, hit him, dragged him behind the store, mounted him, and went to work with a sheath knife. The motive was robbery, but the boy had only change. A cop intervened. The boy survived, though permanently disabled.

The judge set bail so low the criminal could continue his good works. While awaiting trial the creep and an accomplice ambushed a retarded man walking along a lightly traveled highway. The accomplice hit the man over the head with a bottle as the creep held him. They dragged their victim into the woods where the creep stabbed him through the hand and thigh and slashed his back and side with a sheath knife. The motive was robbery, but the victim had no money. The attackers took his shirt and belt. Admiring his tattoo, they threaten to cut it off, but left him for dead. He walked a mile to a gas station for help and lived to testify against the creep, who was sentenced to a total of 15 years for both offenses, to be released in his prime to prey on the weak and the unaware.

Though such predators are tolerated by society and thus mix freely with us, they are so few that their efforts pale before the accomplishments of their numerous part-time competitors.

DRUG AND ALCOHOL USE

Drug and alcohol use are prime indicators for determining the likelihood that violence will haunt your life. It is no coincidence that the best self-defense book available was written by a barroom bouncer. According to a recent survey of men incarcerated for violent felonies, 40 percent had a blood-alcohol level three times the legal limit. In fact, bail bondsmen post most of their ads near liquor stores.

GROUP IDENTITY

Group identity, or reinforcing it at an outsider's expense, is the underlying motivation—or excuse—for many attacks. Most people are attacked by those they know. However, virtually all "stranger" assaults are committed by young men with no empathy for their target. This lack of empathy is critical for establishing the predator-prey relationship. For visually oriented males racial differences offer convenient catalysts.

Whatever your race or ethnicity, be wary when living on the

periphery of or mixing with populations that demonstrate a strong group identity. You might be the only black working in a redneck town or the only white occupying a cell block. The ugly truths are that it's easier to hate somebody who doesn't belong and it's easier to hurt somebody you hate. More important, you can expect no help from those who do not identify with you.

As an example, in the past month I have been threatened by three different pairs of white males driving pickup trucks. All three incidents took place in areas where I was virtually the only white (on foot). On the face this seems odd, but it actually makes perfect sense. These are rural guys cruising into town for their drug supplies. To them I'm a freebie. Painting the curb with my face would satisfy their hatred without risking a group response.

I accept that many black men hate me for the color of my skin. That just as many white men hate me for not hating blacks. That one-third of these hate-filled people will—if *given* the opportunity—act on this hatred; and that few whites, and virtually no blacks, would consider coming to my aid.

Threats by people who will shut down before physical contact—provided you do nothing to worsen the situation—far outnumber premeditated attacks and physical escalations combined because nasty people far outnumber dangerous ones.

Material envy is the spark that ignites most violent crimes. This is the second oldest motivation for physical aggression and the best reason for a Korean grocer not to wear a gold watch in West Baltimore.

SEXUAL ENVY

Sexual envy is the spark for most attacks by whites on blacks and skinheads on long-haired guys. This is the oldest motivation for physical aggression and the best reason not to jog on a country road. If you are handsome, well built, different, or the wrong color, you can expect to be hated. Anything that flags you as an outsider could bring the group identity factor crashing down on your head. Attacks based on this factor tend to be excessively brutal. So, if you look like Lorenzo Lamas or Wesley Snipes, look out for those pickup trucks. Being in the company of an attractive woman will cause this risk to increase geometrically.

In my experience, most of the men who express sexual frustration through violence have five things in common:

1. White skin
2. Poor physical fitness
3. Binge drinking or cocaine use
4. Cigarette smoking
5. Full-time employment

Note that two, three, four, and five all contribute to erectile failure (impotence) and premature ejaculation.

A reliable indicator of your risk is the number of strange, able-bodied males ages 13 to 45 with whom you have daily contact. Count the men you encounter on a typical day. How many appeared physically able to harm you? How many regarded you with curiosity? How many hassled or attempted to intimidate you?

CASE STUDY

9:00 P.M. Sunday, July 5 to 12:00 P.M.
Monday, July 6, 1998

Able-bodied Men Encountered	112
Curious Men Encountered	14
Threatening Men Encountered	3

This really was a typical day for me. As expected most of the strange men I encountered were physically superior to me, and, of those, only a tiny minority—a punk and two drunks, one black and one white—indicated a desire to harm me. The punk and the white drunk were attached to small groups with low cohesion that indicated no desire to back them up. Since their threats were obviously based on their group association, they were unlikely to initiate contact. I ignored the punk and toyed with the white drunk, humiliating him in front of his "friends." The black drunk was a different story. He must have been fired by a white guy that day. Based on his size, condition, and intensity, I assumed he could have seriously injured me in the closed confines of the bus. I declined eye contact and crossed my fingers. He stared at me until I exited, and he did not follow.

After reviewing the numbers I'm convinced that women have a real dilemma. A woman who followed the same routine as I did would have encountered 160 men and women who where capable of harming her without weapons. If attractive, she would get second looks from virtually all of them, making hostility indications less clear. She would have to pay much closer attention to make the same observations that I did.

APPEARING LOST

Being lost or appearing to be lost definitely makes you a target for the opportunistic criminal. The fact that most men avoid asking strangers for directions means only that men have better developed survival instincts than women. Never ask directions from a stranger. Ask vendors, cops, firemen, and shop owners for directions. Asking for directions from someone on a bus or in a bar is not advisable. You never know who is listening.

PROXIMITY TO DANGER

Location is the factor that most people use to determine their risk of violent crime. This just proves that the masses aren't wrong about everything. In fact, all those yuppies fleeing the cities are more right than they know.

The most recent news report I've read on the subject indicates that a suburbanite runs a 1-in-20 chance of becoming the victim of a violent crime over a lifetime. However, the poor slob living in the city runs a 1-in-10 chance over the course of his shorter (men in Baltimore have the same life expectancy as men in Third World dictatorships), unhappier life. This statistic, based on police reports, is flawed and requires examination. Having lived in the city, county, and country, I have observed the following:

1. It takes 10 city cops three minutes to respond to an auto accident and one city cop 30 minutes to respond to a home invasion or assault in progress. In fact, good city cops have a hard time getting backup for dangerous calls.
2. City dwellers report less than half of violent crimes to the police. What's the point anyway?
3. City cops file reports on less than half of the calls they do answer.

I would triple the risk for city dwellers to roughly 1 in 3. But keep in mind that the guys who hit you in the suburbs will be more competent than the scrubs knocking off pedestrians downtown. The talent always goes where the money is.

You don't have to end up a statistic. Only those conditioned to fear and accept aggression will have to bow to the numbers.

In determining your risks, you must be knowledgeable about the local crimescape. The TV news reports are no help. These productions focus on domestic, gang-, or drug-related shootings. Radio reports, which give statistics—such as the fact that Baltimore is home to 210 gangs—are of some use in painting the broader picture. The newspaper crime blotter is the only real source for information on current locations and patterns of robberies, assaults, carjackings, and home invasions. For example, in June 1998, according to the media, crime was declining in Baltimore. However, the crime blotter of the *Baltimore Sun* reported 35 robberies at bus stops in my area. Not coincidentally, I was harassed by men I believed were interviewing likely victims, and my friend was ambushed by two armed punks right next to a bus stop in this same area.

Listen to the AM news on the half-hour, read the crime blotter, and talk to your neighbors, especially cops, cabbies, and small-business owners.

CHILDREN

"The little children punched one another's heads on the sands, the boys punched one another's heads in the streets, and in those days a stand-up fight between men was not uncommon."

—Sir Richard Francis Burton, quoted from Edward Rice's
CAPTAIN SIR RICHARD FRANCIS BURTON

Children should not be expected to provide their own protection. Unfortunately, they sometimes have to. My son's kindergarten teacher was allowing a 100-pound second-grader to beat him and his classmates at recess and after school. It took two 20-minute lessons to arm him with a stiff jab and back-leg round kick—using the tow of the boot as an equalizer.

A week later his grandmothers approached me about a "behavior problem." They had caught him fighting the bully on the "tot lot" (a walled-in patch of asphalt). According to them, this was unacceptable and could even result in him turning out like his father! I was shamed to action.

I informed my son that he was doing something wrong if he had to fight the kid twice. Dad would be picking him up from school until he got this settled, and Dad walks home. The next day I rounded the corner of the tot lot as my boy sent this kid to the asphalt. End of problem.

A child with *any* fighting skill has a huge advantage over his peers and even some adults. I once watched—and laughed—as a 70-pound boy of 8 brought down his sadistic 300-pound uncle with a round kick to the groin, finishing him with an elbow to the temple. The kid had been taking tae kwon do at a school recreation center.

Childhood violence is a bigger deal than people realize. One of the people I interviewed for this book is a black man who had survived military service, gangs, guns, knives, and prison. About the time of the interview he was being harassed by our racist white boss, who eventually fired him, and was being preyed on by his unemployed neighbors, who regarded him as an Uncle Tom for holding down a job.

His life had been a like a B movie, and he had a lot to be bitter about. He had always taken it all in stride, he told me, except for one particular incident, which had just been "too much." It wasn't "the pigs" who had interrogated him, the "shit-stabbers in the joint," or "them 10 stick-swingin'" Panamanians in Panama City who had stolen his leave pay. The incident that had broken him was "that kid at school that wanted my lunch." At work he was a nice guy—until some idiot ate one of his potato chips. . . .

Boys Being Boys

Boys and their schoolyard fights are dismissed by hard-core martial artists: "They're just kids." "Nobody gets hurt." "It's not a real fight." Wrong. We had our older boy drop out of school as soon as he was 16—to save his life. Since he had been 13, school had been nothing but a survival course punctuated by muggings and beatings. Last year, on three separate occasions, I stopped "schoolyard" beatings (one was a serious strangulation attempt) being administered by adult-sized boys. This year I gave boxing lessons to a man who was still dealing with the effects of being physically intimidated as a boy. Every Tuesday, I walk by a junior high school that looks and sounds like a prison.

Males in our society are usually targeted for violence between the ages of 12 and 22. Some of these instances can be dismissed as trivial, even character building, but most are damaging in some way. At this age the pack mentality runs strong. Coupled with a mothering society that discourages combat sports and declines to punish violence, it is no wonder that our teenage sons feel like they're walking a tightrope.

WOMEN

Women are the preferred prey of the criminal class. Why?

1. Young working women are increasingly likely to have more material wealth than their male counterparts.
2. Women generally lack the means to combat an attacker.
3. Women are increasingly isolated, because working women begin traveling alone, unlike schoolgirls who move in groups. The few remaining housewives are alone in neighborhoods emptied of all but toddlers and the elderly. Also, men are less inclined to protect strange women than in the past.
4. Women are not conditioned to understand predation and aggression. A girl who hunts or plays contact sports will greatly enhance her basic awareness.

MEN

Men are the subjects of most violent acts, usually in relation to their own risky or criminal behavior. Muggers, stalkers, and bullies, like the predators of the animal world, rarely target healthy adult males. Male risk factors are based on their own lifestyle and behavior. Men figure into the risk equation of women and children in three ways:

1. Some men prey on women and children.
2. Most men are cowards or weaklings, incapable of providing physical security for their dependents.
3. Society has alienated the average man to the extent that he will not discipline violent boys for fear of legal hassles. Punks do enjoy judicial privilege and protection.

Allow me to illustrate point three. It was an overcast day, and my back was killing me. I decided not to work my day job across town. Instead I headed home on the out-of-town bus used to transport kids from the projects to the schools on the city-county line. This bus was built to seat 45. There were about 70 on it that day. As usual, I was the only white. About a dozen construction workers were seated to my rear.

Five 120-pound punks got on and began beating up a seated boy from their position in the aisle to my right. I had an aisle seat but decided not to get involved. I didn't trust the brothers behind me not to interfere if I acted. They could take care of their own.

The situation got ugly early. The kid taking the beating was sitting next to an old lady. Every time he rolled with a punch, the top of his close-shaved head hit her in the face. She tried to raise her shoulder but was too short. After about 30 seconds her cheek was swelling as her head rattled off the window. She gritted her teeth in silence. The fact that she knew how to take a beating was sickening. We all tried to pretend it wasn't happening. It continued for another minute.

Finally, a woman yelled, "Respect your elders!"

The alpha punk yelled back, "Fuck yo eldas! I ain't got none!"

They continued for another minute before growing bored and starting to talk about themselves. At this point I was nearly insane with rage. The old lady's day was already ruined, so I decided to soothe my hatred with some punk-stomping action. This was far from a noble impulse. It was a simple attempt to satisfy my generic hatred for bullies.

I knew which stop was theirs. I had stopped carrying a knife, so I knew I wouldn't be going to jail—I relaxed. When the bus began to brake I elbowed a punk to my front. He had not participated in the beating but was part of the group, and I needed to trim the odds. I ground my right elbow into his left eye. It was so crowded that his head was buried in a tall girl's book bag—his face literally impaled on my elbow for many seconds as he cried and pleaded with his right eye.

When the bus sped up again, I turned around, hit the alpha punk with a shoulder butt, kneed him in the belly, stepped on his thigh, and walked over him, dragging my handbag across his face as I made my way to the rear door well where I waited, gripping the rear vertical railing bar. A crowd was waiting at our stop, so they would have to file by me to get off.

I waited patiently for my victim. The alpha punk—apparently believing that I had simply been rude when I trampled him—decided to swing by. Holding the bar, I swung into him. My left shoulder caught his chin. I stepped in, pinning his head between my shoulder and the rail. I pushed and ground, as his head squeaked and "clanged" on the square metal railing. While I was grinding his face against the railing I noticed an old toothless dude (looked like Grady from *Sanford and Son*) grinning from ear to ear. At that point I realized that every man on the bus wanted to thrash these punks, but were wary of the law. I wasn't really alone, so I let him walk.

When I stepped off the bus, the five-punk crew just stood there slack-jawed. I growled and limped off, in no condition to fight.

APPEARANCE AND BEHAVIOR

"Yo, caveboy, I look out fo ya. No joke. Yo gots protectin."

—MY FAVORITE CRACK DEALER, who worked one of my bus stops, until a yuppie left his keys—and baby—in his SUV

Your appearance, though superficial, is important to your interactions with strangers. Potential attackers will type you based on your outward appearance and body language. You must accept this hollow reality to read people effectively. The world really is a stage, and image is the biggest attraction.

It doesn't matter if you look like a librarian or a biker. What matters is your ability to read the effect your appearance has on others, especially strange young men.

One effective learning tool is new friends. Observe how their opinion of you alters over a week of casual conversation. Later on ask them about their original impression of you. Another method is watching people watch other people. Look for behavioral cues. Men, especially young men, visibly alter their gait, posture, and expression in response to others. They are as easy to study as rats in a cage. There is no trick to picking this up. Experience and effort are the keys.

I used to get challenged by a young buck about once a week until a simple change in my attire inadvertently stopped all that. October 1995 was exceptionally wet, and I was sick of getting to work—in a freezer—soaked. Besides, the wealthy women uptown were starting to offer me money because they thought I was a homeless guy. I bought a long oil-skin coat and hat. The young bucks stopped breaking bad with me. Why? Does an expensive coat improve fighting ability?

I found out why early one Sunday morning as I headed to a friend's house. His old lady was on a tear 364 days a year, so I stopped at a doughnut shop to get her a half-dozen peace offerings. When I pushed open the door, this old white suit sat up and swallowed hard, regarding me with obvious fear. The girl facing him didn't notice me. But the two Pakistani kids behind the counter dove into the back room. That's when I finally realized I was wearing armed-robbery apparel. Allowing myself to be insulted, I glared at the suit and leered at the woman, who I figured was his daughter or girlfriend. He almost had a stroke, but she wasn't fooled. She smiled and broke the ice for everyone.

Your behavior—actions and attitudes—are all that stand between you and a violent situation, the outcome of which can never be predicted, with possibilities that include your death. A fit, confident, aware, well-behaved man is not likely to be the target of a violent attack. Your involvement in violence, if any, will most likely be voluntary.

MARTIAL ARTS INVOLVEMENT

Your martial arts involvement is the most reliable source of physical abuse, injury, and mayhem. People will find out about you. There will be no shortage of jerks who will try to draw you into fights. If you're big and young you'll have plenty of challengers too. There is a strong undercurrent of adolescent rivalry

in the martial arts world, often encouraged by the "adult" patri-
archs of various schools. Expect to be challenged by twerps and
fighters alike.

I was teaching a young wrestler to box. He did most of his
solo training at a suburban health club. He was observed working on the bag and challenged by a tae kwon do instructor and
a black belt who claimed to compete in Europe. He was getting
pretty nervous about these "karate guys" picking fights with
him. After some counseling he offered to cross-train with both
of them. The Eurotrash declined. The instructor and my young
friend became productive training partners. These things don't
always end so happily.

LEGAL JEOPARDY

Legal jeopardy is a risk you take every time you defend yourself. When the cops come to avenge the scum who tried to shank
you, you lose, pal! I personally think our laws and the people
who enforce them are a joke. Don't take my word for it. Go
down to the local courthouse and sit in the back of one of the
chambers. Viewing criminal proceedings in your locale is the
best way to prepare yourself for the legal hassles associated with
surviving an attack.

I recently saw a repeat violent offender, who had almost run
me over with his van while he was sucking on a crack pipe with
one hand and tossing his girl out the passenger side with the
other, get off with a warning. The state's attorney kept asking
the private defense lawyer for legal interpretations—she didn't
even know what his plea meant—while the public defender tried
to flag down clients, who ignored him, and then pleaded that
they had no counsel! The judge gave them all postponements.

None of the cops who took the stand had taken coherent
notes, filed a report properly, or stood up to 30 seconds of cross-
examination at the hands of the private attorneys defending the
various slimebags. The only man who suffered at the hands of
the judge was the only defendant with a job and without a
record. "Justice" is risk number one.

My experience and research have led me to distrust the law. This book contains dozens of accounts concerning criminal assaults. I also have notes and questionnaires concerning another 40 or so incidents. In virtually every instance a successful defender was jailed, prosecuted, or sued. Of the murderers, thugs, and rapists who were apprehended almost none received any criminal penalty.

An old man does time for jacking up two muggers, and a judge refuses to try a rapist who attempted to kill his victim—who suffered serious head injuries—because he was already up on armed robbery charges!

Most judges and lawyers are ignorant of the dynamics of violence and believe that the government should have a monopoly on the use of force. The cop is the only one who has a clue, but he is no match for a lawyer. If you have a good punch, you need an even better lawyer.

CHAPTER 5

Starting Out

"Boy, walk in the rain, you get wet. Walk in the ring, you get hit."
— "REDS" FOLEY, 1976

"I know what I said—but you won't win with your face!"
— REDS, three minutes later

A martial art does not present all of the realities of combat. Fights to the death on pavement are not part of any self-defense course. However, each art presents at least one aspect of real combat. Consider sumo. This art has been discredited in open competition. The world's best *rikishi* (sumo wrestlers) have been humiliated by opponents lightly regarded in their own arts. Besides, what could possibly be significant about men with the physiques of giant babies engaged in a titanic wedgy contest? Sumo reflects reality in its own way.

Sumo is the most basic, primitive, and ritualized martial art. More important, the duration of the struggle closely parallels that of real fights, as does the unequal size of the combatants. The rules also permit slapping, which is banned in most arts, precisely because it is a common brawling tactic.

When examining an art, look *into* it, not at it. The most important consideration is not the art, but it's application. This makes the individual presenting the art a prime focus of your inquiry. The five prerequisites of an effective coach, trainer, instructor, sensei, sifu, guru, or master are as follows:

1. Intelligence or common sense
2. Curiosity or open-mindedness about his art
3. Kindness or politeness
4. Teaching skill
5. An interest in developing your ability

You are interviewing a potential service provider, not seeking a guru or applying for membership in an invincible brotherhood. You will fight alone. To seek group identity as a condition of your training will leave you "naked" when faced with real combat. Before pursuing an art adopt the following guidelines:

1. You want real fighting ability *yesterday*, not 10 years from now! Any session that does not enhance or maintain your ability or durability is a waste.
2. Minimizing training expenses has value beyond the money saved; it allows you to vary your study and exposes you to fewer scams.
3. Don't commit yourself to an art—or an approach to an art—that is incompatible with your body type or state of mind. Exploration is fine, but forcing yourself to conform to an inappropriate course of study simply because it seems superior is not wise. Theoretically and competitively, some arts may be superior to others. However, allowing your core effort to be spent developing a dead-end is no good. Ninety-pound wrestlers, fat savateurs, timid boxers, squeamish knifers, and overaggressive aikidoists are combative oxymorons bound for the pavement in a real fight.

At some point you will need to separate study from commitment. If you select a core discipline—or devise an art all your own—be certain it fits you.

Before you put on that white belt there are a few prerequisites you will need to be an effective fighter. These are abilities rarely acquired in a martial arts studio and without which you are a safe bet to become dog meat in a real fight. Once you have earned these abilities, your training should be more productive and less expensive.

The prerequisites of the effective real fighter are, in order of importance:

1. Wrestling ability
2. Weapon ability
3. Boxing ability
4. Specialized empty-hand ability: kicking, submission grappling, etc.

   NOTE: The *prime prerequisite* is real combat experience.

Even if you are a traditional, sport, or combat stylist, you're building on a weak foundation if you don't have these under your belt. Like it or not, a skilled martial artist is a brittle fighter if he can't wrestle, knife, or box.

For example, my Chinese boxing coach fights in tournaments and at black belt tests. If an opponent lacks boxing ability he becomes a knockout victim of this fanatical devotee of the Asian way who regards fighters who have not taken the time to learn Western boxing with utter contempt. He does not extol boxing as a superior art but regards it as a basic requirement. In fights without rules, this is even more true of wrestling. As for weapons, practicing knife defense without learning to use the knife is asking for a belly full of steel.

A good reason for pursuing wrestling and boxing before programs intended for self-defense is that sport training is best done at a young age. Get the experience when your risk of injury is as low as possible.

Another reason for accessing sport programs early is cost. If you are under 18, wrestling and boxing should cost nothing. If you are older, these options remain inexpensive. I have only paid once for training in a fighting art: $160 for four months of American karate. What this taught me about fighting was that my ability as a mediocre amateur boxer made me too dangerous for most karate students.

Sport training and weapon sparring feel a lot like real combat and impart contact and timing experience rarely found in the martial arts studio. I have used my wrestling, boxing, and real-fighting experience to obtain free instruction in more than six Asian arts. In fact, my Chinese boxing coach works with me for free as a way of measuring his more exotic skills against what he regards as the "foundation art" of boxing.

Before training under anyone, you should determine the trainer's sports medicine IQ. Nothing compromises fighting ability more than use injuries. If this person requires his athletes or students to do any of the following seek an exemption from the fitness aspect of the program and ask for skill training only. If this is not kosher with him—leave. Harmful exercises include the following:

1. Wrestler's bridge
2. Prone 6-inch leg raises
3. Traditional or Roman chair sit-ups
4. Duck walks
5. Plyometrics
6. Ballistic stretching
7. Hurdler's stretch
8. Any strength exercise done for speed
9. Hitting or kicking "air" for power

Any instructor you choose should also know cardiopulmonary resuscitation and first aid and have some knowledge of nutrition, anatomy, human behavior, and group dynamics.

WRESTLING

"I attribute my otherwise inexplicable good health and longevity to wrestling."

—A BAR PATRON

At some point in a fight it will be to somebody's advantage to wrestle. The latest hysteria to hit the martial arts world is the belief that one should grapple with an attacker, presumably on cracked-glass-strewn asphalt. A friend of mine is a member of a grappling club. Its novice heavyweight outweighed his veteran opponent substantially and was thus able to grapple to a draw. (In a field party brawl that means the fat biker's girl had plenty of time to smack you with a bottle of Jack.) This does not happen in striking arts.

Middleweight pros eat novice heavyweights for lunch. In the grapple you are in constant contact with a larger opponent's primary asset—his weight. Even in the boxing ring, the worst thing about sparring big guys is when they lie on you.

In a survival situation, it will likely be to your attacker's advantage to grapple because of the following six reasons:

1. He is larger than you.
2. Because he is an unskilled puncher, his blows will tend to pull him off balance into you, or he will need to grab you in order to strike effectively.
3. Since he has the initiative he may assume that controlling your body will ensure his momentum.
4. He may be afraid you will escape—nice thought.
5. He may have help on the way.
6. He may be a high school or—yikes!– college wrestler.

You need to be able to counter simple grappling attempts. Since any skilled grappler you face would most likely be the product of a high-school wrestling program, I suggest you study American free-style wrestling or Greco-Roman wrestling. Most untrained fighters will try and take you down from a shirt, belt, or hair grab or waist tackle.

The fighting skills best developed through wrestling are as follows:

1. *Defense against the takedown.* The ability to avoid the tie-up

and takedown against a wrestler on a mat is magnified on pavement. If you can brush off an athlete for even 10 seconds, you should be able to maintain your preferred range against a brawler. Free-style wrestling permits more takedown options.

2. *Escaping and reversing holds, especially those applied from an upright position.* You may not know you are in a fight until that headlock is applied. Greco-Roman is tops here.
3. *Wrestling instills grit and poise.* If you can't handle six minutes of mat munching, you don't belong in a real fight. Wrestling offers exposure to combat intensity.

If you are not inclined to wrestle, you will not be very good. That's fine. Wrestling is preparation for a worst-case scenario. Grinding it out on the asphalt is not a reasonable survival tactic unless you are the aggressor or are severely compromised. Wrestling ability enables you to avoid the grapple, endure it, and reverse and escape holds—providing a stable base from which to strike.

If you are not eligible for scholastic sports here are some angles to work for inexpensive instruction.

1. At the close of the season, approach an athlete about lessons. If you are a martial arts teacher invite him to your school as a coach. Of course you must okay things with his coach first.
2. At the start of the season offer to work as an assistant for a wrestling team in return for lessons.
3. Pay a top wrestler for lessons. Learn to splay, splay, and splay.

WEAPON SKILLS

"I belong to the 'point and shoot' school of self-defense."

—WALT

Weapons are far easier to learn than the rest. But teachers rarely cover weapons until you have trained for years—so they can soak you for all you're worth. Learn the stick and knife. This is where the training videos and manuals are worthwhile. You can even learn useful weapon skills—of the common-sense variety practiced by the untrained criminals you would likely defend against in a real situation—by simply padding some PVC tubing with pipe insulation, donning goggles, and going at it with a friend. Any teacher offering weapon instruction to novices rates highly in my book. (For more information see Chapter 17.)

BOXING

"I expect to hang a sign over your eyes sayin', 'Closed for the weekend.'"

—"Terrible" Tim Witherspoon

Boxing is a cheap and relatively quick method for developing the ability to inflict, avoid, and endure concussive trauma. It is the most well-known and often-televised combat art. There is no need to make a case for its effectiveness.

There are a handful of boxing gyms in most metropolitan areas. There is usually one within reasonable driving distance of a small town. If there are no gyms listed in your local yellow pages, inquire at a YMCA, a fitness club, a health spa, an inner-city ethnic bar, or a go-go bar.

Memberships run from $50 a year to $75 per month. Young competitive fighters often have their fees waived. Some gyms require that you join an association before you are allowed to spar. This is basically a cheap annual liability policy. You should not spar your first month. Suburban gyms that double as kick-boxing gyms are suspect. These may feature contract payments, may be run by a commercial martial arts chain, and rarely have dedicated coaches. A gym run by a civic group, such as an Optimists, Kiwanis, or Boys' Club, or police athletic league will have at least one quality coach. However, the best gyms are the inner-city dungeons that produce the pros. The biggest problem with most of these places is that they have restricted hours. The owners or organizers barely break even, and open up after work for a couple hours only on certain nights.

Before deciding on a gym, attend a local show. Watch the fighters and—especially—the trainers in action. My brother Tony was in town for the holidays, so we went to see a friend compete on a local amateur card. Tony is an accomplished natural athlete who boxed in the army. He was livid over the fact that all the fighters from one gym kept dropping their left hand. He yelled for them to jab from the shoulder, until he noticed the trainer giving pep talks between rounds from his boxing stance: left hand held low! That's when he began rooting for the other clubs.

After observing the ring habits of the fighters and the corner work of the trainers, he rated all five clubs. Though he knew nothing of the local boxing scene, his impressions jibed with my inside information. His ability to critique five programs based on an exhibition of their novice fighters was not uncanny. Any sports fan with an athletic background could have come to the same conclusions.

Before you begin training, consult a boxing manual. The quality of trainers ranges from the stratosphere to the gutter. Also, if you do not intend to compete and have not accessed a "white-collar" program, you will be a low priority. Doing your own homework is important.

Wherever you choose to train, you want to get the most out of your experience. Below are some guidelines for maximizing gains and minimizing injuries:

1. Don't bring a woman to watch. (No joke.)
2. Don't get close to the peripheral characters who hang around.
3. Expect to be undertrained by the coach.
4. Nobody cares if you suck. (They really don't.)
5. No matter your skill, hard work will get you respect with the fighters. With respect comes advice.
6. If you have a martial arts background, do not let anyone know. (You have been warned.)
7. Don't train more than four times per week.

8. Be quiet. Damaged brains are trying to concentrate.
9. Don't swear. Some of the boxers are Christians.
10. Don't adopt a peek-a-boo or in-your-face style.
11. Be a classic boxer or counterpuncher.
12. Bring your own hand equipment. Don't spar until you feel ready. Don't spar every workout. Don't spar with a cold, flu, or headache or when tired.
16. Don't spar without supervision. If this is even going on, find a new gym.
17. Don't spar larger fighters without a chest protector.
18. Don't tee off on the big boys or foul the pros.
19. Don't become a spectator. Watch the sparring while skipping rope or shadow boxing.
20. Never show anger.
21. Don't fight for the gym unless it waives your fee. That means you are a prospect, not a trial horse.

If you work hard and spar responsibly for six weeks you should begin to experience some good will and receive advice. If things are still cold on the personal level or your trainer is letting you get busted up sparring, find another gym.

After you can defend yourself in the ring, spar with pros and heavyweights. When you can give them a little work without getting mauled, it's time to cut back. You can't do this year after year without some real brain damage. Keeping in mind that your aim is real-fighting ability as opposed to ring competition, consider shopping the martial arts market. You might wish to begin cross-training here and nix the dojos. Though boxing will enhance your fighting ability geometrically—to a point—the quick wits of the superior fighter are eventually diminished through excessive contact. You must identify that point of diminishing returns and step back. Your health is the foundation of your fighting ability.

KICK-BOXING

Kick-boxing gyms, if well run, are much like boxing gyms for the novice. They will begin with "hands" training and then ease you into the few effective kicks. In fact, many gyms double as both these days. Here are some specific tips:

- Kick for power, not points.
- Ask to be trained in Thai, free-style, or Chinese rules. When sparring, imagine that you have no groin protector.
- Ask if you can train—not spar—in shoes.
- A chest protector is a must when sparring with kicks.
- Your trainer is the guy to ask about the local martial arts people. He will know who the serious ones are.

MARTIAL ARTS STUDIOS

"No one can make you feel inferior without your consent."
—ELEANOR ROOSEVELT

If you sign up at the nearest karate school you are probably wasting your time and money. Below is the system I use for sizing up training options and scouting for friends interested in lessons or clients in need of quality sparring partners.

Recreational Programs

Recreational programs, sponsored by a city or county recreational council, are inexpensive and usually run by good people. In my area three of the best self-defense teachers work out of school gymnasiums as "employees" of the local recreational council. One teaches jeet kune do and jujutsu twice a week. The cost is $30 for three months! He has to charge five times that at his suburban school just to cover rent and liability insurance. Another man, perhaps the best all-round combat artist I know, drives 30 miles to spar with his students once a week. Yet another is a Vietnam veteran who learned his art in Asia from real masters—who were real killers—and understands the dynamics of urban street violence.

Yellow Pages

The local yellow pages is the place to start. Avoid any outfits that have multiple listings. These are chains, and you would be handled by assistants. Avoid listings that include the words *studio, power, masters, kick* (*kick-boxing* is OK), *ultimate, sport, dragon, tiger,* etc.

Check into the listings that advertise an art as opposed to a generic karate listing. Listings advertising multiple arts or employing the word *practical, universal, united, kwan, dojo, dojang,* or *club* are worth checking out. Schools that advertise pay-as-you-go, no contracts, or free lessons should be considered. Places that also advertise equipment sales usually have a nice training facility.

The Art

The art is an important consideration for two reasons:

1. Teachers who water down their art for commercial or theatrical purposes will go generic. For instance, they will not advertise as tae kwon do but as "sidekicks karate."
2. If there are many competing listings for the same art this indicates that assistants are breaking away to compete against their masters. This is a warning that you will have to put up with a lot of politics and that there will be an emphasis on what looks good.

NOTE: If the teacher of an art also offers a separate self-defense course, he has, by recognizing the difference between art and application, demonstrated a level of understanding far beyond that of his peers. Consider taking any such self-defense course, regardless of the instructor's art.

The Storefront

The storefront tells a lot. Any school located in a suburban strip mall may be assumed to be a commercial operation, based on the high rent. Look at the sign and rate it as an ad. Look at the enticements. If the sign stresses discipline, confidence, enhanced academic performance for kids, or fitness for women, be suspicious. The buzzwords you want to see are *self-defense, practical defense, progressive, combat,* and *survival.*

Most places will have trophies won by the teacher placed in the window. (I prefer seeing trophies won by a student or the school team.) This is seen as a commercial necessity, so don't be too critical. However, if they are too numerous and recent, then this man will probably be more preoccupied with his own image than with your progress.

The Phone Interview

Phoning is preferable to just showing up while the instructor is teaching. During this phone interview, get the basics: cost, curriculum, class size, personal instruction policy, and the teacher's background. Ask for a free lesson or to observe a class. If you have to sign a contract or commit yourself without observing or participating in a free session, go elsewhere. The exception to this last rule is the person who only does individual or small-group instruction by appointment. He should be paid for the introduction, since it represents a scheduling commitment.

The Training Facility

The training facility is crucial. It is a reflection of the teacher's priorities. Do not expect state of the art. However, there are some basics you should insist upon:

- Enough space to conduct the class without students being required to sit out
- Something to hit, such as bags and mitts.
- Protective sparring gear

Mirrors, mats, and practice weapons are big pluses. But if none of the three basics are present, and he is teaching an empty-hand striking art, leave.

The Face-to-Face Interview

The face-to-face interview should go pretty well if the rest checked out. The following are red flags that may indicate a mind-set that is not conducive to proper training:

1. Instruction is conducted by unsupervised assistants. (A chosen successor or paid professional fighter is not a mere assistant.)
2. Individual instruction and scenario-based self-defense training are not offered.
3. Belt-test fees must be paid to qualify for rank advancement.
4. You are guaranteed to achieve black-belt rank after a certain number of lessons or payments.
5. The possibility of your eventually becoming an assistant instructor is presented as an inducement.
6. The teacher interviewing you is wearing a suit and tie.
7. The number of black belts graduated from the school is offered as a measure of the school's success.
8. You observe women and children who are obviously incapable of tolerating contact or defending themselves wearing black belts. This demonstrates a higher regard for forms and acrobatics than for fighting ability.
9. The teacher is in poor physical condition. If due to an injury or advanced age, it is not an issue.
10. You are asked to commit yourself to more than three months of training. This is not even legal in some states.
11. The owner has a moving van, limousine, or catering service as a sideline, and the vehicles are trimmed with his school logo.
12. The studio holds birthday, Tupperware, or graduation parties in the training hall.

If three or more of the above statements are descriptive of the school, leave. Never, ever sign a contract for martial arts instruction.

The following are questions to ask the instructor during the interview or at some point before you make a serious commitment.

1. "Do you have any wrestling, boxing, kick-boxing, submission grappling, or "reality fighting" experience?"
2. "Do you have any experience in bare-knuckle bouts or real fights?"
3. "Have you played any contact sports?"
4. "Have you been in any real self-defense situations?"
5. "Do you have any military combat experience?"
6. "Do you have any bouncing or security experience?"
7. "What about that other school?" (Name another outfit that rated high according to your investigation.)
8. "Is what you teach different than real fighting?" (It has to be.)
9. "Have you trained—or do you train with—people from other styles?"
10. "What other arts are effective for self-defense?"
11. "Can you recommend any related books or magazines?" (This is important. Would you go to a surgeon that didn't read up on his specialty? More important, reading the magazines indicates dedication. You have to plow through a lot of useless crap to find the rare worthwhile material.)

If he offers a positive response to most of these questions, you have struck gold. If he doesn't respond positively to four or more, leave. (Any decent teacher should get questions 8–11 right.)

Observing a Class

Observing a class can be very enlightening. Below are signs of a quality instructor.

1. The instructor teaches by demonstration and explanation.
2. He observes and addresses the students individually and as a group.
3. He is willing to play the bad guy in self-defense scenarios.
4. He does not pose, strut, or swagger.
5. He does not teach all his students to fight identically.
6. He does not date or flirt with the female students.
7. He makes the class sit and watch another student do forms only when that student is testing for advancement. Forms work should be mostly homework.

8. He does not permit, encourage, or require students to train while drunk or high. (This does happen.) He doesn't insult or disrespect students.
9. He regularly reminds students of aspects of real violence.

Below are some flaws common to ill-conceived self-defense training.

1. Kicking to the head is encouraged.
2. Students are only trained to kick barefoot.
3. Sparring partners break contact after one blow, stopping the drill where a real fight begins on contact.
4. Spinning, jumping, breaking boards, and other such stunts are given serious attention.
5. Self-defense drills feature a passive attacker who must cooperate for the defense to work.
6. Techniques are practiced from a nonfighting horse stance. This is done to increase leg strength, and to make retraining of advanced students necessary, which is an intentional flaw—or inhibitor—common to Asian arts.

The Free Lesson
The free lesson, or trial lesson, is a good way to get to know the teacher. His technical proficiency and practical nature can best be measured against others by asking him how to deal with a common threat, such as the side headlock, rear bear hug, frontal choke, right hook punch, or waist tackle.

Costs
Class-based instruction costs range from $20 to $120 per month. Two hour-and-a-half classes per week is standard. You should be able to get your uniform as part of an introductory package. There may also be additional association fees. The best packages offer a free uniform and an individual training session once a month. A three-month prepayment should get you a healthy discount off high-tuition programs. A large chunk of the tuition goes to property rental, so in major real estate markets you can expect to pay more.

Keep in mind that most of your classmates are not there to improve their real-fighting ability. Most are interested in enhancing their self-image, attaining peace of mind, and deluding themselves about the nature of combat. For the men, the biggest attraction is the opportunity to spar without bleeding or facing an actual assailant. Expect to have a conflict of interest with your classmates.

With this in mind, here are some tips for getting the most out of a class setting:

1. Tell your teacher that you are not interested in competition or belt rank and that you want to spar with the black belts. The better black belts may be as capable as some of the talented amateurs at the boxing gym.

2. Don't tell the other students you can box and avoid the boxer-versus-kicker debate. Take it easy on them while sparring.

3. Don't try to beat or control the teacher in sparring. Use him to work on defense and counters.

4. Some of the teachers, most of the black belts, and virtually none of the others will be capable of handling head contact—if it is even allowed. Be prepared for emotional sparring sessions. The fact that a lot of kickers "spaz" when they get tagged can help prepare you for the real deal.

5. Try to find a serious training partner to work with on the side, especially if you won't be sticking around.

6. Ask the teacher for home training tips.

7. Good teachers spend a lot of class time conditioning their students. This is necessary because most martial arts students are small or sedentary people with little or no sports background. However, all of this is a waste of your time. You can exercise with less risk of injury and better results on your own. In fact, if you lack the character and self-motivation to condition yourself adequately, you do not have the will to prevail in a disadvantageous combat situation. So, if you have a good teacher, make arrangements for private instruction.

Small Groups

The small group setting is probably the best learning tool. The ideal arrangement is one novice who pairs with the teacher and two advanced students who pair with two intermediate students for drills, sparring, etc. Having a teacher who works with 10 students in two separate two-hour classes, as opposed to teaching those same students in a two-hour class, maximizes your training experience and should be well compensated.

Private Instruction

Private instruction is the best way to learn if you are self-motivated. For a personal trainer to make any money without charging a high fee, he must leave the time-consuming physical conditioning to you. This permits him to work in smaller time blocks so that he can accommodate more than a handful of students.

There is a glut of qualified teachers. This means you need not pay high rates. The top hourly rate should cost half as much as a therapeutic massage. These people are earning tax-free income on the side, doing something they love. They should be willing to work for a union-scale labor rate. I charge $10 per session, which lasts between 40 minutes and two hours, depending on my client's condition.

Seminar Study

Seminar study is most beneficial if you are proficient in two or more arts or if the seminar is on weapons. Attend seminars by people who do a lot of them. Rate the cost of a six-hour seminar as if you were paying for six lessons at your school. Take a notebook and pencil.

Becoming Your Own Teacher

Becoming your own teacher is the long-term goal. After you have attained a moderate level of proficiency in wrestling, weapon use, and boxing, and have gone on to excel in one of these or another art, you should develop a maintenance and enhancement program. Don't just practice the same stuff for 20 years. Below are some inexpensive suggestions for staying sharp and continuing to grow, based on my own experience. I currently follow all of this advice without spending a dime.

1. Teach or train young fighters and friends interested in self-defense. This will compel you to review your methods and reflect on your art.
2. Develop a network of training partners. These may be people you train or spar with only once a year. An experienced training partner is your best mirror. Keep in touch with the talented people you trained and then train with, or under them.
3. Make occasional visits to gyms, dojos, and competitions and talk to some of the handlers about their students, programs, and facilities.
4. Find a free coach. Train your own. I work with a guy once a week, who, for a cold beer, will happily make 40 minutes of my life a leather-eating hell.
5. Employ an experienced teacher to develop and review your skills periodically.
6. Occasionally pay or barter for a lesson in another art. My next move will be a trip to the local kempo school to work on some upright grappling.

If you are new to the martial arts and really are starting out, keep in mind that some—and probably most—of the teachers out there have been where you are. The best will be those who have not forgotten what it was like to get started.

If you have some significant training or experience, be prepared to encounter elitists, idiots, and egomaniacs who have managed to use their art as a refuge from reality and adulthood. Unfortunately, many use their art as a means of maintaining a permanent state of adolescence. But, for every 40-year-old boy out there fantasizing about streetfighting heroics, there is a real man who has something useful to offer. Find him.

CHAPTER 6

The Fighter's Body

"One fifty-three? Hell, I screw girls bigger than that!"

—SICK RICK

Face it: fighting is physical. Your body will have to do a lot of work before you can claim to "know" anything about fighting. Where do you stand? What is your physical potential?

Women have weaker joints and higher body-fat ratios than men. Lack of testosterone also inhibits effective aggression. Women are also more susceptible to injuries. Recent studies of female army personnel have shown high ratios of lower body injury among female soldiers, and recent Marine Corps data show female stress fractures at 9 percent, in contrast to 2 percent for men. But take heart, ladies: the deplorable physical condition among U.S. men ensures the exceptionally conditioned woman physical parity with an average man of equal size.

MUSCLE

The long-running debate over the value of muscle developed

through deliberate strength training is dead on the level of sports medicine. However, the opposing myths still prevail among athletes and the general population. The debate is best illustrated by a recent call from a young man I once trained.

This person boxes during the week and kicks on the weekend. For an amateur show the competing clubs all share the same—usually improvised—dressing room. While wrapping for a fight he noticed that the welterweights and middleweights from other clubs were arguing over who would "beat on the white muscle boy." They figured he couldn't fight because he was white and muscular. He knocked out one of the middleweights.

Within a week he was competing on a kick-boxing card. His opponent saw him with his shirt off and tried to back out of the fight! My former pupil had to promise not to hurt his opponent to get the fight. He held back and still took the guy out. Not because he is built like a Greek god, but because he hits like a heavyweight. Both of his opponents had been wrong for different reasons and were led to stupid conclusions by men who should have known better.

Since I am a "bone rack" you might expect me to take a hard line against bodybuilding. No way. I like beating on muscle boys precisely because I'm jealous of all that active tissue! I'd kill for two pounds of intercostals to shore up my rib cage. Below are the pros and cons of adding muscle to your fighting frame.

Pros of Adding Muscle

1. Grappling strength
2. Marginal increase in striking power
3. Joint stabilization and injury prevention
4. Shock absorption
5. Increased bone density

Three men's magazines offer excellent advice for those not interested in the perverse bodybuilding scene.

Cons of Adding Muscle

1. Decrease in stamina (you do have to carry it)
2. Possible decrease in speed, flexibility, balance, and range of motion if you acquire additional muscle mass by just strength training and not maintaining your athletic ability

A number of current champion boxers are successfully moving into higher-weight classes with the aid of weight training. Evander Holyfield is a virtual advertisement for supplemental strength training. The reason most boxing trainers are so dead-set against "being on weights" is that it's dangerous for mediocre fighters. Boxing is a weight-class sport. A fighter moving up in weight is in danger of colliding with a monster with larger bones, who is sucking 20 pounds to make weight the day before the fight and then rehydrating to his original weight before fight time. (Just add water—instant middleweight!) This can be real ugly. Some fighters build careers on sucking weight to crush little guys. It's not that the muscle is inhibiting; it's just that the extra weight is pitting you against a bigger fighter.

Weight training is a must for injury prevention and rehabilitation. My shoulders are rounded from years of boxing. Hitting doesn't build a balanced musculature like wrestling. My therapist demonstrated that my pectorals were too strong for the opposing muscles in my upper back. This muscular imbalance became almost crippling—not to mention noisy. Had I supplemented my boxing routine with exercises to strengthen those weak areas, I could have avoided this. Find some musclehead who would like to learn how to fight to act as your personal trainer. Many are permitted to bring a guest to their gym.

BONE

Bone is—physically, at least—half the show. Honestly, there is little you can do about it. Weight training can help, but it's pretty much up to nature and the quality of your diet as a child. Premature puberty can prevent bones from lengthening to potential.

The length and thickness of your bones will determine how

much weight you can effectively carry. I'm talking size, and size is, well, a big deal. As much as we'd like to make fun of hulking muscleheads who can't wipe their ass, we've got to admit that, when all else is equal, the big man wins. Bigger bones permit you to develop more muscle and hang more fat without degrading your athletic ability. Last, but not least, big bones break little bones.

Study the bodies of athletes and the people you meet. This will help you determine how you rate relative to possible attackers or opponents. Note the thickness of the wrist, ankle, fingers, forehead, and neck. I work with a guy who has wrists twice as thick as mine, and seeing them was a sobering observation for me. (He does claim to be the first member of his family—subspecies really—to walk upright.)

HEIGHT

Height alone is not an advantage. A tall person is easier to hit in the throat or chin, and those long legs are easily grabbed. (In examining more than 300 fights, I have identified only three blows to the neck, all sustained by a tall opponent.) A tall puncher also stands a greater chance of breaking his hands on the top of an opponent's skull. What height usually offers is a superior bone structure and reach. A tall man with short arms has problems.

I was once approached by three young bodybuilders about boxing lessons. I took them—with their new gear—out to a city park to spar. The big boy was an excellent student, but he had short arms, shorter than mine. The medium-sized kid had longer arms and broke the big guy's nose within 10 seconds. Trying to protect your chin and long torso with arms that barely hang to your waist can't be much fun. As he bled on his gear I suggested a kicking coach.

The optimal height for fighters is between 5 feet 10 inches and 6 feet 4 inches. If you are shorter than 5 feet 6 inches or taller than 6 feet 6 inches, you can expect to be frustrated by certain body types and fighting styles.

REACH

Reach is not just the length of your arms. A boxer's reach is measured from fingertip to fingertip. Why? Because shoulder width enhances punching power. Reach is always a good thing so long as you use it. Your reach should equal your height. If your reach exceeds your height by more than 2 inches, consider yourself lucky. If you are on the short end of the equation, the disadvantage can be minimized through specialized training.

HANDS

"Another potential problem is that you are at your instructor's mercy in class."

—BILL WALLACE, *Black Belt*, April 1998

Hands are all-important. The bigger they are, the harder they are to break. Grip is also a consideration. This is where inherent bone structure really counts. But there is room for improvement. People tend to concentrate on developing the muscles that close the hand, ignoring the extensors that open the hand. This is fine for grappling strength. However, for strengthening the fist, the opposing muscles should be well developed. Don't just squeeze a ball or hand grip. Roll golf balls in your hand and practice opening the hand with rubber bands around your fingers. If you do knuckle push-ups, understand that this is primarily to strengthen the wrist. Wear work gloves and start out doing them against the wall.

If you are a hitter, hand conditioning is a priority. On off days soak the hands in hot salt water to toughen the skin. Some of the 27 small bones of your hand are dislocated every time you punch. Applying ice will minimize damage to the tissues that move and stabilize these small bones.

Do not attempt to toughen the hands—*or any joint*—by striking hard or heavy objects without protection. Bone "toughening," "hardening," or "callousing" does not really occur.

Putting bone under stress without fracturing it will eventually increase bone mass, developing a stronger bone. This applies to muscle as well, so long as you do not bruise the tissue or rupture blood vessels. But impact injuries to tendons, ligaments, and cartilage do not result in toughening. Connective tissue heals poorly, if at all. Go ahead and toughen the large simple structures, such as the shinbone, but nothing complicated. Mother Nature gets mad when you crinkle her blueprints.

Honestly, the reason many kung fu and karate people get away with hand toughening is that they don't hit that hard. They depend mostly on kicks for power. The ones who do punch hard often end up with bad hands in middle age.

You must also consider the shape of your fist. Ideally, it is thick and has two large knuckles of equal size. In the bare-knuckle era this "mallet fist" was a prerequisite for the aspiring prizefighter. I have prominent index and middle knuckles. But the middle knuckle is so much larger that it absorbs most of the force of each blow, even when the fist is taped and padded and the punch is "corkscrewed" properly. We will take a closer look at the fist later. However, if you have a structural problem all you can do is train around it.

"If you engage in sports you will eventually develop a medical condition related to that sport."

—Dr. Dean Edell

I have had only 60 percent use of my right Achilles tendon since rupturing it 20 years ago in a fight—but that hook-kick did look good! After breaks, fractures, sprains, and bruises, my right hand is almost worthless—thanks, in part, to "toughening" methods prescribed by martial arts teachers. My shoulders require six hours of therapy and strength training per week just to keep them operational. Torn jaw ligaments have forever deprived me of my favorite low-fat food—burnt pretzels. I am only 35 years old! Don't listen to the macho men as I did. If I get thumped by a couple of punks on my way to work tonight, it may be because I haven't been able to put together six weeks of hard training or spar regularly for more than five years, all because of injuries. The injuries weren't all self-inflicted—the 10 concussions weren't—but many were.

OCCUPATIONAL INJURIES

Occupational injuries, for you blue-collar types, are probably your biggest worry in regard to injury prevention. People assume that working with your hands will keep you fit. Unfortunately, working as a laborer almost always results in a chronic condition related to 40 or more hours of doing the same thing for years. If you are such a person or if you are a computer operator prone to wrist problems, you must factor your job into training. Fully one-third of my training is devoted to counterbalancing occupational stresses on my body.

"CHIN"

"The front of the skull is relatively tough. But a blow just above the jawbone can break the skull even if it's delivered by a strong child with a big stick."

—PROFESSOR RICHARD HOLMES

"Chin," or a fighter's ability to endure head strikes, is a complex and important asset. A true attack often starts with a blow to the head, and the inability of most people to take a punch accounts for the short duration of many fights. Now, the fine art of getting hit in the head is something—probably the only thing—that I have mastered. The how of it will be discussed later. Your baseline ability to handle head blows can be determined by rating yourself or your opponent according to the following criteria.

1. *Development of the neck and minor muscles that attach to the*

skull and operate the jaw. A doctor in Las Vegas determines the odds of heavyweight fights by comparing neck measurements. (Makes sense. They all hit hard, and all get hit.) Be careful working the neck. Try head rolls, isometrics, or resistance machines. Forget the bridges and head straps. To strengthen the jaw many boxers chew gum. Be careful not to chew too much on one side. This could cause TMJ (feels like an earache). If headaches develop from training, it is probably the neck. Get a massage from a certified therapist.

2. *The thickness of your skull.* This can be estimated by checking the thickness of your wrist and ankles. However, the best method is to look at how far apart the eyes are. The closer together your eyes are, the thinner the skull.

3. *The shape of the skull.* Big-looking domed brain cases are more fragile than sloped or pointed skulls with heavy brows. Examine the head as you would the armor of a tank. Thickness isn't everything. Ideally you want a low crown, wide-set eyes, and thick forehead, balanced on a neck that is thicker than the skull.

You probably rate low on the above scale. (You *are* reading.) Not to worry, structure is only half the battle. Knowing how to get hit—and that it's not the end—is the other half.

WIND

"Wind," or the cardiopulmonary system, is an asset that is mostly what you make of it. It's nice to know you can last when you start tasting that bloody snot. The rib cage is your engine housing. Do not neglect it. Rib injuries are slow to heal. My wife once had to roll me out of bed for three weeks so I could crawl to my feet. However, the worst part about it was working with a very good amateur comedian. Sneezing, laughing, and coughing became dreaded events. The left side does not hold up as well as the right because the lower rib is just connected by cartilage. Having sustained bruises, fractures, and torn cartilage, I suppose the worst rib-cage injury was having the cartilage above my heart compressed. The doctor said that the only way he could fix it permanently would be to shove his hand down my throat and pop my chest out like a ding on a car fender. Instead, he arched my back and made me sound like a giant piece of fried chicken and got me off the table, but it will never be right.

The ability to breathe without opening the mouth is important. This can become a problem if you spar regularly. As much fun as it was to clear my nose in the opponent's direction, I got mighty sick of all the premium chow I ate tasting like nasal meat. Bloody milkshakes are the worst. I tried snorting hot salt water. This was worse than getting hit, but it stopped the bleeding.

BALANCE

Balance is a prerequisite for just about everything. Being short, being female, and having huge feet all help. I never gave the muscular component much thought until attempting to walk again after a back injury. I couldn't walk a straight line to save my life and couldn't get my pants on standing up.

The doctor explained that my interior skeletal muscles had all but wasted off the bone (atrophied). Muscles that I couldn't see, and the gimpy exercises used to develop them, became the focus of my life for months. By sticking with these exercises, mostly interesting ways of standing on one foot, I have since improved on my original balance.

FAT

Fat drags you down, but if you have the frame to hang it on and the will to use it, it will drag your opponent down as well. You are used to it; he isn't. Tall, aggressive fat guys are scary creatures.

As a welterweight boxer in high school I held fat boys in contempt. They were easy on the hands, and when they cried the tears were highly visible rolling over those puffy cheeks! The only drawback about beating fat boys was that they never had a girlfriend hanging around to cry over my handiwork. (An old friend recently reminded me that I had been "one mean dick-head" in adolescence.)

One night I was at a party when the junior varsity heavy-weight wrestler showed up. He went about 5 feet 10 inches and 250 pounds. He was also highly intelligent and inclined to remind me how intelligent I was not.

After some real or imagined slight, I smacked him with an open-handed left hook. His face, lips, breasts, and gut shook like gelatin, but the waves broke at his belt. His legs were thicker than my waist and rock solid. He was also quick on his feet—I didn't even have time to say, "Oh shit."

He crouched, grabbed me around the waist, and heaved me over his shoulder as he twisted (a suplex, I think). I landed flat on my back on a concrete floor, ears ringing. I tried to suck in some air, but he was sitting on my chest, trying to pin my hands. I remembered—from reading *Sea Hunt* novels in special education class—that I would only have two minutes without air before I blacked out.

He tried to pin both my hands, but he didn't like getting hit in the nose—and I was working his face like a speed bag. He couldn't match hand speed with me, so he tried covering with one hand while attempting to pin both my hands with the other. When that failed he went for the hand that was hitting him with both of his and started getting hit on the other side of the face. We played this retarded game of gotcha for so long I began to panic. I was dead. One head butt would have cracked my skull against the floor. Finally, after about a minute, he got up.

What saved me was that he hadn't been hit before. His strength had taken me down, but it was all that fat that had kept me there. No matter what mistake he made, I could never bridge 60,000 Twinkies! We were both so embarrassed that we acted like we were good friends so that everyone else would think we had just been playing around.

STYLE

Style is a consideration regarding the possibility of training injuries. Some arts are more acrobatic or strength oriented than others. If you are built like an apple, the acrobatics of tang soo do may enhance your confidence but will result in needless injuries. If you're a stick, judo might help develop strength and balance but will certainly result in your sustaining more injuries than your stocky teacher.

Most people holding teaching rank will have a body that is compatible with their art. Perhaps the best example can be found by reviewing the photos of wing chun and contemporary jeet kune do sifus. These are trapping arts. The top 10 guys, regardless of race, would be almost indistinguishable without their heads. These men promote their arts as ultimate combat systems. For them, they are probably right. They stand between 5 feet 6 inches and 5 feet 10 inches, and are on the muscular side and built like a hybrid boxer/wrestler.

The problem with this phenomenon in any art is that it leads to ignorance of injury. A stocky sifu who has only experienced injuries in the pursuit of tae kwon do will assume that wing chun is safer. For him it is. But the tall, skinny kid he is trying to convert from long-hand kung fu will probably sustain damaged forearms and hands from trapping with thick-boned initiates. He will also be punched in the chin too much, because of the guard that was developed for shorter men.

A style designed for your body type will limit injuries. Also, a teacher with experience in recovering from injuries will be able minimize your injuries and help you recover from those you suffer. A fighter who has never been hurt is blessed, lucky, or hasn't fought much—probably all of the above. Don't expect some guy with a freakazoid body to take precautions that will minimize your injuries. When you are hurt, don't be surprised to hear a "pain is good" speech. That's his way of saying "welcome to the Stone Age."

An accurate, objective appreciation of your physical assets and deficits and those of an antagonist will enhance your training and the application of your art.

Take a final reality check concerning your body—which is your fighting tool. It takes a huge skill advantage to avoid injury against a larger, determined aggressor. If this determined aggressor is twice your size, or has any skill, you will also need a big psychological advantage if you hope to survive intact.

CHAPTER 7

The Fighter's Mind

"Bedford had plenty of sense but would not apply himself. He thought more of wrestling than his books; he was an athlete."

—JOHN LAWS

What a messy subject. The psychology of the effective fighter, and the use of controlled aggression, is worthy of volumes of academic offerings. What follows is my gut-level contribution to this high-minded discussion.

The fighter's body and mind are analogous to the general's army, complete with transport (legs), supply (blood), arms, and intelligence. The brain is your command and control center housed in the bunker of your skull. Your conscious mind is analogous to the general, your subconscious his staff, your instincts their tactical doctrine. A veteran fighter is his own general and often becomes as dispassionate about injuries during a fight as a general at war taking acceptable losses.

Stupid fighters are slower and less versatile than smart fighters. The reason you will probably not see a good academic study on this subject is that educated people reject the idea of the smart fighter. For evidence they point to uneducated boxers, who have sustained chronic and acute brain damage for decades. Fighters age faster than most athletes because of diminished motor function resulting from head trauma.

Prizefighters acquire brain injuries like soccer players pick up knee injuries. What rational person would suggest that soccer selects for weak-kneed players? In the end, professional-level sports tend to trash the attributes they attract. People who do well dealing with violence—in or out of the ring—must possess keen mental functions appropriate to the circumstances.

Academics—and there are some promoting certain martial arts—accept only their brand of intelligence, although most are physically "illiterate." The successful fighter or athlete is wired for action rather than contemplation. The support system for this functional state of being must include simple answers to the "what ifs" of combat and battle-tested solutions to common hazards.

Sedentary people are rarely able to defend themselves against an aggressive slob, who is also in poor condition, primarily because they have not been prepared to deal with the dynamics of aggression through sports or experience. Part of the problem is a lack of appropriate answers to physical dilemmas. There is, however, more to the mind than intelligence.

EMOTION

"Put my mouthpiece back in. I'm gonna go knock him [Tyson, the ear-biting boxer] out."

—EVANDER HOLYFIELD, June 28, 1997

Fear and anger are opposite reactions to aggression. Both will inhibit intelligent action in the face of danger, and both may be harnessed to deal with aggression. The emotional goal of the survival fighter is identical to that of the combat athlete: sustained, controlled aggression. The behavioral mechanisms used to channel these instinctual responses are courage for dealing with fear and will for dealing with anger.

If you have never dealt with blood-chilling, palm-sweating fear or homicidal anger, or if you have experienced these emotions and remain puzzled, consider the following diagram.

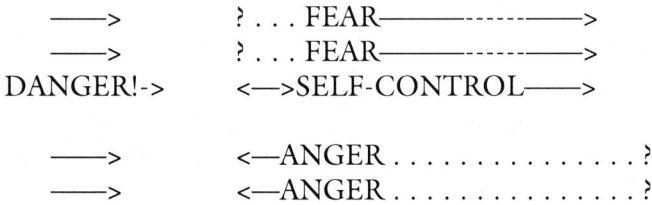

```
——>              ? . . . FEAR——————------——>
——>              ? . . . FEAR——————------——>
DANGER!->        <—>SELF-CONTROL———>

——>              <—ANGER . . . . . . . . . . . . . . ?
——>              <—ANGER . . . . . . . . . . . . . . ?
```

Fear

Fear usually comes first. In a contact situation it is almost always a disastrous reaction. If you have the room and ability to run, fear is your friend. If flight isn't a practical option, you are going to choke on your own adrenalin unless you can manage your fear.

Anger

Anger is what the aggressor usually has going for him. Certain people are wired to channel fear instantly into intense anger. (All the criminal attacker has to do is channel his reasonable fear of doing time into anger for his target.)

Aggressive people are rarely the targets of unprovoked violence and are never targeted by for-profit criminals. A short fuse and the ability to project internal anger generally protect the rare natural fighter from attack. However, he is often a danger to himself, ending up shot, stabbed, or imprisoned.

Self-Control

Self-control is the means by which the fighter suppresses his fear or channels his fear into anger. Uncontrolled fear and anger will clean you out in a hurry and leave you shaking like a leaf. Successful athletes, soldiers, and criminals know how to keep the lid on the rage so they can apply sustained aggression, thereby reserving the ability to go berserk, if necessary. Below are the methods I use to prop up the inner coward and leash the beast within.

Familiarity

Familiarity is a reliable tool. If I'm hit or grabbed by surprise, I instantly relax and become dispassionate. Early on most of my opponents and sparring partners were bigger, badder, or better than I. My work with them was self-defense. Been there, done that. Time to go to work. Under bad circumstances I do not suffer the dread of the unknown that paralyzes the novice or the ego crisis that shocks a dominant trained fighter. I'm a loser. Getting the raw end of a rotten deal puts me in my element and makes me more dangerous.

A more user-friendly way to put familiarity to work is applicable to challenges. When challenged, take emotion out of your end of the equation by ritualizing the encounter and treating it as sport combat. To keep calm while his adrenal gland trashes his cardiopulmonary system, fool yourself by rolling the wrists, cracking the knuckles, shaking out the shoulders, and pacing as if warming up for a workout.

When the action starts, you have a huge edge in endurance. Play for the draw, showing respect—even if he sucks—all the while looking to provide him with an honorable out. The goal is to make friends with him after the fight. This short-circuits the fear-anger process, keeping you out of jail, out of the emergency room, and off a humiliated man's hit list.

Goal Orientation

Goal orientation focuses the mind and suppresses panic. The goal is usually to kill my enemy. I have only used this tool twice with humans and in each case failed, thanks to the incredible efforts they were willing to spend to survive. As soon as it figures out what you are up to—especially if it's a dog—the episode goes from self-defense situation to exhilarating hunt in a hurry. So long as you haven't cornered it, serious opposition is less likely than flight. In fact, I use large dogs to maintain the anger pump, which is primed by that primal fear of the deep-throated growl.

My full-time pedestrian status in a city plagued by pet neglect, drug dealers, and dog fighting, results in regular rottweiler, pit bull, and Doberman pinscher encounters. Just recently, in fact, I was attacked. The initial growl, emanating from behind a car, triggered the fear response. However, being an experienced dog-stomper and having been mauled by a dog as a child, the switch to anger was *almost* instinctive. I controlled the anger by adopting the kill goal. I kicked for the throat but only caught the neck. At this point my self-control became crucial when the fat city-hick owner threatened me. If I had initially let the anger counterresponse take over I would have gone for him too.

The cool focus of the hunter battled the rage deep inside. I had been walking in the middle of the street to avoid sidewalk dog fights, and gelatin man wouldn't let it go. I wanted to work him over. When I got home and found out he had insulted my wife previously, I wanted to kill his dog and feed it to him. These savage urges were, thankfully, not given reign.

Self-Hatred

Self-hatred is my most reliable survival tool. It doesn't take a conscious effort. It just happens. So, I guess, as a tool it leaves something to be desired, like using a malfunctioning amusement park ride for everyday transportation.

If I get caught unaware I will feel fear in a big way. If the aggressor is larger, younger, or fitter than I, that fear will be intensified. When I have hit the bottom of the fear curve—it takes about a second—I get intensely angry at myself for being a wimp, a bone rack, a failure in the ring, a joke on the mat—and for being a 35-year-old stock*boy*! "Why live? Life sucks! My piece-of-junk body is going to pay for all the times it failed me! I hate him for reminding me of my fears, so I'm taking him to hell with me!"

This is followed by growling, very basic techniques, an urge to jump up and down on his head, memory lapse, loss of sensation—which makes me work harder so I can hear the impact I so desperately want to feel—and loud ringing in the ear, which intensifies the insanity.

The episode will be followed by uncontrollable shakes, guilt, embarrassment, and a passive/suicidal state of mind. If I use a weapon, I only get the shakes.

The first sign is usually the ringing in my ears, low and distant at first. Last year, while recovering from a secondary back injury (which figured to cost me my job), I was spotted limping away from the bus by a very good-looking young man. I just know he was a karate guy. He was built like a welterweight boxer, but had strong legs and was handsome. He was showing off for his girlfriend when he tried to pick a fight with me—by comparison, a lame old man.

While he was breaking bad with me, I decided that having this punk kick my ribs in, and then my losing my job for being late, wasn't an option. I had free legal council through the union, and if I was going to lose my house, I might as well reside at the city jail as the *victor.*

As he continued his finger-wagging scolding I relaxed as the ringing in my ears drowned out his voice. He didn't notice as I shifted the grip on my spare jacket in my left hand or slipped my right hand into my rear pants pocket. I wasn't afraid or angry anymore. I was committing suicide and taking him with me. His girl noticed my shift and interceded. She deftly shut him down, and forced a smile at me as her eyes teared up. I heard the traffic again and clicked off. Weird. I walked off before the shakes set in.

Fear Over Fear

Fear over fear is useful for dealing with group attacks, dangerous training, and competition. It is very simple. I do fear pain, but I fear injury more; and I know that flinching from the oncoming pain will make injury more likely. From here the scale progresses. I fear defeat more than injury, death more than defeat, incarceration more than death, and humiliation—loss of property—more than incarceration.

Well beyond the scope of my nasty little world, the ancient martial artist was required to prioritize his deepest fears when he contemplated defending his honor and perhaps his very way of life with cold steel. Looking into how these men faced mortality is worthwhile. There is no shortage of dope fiends willing to kill for 10 minutes with your credit card.

Visualization

Visualization is a type of familiarity tool that develops the nervous part of the reaction process. (When I see myself throwing a left hook, I invariably feel pain—and sometimes spasms—in the muscle that I once tore stopping a man with that same punch.) This exercise will help develop awareness to some extent. It may not make a huge difference. But a little of anything helpful is a big deal when it comes to avoiding concrete burns. The two prerequisites for effective visualizations are as follows:

1. Full-impact, continuous-contact experience
2. Reliable information on real violence, as supplied in the later chapters of this book

You can develop a real-violence scenario "written" frame by frame in your brain. I have been working on a scenario for three years. Of the hundreds of times I have played out the possibilities in my mind, I have only concluded the "action" twice. I will use this scenario as our working model.

1. *Circumstances that you regularly experience should form the basis of the exercise.* For me, it's getting off a bus, in the city, at night with two to four (make it three) hostile young men.
2. *The environment in which you actually operate should serve as your stage.* Mine is always a sidewalk. I select one of the actual bus stops I use in high-crime areas. This gives me eight likely venues for my imaginary encounter.
3. *Your preparedness should be low.* How could that happen to you? In my case we're taking uncharacteristic aggression because of a domestic or work-related hassle. This establishes your state of mind.
4. *Identify the enemy through role assignment, body typing, and character.* The leader is 17, tall, athletic, and arrogant. The hitter is 16, tall, fat, and aggressive. The follower—not even part of it unless I go down or fly into overkill—is 15, short, thin, and afraid.

5. *Supply a catalyst and establish the relative senses of justification.* Both parties will be (a) righteous, (b) conflicted, or (c) wrong, and aware of it. Is your attacker (1) a punk who feels you owe him; (2) a violent alcoholic, who hates sleeping it off in jail; or (3) a guilt-ridden pot-head incapable of sustained focused aggression? What about you? The bloodiest fights are between parties who both feel justified.

   In my scenario I'm asking for trouble with some punks who I figure deserve it, who likewise feel justified when I bump shoulders with their leader and say, "Punk!" (What else am I supposed to say?) This is a potential bloodbath. Fantasy is so cool!

6. *Assign positions.* Are you surrounded, cornered, cut off, or in his face? We're in a nose-to-nose stare-down.

7. *Determine initiative.* I'm overdoing the stare-down and give the hitter an angle.

8. *Visualize the action act by act.* The fat kid pushing is an entire act. He either (a) fails and gives me the initiative, (b) has some success and maintains the initiative, or (c) succeeds in injuring me or worsening my position, giving the others an opportunity to jump in. I figure this kid shoves me twice, and I get hit once by the leader before I pivot off a trap to his elbow.

The possibilities are endless. A scenario built on individual acts advances by the second. Try at least three results for each act before advancing. Below are some tips.

- Never write your responses down.
- Limit your actions to trained or natural responses.
- Use spontaneous situations.
- When you "get set" in a stance or use a technique that requires chambering, as do many kicks, the initiative passes to the enemy.
- Experiment with worst-case results that include serious injuries. It is too easy to be Chuck Norris and skip the rough spots. Being Homer Simpson is far more instructive.

FAMOUS LAST WORDS

"A balanced lifestyle is for people who aren't going anywhere. People who accomplish things are people who are mad and pissed off."

—MAN AT PAY PHONE

Awareness of justification responses, based on knowledge of your antagonists' worldview, is important. The ability to avoid giving away that sense of justification will reduce the intensity of an encounter and the likelihood of a worst-case scenario. To illustrate this point I have selected four brutal incidents from the violence survey, for which I was provided with the dialogue that touched off or intensified the encounter.

Bar in West Baltimore (think South Central Los Angeles) at night

A drunken hippie not satisfied with the promptness of the service said, "What nigger do I have to blow in this joint to get a six pack?"

When he failed to emerge from the bar, his friend entered, watched, and waited as a muscular black man bounced the man's face off the bar for a prolonged period, reckoned as "minutes." The witness retrieved the beer, his hippie friend, and his friend's glasses, in that order.

Street corner in East Baltimore at night

The subject was irritated with a group of young men who failed to respond to his request for directions. Noticing that one was black, he said, "Well, you all can't be too smart if you're partying with niggers."

When the group turned to face him, he said, "Oh, you *are* niggers."

He was knifed.

Bus in West Baltimore during the day

A drunken redneck, who was the only white man on the bus, said to the former convict across the aisle, "What the hell are you looking at, you goddamn dumb nigger?"

Every brother on the bus got in his licks as the drunk was passed to the rear. The finale saw the white boy achieving airborne status as he was launched from the rear of the bus. However, this experiment in redneck aerodynamics ended in disaster when the flannel landing gear failed on contact with the concrete runway.

Bedroom in East Baltimore at night

A man who "preferred combat in 'Nam to this bullshit in the States" left work sick. When he tried to get in bed he noticed a very large man lying next to his wife. He didn't care who his wife was sleeping with, but he wanted to lie down. As they woke, he drew his .45 auto from beneath the mattress and told the man to leave.

His wife's boyfriend replied, "If you don't leave I'm gonna shove that gun up your ass."

In one of those rare cases of true courtroom justice the husband was sentenced to a year of parole and ordered to pay for the boyfriend's knee-replacement surgery.

So, be careful what you say to people, especially racial or ethnic slurs and never insult someone who is armed. In either case, you are insulting a man's core identity. You are also inviting his peers and associates to join in the fun.

THE CONCEPT OF CRAZY

"Well, I think . . . some of the professional duelists, certainly in the 16th and 17th [centuries] clearly [were] psychopaths."
— SIDNEY ANGLO, author of *The Martial Arts of Renaissance Europe*

Among primitive people (including most American city dwellers) insanity is believed to imbue the afflicted with magical powers. Although clinical insanity is a factor in that deranged men are turned loose from institutions daily, it is not the focus of this discussion. The concept of crazy is more relevant in terms of your being selected as a target. It is child's play to avoid the deranged brute as he staggers across the street mumbling to the birds and "shooing" away cars.

The primitive urban youth will regard you as crazy—and not worth a bullet that would liberate you from your obvious living hell of a life—because of the following:

1. You take unreasonable risks, such as dating his sister. In other words, doing stuff that most people would think stupid.
2. You regard physical comfort as a low priority. Walking more than a block is a good example.
3. You exhibit inappropriate emotional responses (e.g., you are cool under stress or agitated under normal circumstances).
4. You have no fashion sense. (I used to remove the tongues from my old sneakers and lace them over my new shoes to keep my feet dry at work. Needless to say, this looked terrible, but it preoccupied many a punk as he gawked wide-eyed at this footwear abomination and avoided me as if I was a leper.)
5. You do not demonstrate or seek a group identity. Number five is important. Members of ethnic or racial minorities, especially males, often have a strong attachment to their group identity. Thanks to the racist proclivities of the dominant group they are also provided with rational reasons for maintaining a stance rooted in blind hatred.

A predator prefers predictable prey. Viewed from the tribal perspective of the illiterate urban criminal, absence of companions (and especially of group association) is crazy. If the subject of their attentions seems vulnerable or is female, he or she will be cut out, like a sick prey animal taken from the fringe of a herd. However, healthy, aware males will be suspected of being armed.

As an example, I was a night-crew supervisor at a city supermarket. My racist Australian boss openly despised me as low-grade white trash, redeemed only by the color of my skin—my only qualification for supervising seven black men, mostly convicted felons. Initially, the crew hated me, viewing me as the errand boy of the mythical "Man." I didn't realize that I had been upgraded from "dumb white boy" to "crazy white man" until the boss hired a white guy. We also had a new brother who had been processed directly from the boss to my assistant (whom the boss liked because he was an athlete, and Australians love ball players). The new white guy and I overheard the new black man and my assistant discussing work in the next aisle.

"If you ain't the boss, who is?" asked the new guy.

"The white man," responded my assistant.

"Which one?"

"The crazy one."

The new black employee came around the corner, walked right by the other white guy without a glance and said, "So you The Man. What up?" The white guy became noticeably uncomfortable and quit.

One of the crew explained that I was considered crazy because I had no friends, did not associate with other white people, was loyal to a man who despised me, and was fair to men who hated me. I was acting against my own self-interest by serving and promoting enemies and not associating with those who might accept me. (The whites on the other shifts and those who cycled through our shift called me *bwana*, "Jungle Jim," and— my favorite—"that dumb white nigger.") According to him and other convicts and street people I have known, these personal characteristics became physically evident.

MARTIAL ARTS MIND-SETS

"A man has to live by a code."

—SAM BASS

Delusion

Delusion is the most common state of mind among practicing martial artists. The need to believe in a style is the primary indication of weak will among "fighters." Like it or not, most of your training options will put you side by side with these wimps. This childish belief in an invincible style is often fostered by egotistical teachers. But in some cases a good teacher feels obligated to let the delusion stand. If you talk to enough teachers, you would be surprised how many do not believe in their students' ability to defend themselves, no matter how skilled they become.

This is due to the fact that those who rise to teaching rank are aggressive—or at least assertive—and that your typical student is more timid than the average person. Face it, most people engage in martial arts training because they doubt their ability to deal with violence. Also, many children who cannot handle contact sports take up karate instead.

There are, however, two sides to the confidence equation. A traditional sensei recently confided to me that his students were wimps. They picked up the techniques, he said, but couldn't execute them under pressure and had no stomach for contact. I responded that this lack of confidence was to be expected from those who are induced to sign up, in part, because karate is promoted as a confidence builder. I also pointed out that the young men whom I train to box usually present the opposite problem. These natural fighters won't pick up technique unless you beat it into them. This stems from their aggressive nature, which, coupled with a successful career as a schoolyard or street corner brawler, imbues them with misplaced confidence.

My advice for men such as this sensei who are truly concerned with developing their students' fighting ability is to find a place in your program for the aggressive young men who would otherwise gravitate to combat sports. This way you can always point across the hall to a reasonable facsimile of what your self-defense students are preparing to face. Each karate school should have at least one combative athlete.

Combativeness

Combative students of the sort we have just used in contrast to the deluded type are generally more capable of defending themselves the day they sign up than the average student is at black-belt rank. They often play contact sports and are mostly ill-served by the mainstream martial arts.

Once a person has reached the age of 15, brain development is set, and the individual can safely engage in head-contact within reasonable limits. Even so, most teachers refuse to initiate their young students into this most personal and pervasive aspect of real violence—something the young ones have a natural urge to understand. The result is that most young men leave the conventional market for home-based video and book training with their peers, even forming their own clubs, which usually dissolve when they hit the legal drinking age. This is a major missed opportunity for the martial arts industry and civil society.

I recently gave boxing lessons to a 47-year-old karateka who had taken karate in the late 1970s. Although he still practiced his forms and did his stretches, he never pursued his art in a formal setting beyond brown belt. When his school had closed he did not look for another because he assumed that all schools—as had his—would only permit black belts to spar full contact. Three years of watching others fight had diminished his interest.

After his first session he was enraged over how poorly three years of attending classes religiously and decades of following up faithfully had prepared him to deal with a fluid striking situation. After his second lesson, he was knocking karate and discounting the value of kicks. (I do neither.) After his third lesson he was ecstatic about the contact mitt training. I literally watched the bitterness wash away with the sweat as he went at the drills with the wild-eyed enthusiasm of a child, finally able to get a taste of the combat training he had instinctively craved as a young man. Watching this man come alive before my eyes convinced me that our culture lacks—even suppresses—important masculine rituals.

Artistic Expression

Artistic expression is a beneficial form of study. However, a certain number of students will retreat into this refuge rather than face reality. Then, again, there are those who practice their art exclusively as such and have no delusions about their chances in a real fight. Such people can be useful training—though not sparring—partners.

Practicality

Practical martial artists often evolve from the other types. The practical survival-minded martial artist is whom this book was written for. For this person, the arts offer a menu of options for countering violence.

THE SUBJECTIVE MIND

"Trust? Trust is the condition necessary for betrayal."

—WALT

I have noticed that the kind of guy who keeps his word despite the inconvenience tends to keep his head in a fight, no matter the hardship. The thing we call courage or heart, and that generals call morale or élan is hard to peg. I suspect it is linked to the expectations we set for ourselves. However you cultivate your fighting spirit, once you have found it, you will recognize those who have it, unless you have become consumed by your own ego—the fate of many a martial artist.

I have one final bit of advice concerning your mind-set: determine whether your fighting spirit is social or antisocial. This concept is best illustrated by a recent discussion with an instructor who specializes in teaching children. I believe he was quite horrified when I informed him how I had taught my 7-year-old son to handle threatening groups.

My boy wanted to know how to handle a bully who was backed by a group. I told him that if the bully would agree to meet him alone, then he should fight fair, as in a match, and that he should not brag about winning. If the bully could not be separated from his supporters and persisted, then he, my son, was obviously the subject of a hunt. I explained group dynamics to him by referring to animal behavior, since he is a big fan of nature films and books. I explained that it was ethical to hunt the hunter and stupid to challenge him.

I directed him to ambush the bully as they sat in class, where the bully would be separated from his crew and off guard, under the supposed protection of the teacher. The preferred means would be a double-eye gouge from behind the seated prey. If possible he should jump up and down on the boy's hands, feet, or face to seriously maim him. If successful, this act would protect him from bullies for years, just as I would protect him from the school authorities who were putting him in danger to begin with.

This is a classic predatory response to threat, advocated by a father who has done better with violence on a predatory (antisocial) level than on a competitive (social) level.

The sensei advocated the heroic strategy of calling out the bully and defeating him in front of the group. I discounted this approach because it would place my boy in the path of a probable group attack. One slip and he's on the ground getting kicked by five kids. I would not put a kid in that position unless he had Jackie Chan's choreographer.

I was, at first, critical of the sensei's judgment. However, on reflection, I realized that he could not possibly arrive at another solution to the problem. He is a large, dominating, gregarious man, a salesman by trade. He has spent his life manipulating the representatives of corporate enterprises. His martial art is steeped in Asian notions of hierarchy and honor, and his training and instruction have been entirely class based. Also, his idea of schoolyard violence was formed in the 1960s, a less predatory era.

He is as social as I am antisocial. Our worldviews have been shaped by vastly different physiques and life experiences. His solution to group threats would probably be as right for him as mine has been for me.

Which one of us do you side with? Such a question put to a prospective teacher may be a prime indicator of compatibility.

RECOMMENDED READING ON FEAR AND AGGRESSION

"Try to work in a casino environment with this t'ai chi attitude and people will eat you alive."

—A CRAPS DEALER

---

1. Pentecost, Don. *Put 'Em Down, Take 'Em Out: Knife Fighting Techniques from Folsom Prison.* Boulder, Colo.: Paladin Press, 1988.
2. De Becker, Gavin. *The Gift of Fear: Survival Signals That Protect Us from Violence.* Boston: Little Brown, 1997.
3. Goleman, Daniel. *Emotional Intelligence.* New York: Bantam, 1995.
4. L' Amour, Louis. *Flint.* New York: Bantam, 1960.

CHAPTER 8

Real-Fighting Ability

"He's big, and he can move. What the hell are you going to do?"

—SENSEI STEVE

Physical self-defense is a question of fighting ability. Developing it gives you an edge—no more. Recognizing it in others will sharpen that edge. Friends experienced in real fighting, who do not bullshit you, offer information for putting your training in context. Martial artists rarely fight. Fighters rarely practice a martial art. Bridging this gap is the essential ingredient in your recipe for surviving violence.

What is a fight? What does it mean to fight? *Webster's College Dictionary* offers 17 definitions, including (2) any contest or *struggle* (my emphasis) and (6) ability, will, or inclination to fight, strive, or resist.

Fighting means preserving our physical autonomy by combating intimidation, deterring threats, and countering full-blown violence. Shutting down a punk through force of will, foiling him with street savvy, and grinding away his acne on the sidewalk are all methods of self-defense.

Your enemies are drawn from the protected juvenile and criminal classes. Thumping punks, like any pleasure, can become a deadly addiction. Defend yourself by more subtle means when possible.

If you ask an experienced fighter how many fights he has had, he may be hard-pressed to give a number. Everyone has a different sense of what a fight is. If asked how many fights I've had, I would say a dozen. Six of these would not be considered fights by certain people. I have also been in an additional dozen or so fight situations—knife pulls, push-downs, etc. Of those, perhaps six would qualify as fights according to another's standard.

There is also your opponent's perspective. Wrestling George Foreman for the last hamburger at a buffet would probably rate as the fight of your life. But for George it would just be another meal.

To most a fight must include blows, throws, and blood. By this measure Rickson Gracie, the hit man for his grappling clan, would never participate in a fight since he relies on the choke. The common conception of a fight actually occupies a very narrow band on the vast scale of human violence. "Fighting" is halfway between name-calling and fire-bombing.

Consider rating violence by intensity, remembering that fight and struggle are the same thing. Rate violence from 0 (avoidance) to 10 (resulted in death). Let's put you in a hypothetical scenario, with three possible outcomes. We will start with a 9, do a 6, and finish with a 3.

SCENARIO: You own a carpet installation business. One of your men shows up drunk for the third time. You are both standing in the living room of a small town house. Your loyal but gutless assistant is standing in the kitchen doorway behind you as you fire the drunk, who responds by drawing his razor knife and directing a backhand cut at your throat.

Option 1: You draw your blade and are the victor of the ensuing bloodbath, primarily because his alcohol-thinned blood pumped out faster than yours! Among your rewards are a lost contract, ruined carpet, increased insurance premiums, criminal charges, and a lawsuit. Congratulations!

Option 2: As he draws, you break his jaw with a reverse punch. All you get out of this is the lawsuit and insurance hassles.

Option 3: You duck the backhand cut. He follows up with a lunging upward slash, which you sidestep, causing him to pitch headlong into the kitchen doorway. You hold him down as your assistant calls 911.

Most martial artists fantasize about #1, recommend #2, and would regard #3 as a missed opportunity for glory.

Now, let's look at a potential 10 that became a 1.

SCENARIO: I was working with Muscles, a short, walleyed, 20-year-old bodybuilder. He wore a tank top, shorts, and very thick glasses. He did little work. His time was devoted to posing in the produce-case mirrors, "grazing" on massive quantities of high-grade chow, dead-lifting loaded pallets of canned goods, and threatening to kick my skinny ass. He challenged me to a fight every night for three weeks. I declined, admitting that I was no match for "His Massiveness." One night he found graffiti in the toilet depicting him being sodomized by his father. He needed a fight, and I was the only other cracker on the shift.

I was standing in the produce prep area—concrete floor, cinderblock walls, steel tables, and hauling equipment—talking to Leroy "Slick," when Muscles strutted in, framed himself in the doorway, and kissed both biceps. Leroy suppressed a sneer, as I hid my grin with a handful of crackers. As I bit into the first cracker Muscles shoved me. I rolled back on my heels as the cracker lodged in my windpipe. He had finally made me mad. He ran such a personality deficit that it had taken him three weeks to tick me off!

Leroy mumbled something about "crackas en tamata soop," as Muscles squared off in his "fighting" stance: legs spread, elbows out, chin high.

I stepped back, coughed up the cracker, and brought up the right fist—making powder out of the saltines. Leroy exclaimed, "Boy, I hope you fighten' betta then yo cussin."

Muscles stepped in, and I faded right. That's when I noticed him tilt his head back and squint through the bottom of his thick glasses. As he waddled forward, Leroy said, "Oh gawd, boy!"

As Muscles began to lean into a swinging right hand, I shot out the left and plucked off his glasses. Leroy began hissing his "Slick" laugh, as Muscles stood frozen in a daze. I put the glasses on the table to our left and returned to work.

Muscles later brought me a letter addressed to my family, apologizing for killing me over a "debt of honor." He asked me to keep it on my body so that his motives would be understood when he went over the edge. I laughed hysterically as he described what a killing machine he was. The laughter broke him, and he began to sob about being deprived of his test of manhood. What a mental case.

The pathetic near-fight could have been tragic. I don't play around with a guy strong enough to break my back. If not for the glasses option, I would have tattooed him. He was walking into a knockout, and there wasn't a soft surface in sight. I doubt that he knew how to fall. He was five punches from a head injury, and I was just as close to being unemployed. A worst-case scenario would have had me doing time for manslaughter. Muscles offered an opportunity to be far more dangerous than I ordinarily am. Declining that opportunity and achieving a low-intensity resolution, rates as my most effective use of fighting ability to date. At his age, I would have gone for the knockout, primarily because I had not yet acquired the poise to employ fine motor skills under stress.

This strikes to the heart of the who-can-beat-whom foolishness that plagues the martial arts. James LaFond at 35 could never beat James LaFond at 16. The kid was stronger, meaner, faster, tougher, etc. However, the kid saw the judge or the doctor as a result of almost every fight opportunity. Based on the fact that I am presented with one to five fight opportunities a week—at least one of which could be construed as self-defense—it is obvious that my youthful fighting ability would have gotten me killed or permanently incarcerated had I not evolved into my current despised state. (Most men I know think I lack self-respect because I shrug off threats and insults.)

Let's look at this rationally. Two fights a week—less Thanksgiving and Easter with Mom—for 20 years add up to 2,000 brawls—400 of which would have been knife fights! The macho men talk tough, but they don't walk where I walk. Even the Brazilian champions with confidential records don't claim more than 400 wins.

Are you going to be your own prizefighter or your own bodyguard? In our complex world effective aggression is best balanced with cool application.

COMBAT STUDIES

"What makes the champions is the ingredient of adapting."

—DAVE BONTEMPO

The ability to consistently adapt to spontaneous fight situations requires the following characteristics:

1. Awareness of hazards
2. Poise under stress
3. A healthy body
4. Familiarity with limitations imposed by surfaces, attire, and obstacles
5. Fighting ability
6. The ability to recognize these traits in an adversary

The remainder of this chapter is dedicated to understanding points four, five, and six.

Critical observation of full-impact, continuous-contact combat sports can enhance your understanding of unarmed combat. Understand that athletes will always "game" the rules to win within the limited context of their sport. Ring and cage combat yield many useful lessons. These sports speak clearly to the primary dilemma facing the survival fighter: going to the floor.

We have already established that it will always be to one party's advantage to grapple and that in a self-defense situation this advantage will likely lie with the attacker. This same dynamic applies to sport combat. In boxing, this results in clinching. In ultimate fighting, the padded cage encourages grappling and discourages striking.

The misreading of ultimate fighting contests has resulted in martial artists—usually ignorant of combat dynamics—crowding submission seminars in the mistaken belief that most fights go to the ground, where they are decided. In a dozen fights I've been to the floor only twice. (See Appendix 3 for frequency of decisive ground fighting.)

Ultimate fighting is an almost perfect simulation of fighting in gravel, on sand, or on grass. The only corrupting factors are that the cage is enclosed, gouging is banned, and the crowd does not kick you when you go down. (Time limits are realistic.) Being only three factors removed from reality is very good for a simulation. The problem with using ultimate fighting as a combat model is that fights in the United States almost never take place on grappling surfaces. When a real fight goes to the ground, hazardous surfaces and booted bystanders tend to bring both fighters to their feet.

Ironically, the best simulation for barroom and sidewalk fighting—the two most likely venues in America—is boxing. By boxing I mean all forms of ring combat, including Pancrase or "shoot fighting." Pancrase is the best legal unarmed combat simulation to date. It is a Japanese sport based on ancient Greek Pankration, which was the first comprehensive martial art and is believed by some scholars to be the ancestor of the Asian striking arts. I recommend viewing all forms of ring combat. Boxing is my focus because it is televised weekly and is an art which I have studied closely.

All combat sports are conducted within a space roughly equal to that which a crowd will grant two combatants: close enough to hear them breathe and see them bleed. Modern Western boxing began as a means of countering wrestling tactics on the cobblestone streets of 18th-century London. It's intermediate stage was a form of 19th-century American bar brawling. It now exists in three sport forms: amateur, pro, and Olympic. As self-defense arts, amateur and Olympic boxing are almost worthless, and pro boxing has many serious deficiencies. One could write a book on modifying boxing for survival applications.

Despite these drawbacks, pro boxing remains a viable combat study for three very good reasons.

1. The opponents attempt to injure one another and, in doing so, risk—and sometimes succumb to—death.
2. It is always to one fighter's advantage to clinch.
3. Being a thoroughly corrupt sport, almost all bouts are completely one-sided. The name fighter's skill advantage is roughly equal to the martial artist's advantage over a drunk or deranged attacker. Because of a relative lack of striking skill, the favored fighter's opponent—like the self-defense student's attacker—will be compelled to clinch repeatedly. Although boxing was once an antidote to wrestling, the

modern boxer is rarely able to avoid or break the clinch. (Each of the classic Muhammad Ali–Joe Frazier bouts would have gone to the floor within seconds if they had been ordinary fights.) The fact is, even the greatest boxers of the modern era would not be able to avoid the takedown of a high school wrestler. There are, at the time that you read this, probably 10 scholastic wrestlers in your state who could defeat boxing's current heavyweight champion of the world in ring combat by submission.

What does this have to do with you? You are probably not a boxer. As one who has trained with professional and amateur boxers, scholastic wrestlers, and high-level martial artists of many styles, I will tell you that boxers are better at avoiding the clinch than are karatekas, kung fu stylists, or even kick-boxers. I will also inform you that only one of every 40 boxers whom I watched in action over a two-year period demonstrated the ability to avoid the clinch of a *less* skilled opponent.

If a man wearing giant mittens can grab and hold your naked, sweating torso, how do you expect to avoid a grab for your flannel shirt?

Watch a boxing match from the following perspective. Pick your man: the full-time professional name fighter. That's you. The part-time local fighter—who delivered beer all week long—is simulating your attacker. He is trying to get close enough to clinch and maul your man. When there is a break, begin counting your man's punches. Stop counting when their torsos or shoulders bump or when they tie up. Three to five punches is the average. Many heavyweight fights never go beyond a two-punch sequence. When a fighter gets off more than five punches consistently, he usually wins, often by knockout. The other factor is the percentage of punches landed. The ESPN geeks will track this for you—30 percent is to be expected; 60 percent typically results in a knockout.

Don't get depressed thinking about a grappling attack. Boxers, although better at avoiding the clinch than karatekas (because they use lateral movement), do not train to avoid it. You can. Examine these mismatches for the missed opportunities and the chance to see that one-in-forty fighters stay out of harm's way. You won't have a referee.

THE ATHLETE

"When the bell rings you find out exactly what you got."

—Mills Lane

Applying, avoiding, stopping, deflecting, or redirecting force is an athletic act. Sorry, but any dynamic physical expression, regardless of the aesthetics and philosophy of an art, is not fundamentally different than being a bully on a playground.

According to my research, self-defense students lacking significant experience with contact sports or violence only succeed in defending themselves 25 percent of the time. These successes were responses to physical harassment, not serious assaults.

By contrast, scholastic ball players prevailed in more than 50 percent of brawls and survival situations. Athletes with self-defense training or experience with violence prevailed in more than 70 percent of encounters. Combat athletes prevailed in more than 95 percent of encounters.

To a certain extent these are not fair comparisons. People who pursue dangerous sports are psychologically and physically better suited for contact than the general population. No matter how she trains, Celine Dion will never be able to fight off Andrew Gollata. Most of us fall somewhere between the 90-pound singer and the 240-pound boxer. So we should, if nothing else, be able to spot the athlete in order to deal with him.

I can spot a swimmer, lineman, wrestler, soccer player, etc., at a glance. Each sport or position on a sport team attracts and selects for an ideal body type. In addition, the activity encourages development in line with the ideal body type, as well as injuries to less suitable physiques. Sports are Darwinian social rituals.

Many body types are dual purpose. Professional quarterbacks and basketball players under 6 feet 4 inches are perfectly designed for punching. Trash sport skaters and cyclists would do well as kick-boxers. Swimmers are well designed for submission grappling. Power lifters are built for control-based grappling, like Greco-Roman wrestling. My pick for the athlete most suited for real fighting is the hockey player.

Sports also develop instincts, balance, coordination, aggressiveness, and tactile sensitivity.

A former roommate of mine, Big Foot, was 6 feet 6 inches and 320 pounds. He walked with an apelike gait: shuffling, knuckles forward, elbows out. He had no martial arts training and had been in only a few fights, most with his 100-pound girlfriend. He had played high school and college football and thus understood aggression, contact, leverage, and momentum.

This knowledge came in handy when Big Foot was jumped on a dock by three guys who averaged 6 feet and 180 pounds. One grabbed each arm, while the tallest attempted to apply a hold from the rear. Big Foot intentionally relaxed and fell back against the cinderblock wall three feet to his rear, cracking the sternum of the tall kid and pulling the other two off balance. He pushed one away and scooped the other up and dunked him in a trash can. He then advanced on the remaining punk with one giant stride and accepted his groveling submission.

As much as this sounds like a Three Stooges skit, keep in mind that Big Foot's ability to react instinctively had been honed on the football field. He had no techniques beyond those available to children on the playground. What he had was pure application. You are better off being able to apply a simple shove than you are knowing 20 strikes, but lacking any experience applying them. Also, this scenario points out the folly of attacking a man who can drink two cases of beer on Saturday and not piss until Sunday.

You don't stand to be in 10 to 20 violent encounters. Even if you live in a city, you are probably looking at one or two opportunities to defend yourself or someone else over a lifetime. If you are unprepared half the time, those one or two chances to apply your fighting skills are 50 percent likely to be disasters. You don't want to live with that. Building on your strengths and working around your weaknesses will take you further than will a quest to become the perfect fighter.

The ability to size up others will permit you to be your own matchmaker in situations that allow discretion. You probably know someone who is good at assessing the likely fighting ability of others. A part of his ability may be related to his knack for sizing up athletes. Perhaps he is a sports fan who has been in, or witnessed, a couple of brawls.

RELIABLE SOURCES

"Bullshitting people is an art not a science . . . and this shit is the paintbrush."

—A STONED POTHEAD

My experience prying relative combat information from witnesses and participants was developed primarily through the collection of more than 320 violent incidents between early 1996 and late 1998. About half of the people I know or work with have had at least one experience. Of those, about 20 have been involved in more than five violent encounters. Of these experienced fighters, about a quarter could be described as habitual or compulsive fighters with fights numbering in the dozens. Two of these individuals have participated in over a hundred fights, almost all alcohol related. As you can see, getting the information was only a matter of time and effort. It is there to be had.

If you intend to teach your art to others for the purpose of self-defense, it is your responsibility to gather and evaluate material on past and current personal violence in your locale. What I have, primarily from Baltimore, may reflect some regional or cultural trends that I have not identified as such. (Any reliable firsthand or eyewitness accounts forwarded through the publisher will be used to update my ongoing survey. See Appendix 3 for format of particulars.)

Women
Women tend to be reliable sources, but they may not be familiar with fighting terminology or concepts. Be patient and ask the same question from various angles. They may need to

demonstrate actions rather than describe them. If you let them hit you, the interview goes much better.

Criminals

Criminals prefer to talk in the third person. Be prepared to converse in "what ifs" and "maybes." Getting too detailed on certain points will be like trying to extract direct testimony from Bill Clinton. These guys are a pain in the ass but are worth the effort.

Potheads

Potheads who smoke a lot tend to lie and twist the truth more than any other group I have interviewed. Get them when they are straight. Don't waste your time while they are smoking. Concentrate on fights they have seen. Don't expect reliable first-person information.

Alcoholics

Alcoholics are sitting on most of the nation's wealth of material in relation to personal violence. They tend to be the most honest group but have big empty spaces between their ears. The quality of their anecdotes are often low concerning details, primarily due to memory loss. What happens to a drunk when he is sober usually burns itself into his brain. Ask for that stuff. What you want from him concerning drunken brawls is the cause, especially the specific trigger, that sparked the incident. This will aid in your avoidance study.

Athletes

Athletes of any kind give very clear accounts unless they were drunk when the violence occurred. They are used to taking in and processing information while in a heated contest. They've got a built-in VCR; just rewind and press play.

Martial Artists

Martial artists are a mixed bag. In large part it depends on which of the above groups they belong to. Here are some prime bullshit indicators.

1. The focus is on what the martial artist did. To judge by his account the other guy just stood there.
2. He never talks about how something felt or sounded. All of the details—like how his pivot sounded so strange when the glass underfoot ground on the asphalt—are absent. In other words, nothing strange, weird, or surprising happened. Unless the guy is a really boring bouncer, it shouldn't sound like a day at the office.
3. He recounts a lengthy prefight oratory, in which he honorably gives ample warning about the doom to befall his hapless foe.
4. He relates how he stopped just before a finishing blow and said something right out of a B movie—and remembers what he said!
5. His actions sound too well choreographed. He lays the whole thing out in perfect sequence and never has to retrace his steps to point out something.
6. Everything that he says is related according to the terms of his art. When a seventh dan tells me, "I grabbed the bastard by the collar and pushed him against the wall," it rings true. If, instead, he says, "I shuffle-stepped to zone 3, reentered for contact-penetration, and struck the carotid artery with a ridge hand," I'm already looking for the door.

Any admission that he used a brawling tactic, as opposed to a technique prescribed by his art, indicates authenticity. Any humor or guilt associated with the incident or memorable details about the location or context are a sign of veracity. Firsthand accounts are the best sources because you get to find out what was going through at least one participant's mind. Combining the fighter's story with other firsthand or eyewitness accounts will help paint a clear picture. The teller usually knows much more than he initially thinks will be of interest or qualifies as substance.

I once transferred to a new work site less than a month after a fight between the most feared member of the crew and the most hated. There were witnesses and two competing claims to victory. As the most feared and most hated member of the union, I was asked to adjudicate the dispute over the fight.

I called for a rematch. But before I could buy a disposable camera, Nasty Nick—de facto boss—pointed out that "those two idiots throw more freight than the other five fuckers here combined." Not wanting to make up for the production shortfall that would follow their suspension after a rematch, I conducted my investigation as if I were a United Nations inspector. The funny thing was that they both felt that they had lost but would only admit it to me.

Mr. Feared was 22, 5 feet 10 inches, 190 pounds, a smoker, and a karateka and an aikidoist. Mr. Hated was 22, 6 feet 2 inches, 180 pounds, athletic, and a jerk. He bragged about leaving his flat-chested wife for someone better endowed. They reconciled only when his wife agreed to breast augmentation.

The two fighters were arguing in front of the store after the shift one morning. Mr. Feared—who is no longer feared—was down curb when he hit Mr. Hated—who is still hated—in the throat with a knifehand. Injured and terrified, Mr. Hated reached over Mr. Feared's head and grabbed the hood to his sweatshirt, which he pulled over Mr. Feared's head and down, while driving three uppercuts to the face. He then spun (athletic guys will pull this stuff out of their hat without thinking) the dazed Mr. Feared and ran *screaming* to his car.

Mr. Feared, demoralized when his lethal weapon merely energized his enemy, threw years of martial arts out the window and roared like some wounded beast as he charged Mr. Hated's car. Mr. Hated had started his car and was attempting to roll up his driver's side window as he began to speed off, cutting off an elderly couple as they walked toward the store front.

At this point Mr. Feared intercepted the moving car, grabbed the now half-open window, as Mr. Hated yelled, "Get away!" and pulled back, shattering the window. As Mr. Feared growled obscenities at the fleeing Mr. Hated, the elderly couple ran for cover.

I declared the spectacle a draw.

Eye-Witness Accounts

Eye-witness accounts offer valuable lessons. I once worked with a fugitive crack dealer from Harlem. He claimed to be a witness to the brawl in which Mike Tyson broke his hand on Mitch Green's face. He gave a colorful account, including an imitation of Mitch staggering into traffic "like a dog hit by a car."

Since I had heard from others that the fight occurred outside a restaurant and this crack dealer said it was in front of a clothing store, I doubted his story. What made me want to believe it was the detail.

The crack dealer's version was that Mike's bodyguards had stopped Mitch. "Then Mitch said somthin' 'bout [Mike's] mamma. Mike ducked under this big dude's arm, took off his drivin' glove, and cracked [him]! Jus like in the rang! But sounded like a bat breakin' off a pitch."

The detail and the sound: I had heard that bat-breaking sound when I broke my hand on a skull. But who goes shopping for clothes at 4:00 A.M.?

Then I read a story in the *New York Post* that referred to Mitch as "the guy Mike Tyson hit in the eye outside a Harlem boutique." It's a small world. In my experience, excepting some potheads and egomaniac martial artists, people only lie about violence in court.

SIZING UP OPPONENTS

"He hits too hard? That's it? All night long you guys have been comparing style, training, experience, ya-ya-ya; and neither one of you would fight him, just because he hits too hard? What's the point?"

—A BEFUDDLED BOXING FAN

The ability to objectively measure yourself against an opponent is of inestimable value. An easy method is point/counterpoint. This method is best illustrated through the words of "The Link" (as in missing link), a savvy man to whom I often turn for advice. In this instance I asked The Link to handicap a fight between Vinny and Stan, both on my crew at work.

Vinny owed money to every man on the crew. I waited for

him after work, and demanded my 10 bucks. He returned to work, borrowed it from someone else, and handed it to me. That night he got into it with Stan, a major creditor. Stan's primary girl (a co-worker) had shamed him into getting his money back by pointing out that "little Jimmy" had. Since I had come close to fighting both of them, she asked me if her man could take Vinny. In turn, I asked The Link.

"Vinny's young. Stan's big. Even there.

"Vinny's strong. Stan's mean. Even there.

"Vinny's Italian. Stan was a marine. Even there.

"Vinny's on crank—now. Stan's pissed. Even there.

"Vinny smokes. Stan's bangin' three broads. Even there.

"Short fight. But Stan's gotta go home with that psycho-bitch, and she hates Vinny. Stan inside a minute. But if it goes to the floor, it's a draw."

Vinny brought in his old lady's check book the next night.

Later that month Stick (35, 6 feet 4 inches, 165 pounds, former boxer) challenged me to a bare-knuckle fight just for the hell of it. The crew assumed I'd win, so I wasn't under pressure to fight. I thought I'd have trouble, so I consulted The Link.

He said, "Three to two, you. But one of you bone-racks'll cut. He's underweight in the USA—messes with whores. Your call."

I called it off.

You probably don't work with a bunch of thugs, but the occupation of your opponent is a major factor. In fact, in the case of a criminal, you will meet while he is working. At bars, stop lights, and parking lots, you may have a moment to size up your adversary. Learn to read people. Something as simple as a belt—what kind and what's on it—can be a reliable indicator.

Real for-profit criminals do not wear oversized beltless pants or new unlaced athletic shoes. That look is an attempt to project a criminal image. This person is a wannabe who equates fear with respect. Jailers relieve inmates of belts and shoelaces to prevent suicide and strangulations. Modern life has become so symbolic that even the aspiring criminal retreats into imagery. Imagine one of these punks trying to hump a TV set down a fire escape with his pants around his knees! The beltless criminal is as absurd a figure as the martial arts movie star.

Unskilled laborers tend to be mean, fast, weak in the grapple, and very likely to use an improvised weapon. Skilled laborers tend to be larger and slower and have stronger hands. Sales and management people are the only other demographic group inclined toward violence. Many managers and salesmen in retail and construction are former scholastic athletes. Tall aggressive men tend to dominate these fields and may be assumed to have some basic skills.

For sizing up an adversary I use The Link's system. What jumps out at you? Is he big? Well, are you faster? Is he mean? Do you have the guts to tough it out? How much sizing up can you do? You may only get to "he's big, but I'm fast." That's a start.

Visual Cues for Identifying a Fighter

- Athletic build
- Light, balanced stride in a small man
- Easy, swinging stride in a big man
- Absence of strutting or posing
- Economy of motion
- Signs of awareness
- Relaxed or focused demeanor under pressure

The sizing up never stops. When the struggle begins, no matter how brief, you will find out things about him and you that you might not have known. Things may appear to happen in slow motion. For me, it's like having a split brain. I'm fighting on instinct but still trying to think and adjust.

In my view smart fighting is training to break contact instinctively, so I have a moment to choose a course of action based on what I just learned about the enemy. Once I set course, I rely on instinct and training until there's another chance to readjust.

Real people offer reliable insights regarding real violence.

Mobility

"Fixed expectations make for fixed responses."
— JOHN KEEGAN, *A History of Warfare*

In other words . . .

"A 120-pound martial arts master ain't worth a fuck when yer layin' on 'im."
— BIG "BOSS" JOHN, on cage combat

Mobility, in regard to combat, is more than movement. It is more than speed, more than grace, more than timing. It is your ability—relative to your opponent's—to adapt to and control your interactions. This advantage may be attained and maintained in different ways.

A muay Thai fighter might damage his opponent's leg. A jujutsu stylist may use leverage. A wing chun man will literally stick to his man. A boxer may dominate the action by setting and then breaking the rhythm.

The value of mobility should not be underestimated. Envision a dangerous fighter. Glue his feet to the floor. How dangerous is he now? Mobility is the supreme athletic expression. It is also the basis for smart fighting. The great captains of history were those who led armies to victory with mobile tactics, usually against enemies relying on static defenses and a predictable lineal offense. Did you know that "ring generalship" is one of the points by which boxers are judged?

Failure to develop superior mobility will result in your going to the floor precisely when your opponent decides that floor fighting is to his advantage.

STANCE

A balanced stance is the basis for effective footwork. Every art—if properly taught—promotes a balanced stance as a first principle. The many fighting postures vary less than one would expect. Although each style favors unique hand and foot positions, most are wedded to a simple modified crouch. To be effective, your stance—or posture is more appropriate—must meet the following criteria:

1. Requires no forethought
2. Needs no preparation
3. Permits movement in any direction

Setup Stance

The setup stance is the basis for most effective sucker punching. It is a compromise between being in your fighting stance and just standing there. You are not squared off, but have one foot back. At least one of your hands should be above the belt line and between you and the antagonist. You should be doing something distracting with your hands: pointing, waving your target off, brushing lint off your sleeves, etc. Simply talking with your hands is a great gambit. The most important aspect of the setup stance is a balanced foot position that will prevent you from rolling back over your heels if you are hit or shoved.

Horse Stance

The horse stance is the novice training posture in many Asian arts. It is also the reference stance for many forms. Its only practical purpose is to strengthen the legs. There is, however, a great deal of ritual significance attached to it. It is therefore integral to the "art," and you may have to put up with it if you are learning from a traditionalist. However comfortable you become in your horse stance, keep in mind that it is not a fighting stance.

FOOTWORK

Effective footwork is the basis for effective fighting. Most arts teach specific patterns and angles of approach. Some prescribe intricate approaches based on a compass of six or more directions. Whatever the style, the objective is the same: continuous balanced movement, providing you with superior angles for attack and defense. Despite the various attempts to systematize footwork, the most effective fighters are usually self-taught in this area. The way you move is very personal. Being a basic expression, it is not easily separated from your mind-set. If you are not a natural athlete you should be taught to move according to some plan. But, eventually, you should cut loose and do your own thing—provided you continue to test it against credible opposition.

As an example, there was a workplace dispute between my short, skinny self and Big Rich, 6 feet 4 inches and 250 pounds. I challenged him to meet me on the parking lot—and waited three days in a row. He declined, weathering the humiliation heaped on him by our simian co-workers. They were a hierarchy of brutes. Big Rich was the beta male, second only to the 320-pound alpha male—a redneck bar fighter of some ill repute. Later that week Big Rich was standing on a milk crate, rocking a stack of seven cases of six 48-ounce jars of applesauce on a rack three feet over his head. (This was standard practice with these guys.) He rocked until it buckled and then slapped the second case, causing the third case to slide out, which he caught with his right hand as he steadied the rocking pile with his left. The top case slid off the stack—five feet above his head—and fell, slamming into his forehead with a grinding chink of glass. He grabbed that case with his left hand, read the label, and threw it back on the rack. I walked up to him laughing and shaking my hand. He gave me quizzical look and asked, "What the hell is your problem?"

"I'm sure glad we didn't fight."

"Fight? I figured you was gonna shank me."

"So you think you could beat me?"

"What beat'n? I'd juss grab yer lille ass n' break ye."

After some discussion he admitted that he wasn't much with the fists, and I agreed that I'd get crushed if he grabbed me. What would decide the fight would be his ability—or lack thereof—to grab me. So, being one evolutionary step ahead of our knuckle-dragging co-workers but not yet castrated, we decided on a manly contest for three rounds at a go-go bar.

We met at a vandalized basketball court. The only rule I demanded was "no break'n lille guys." We also agreed that there would be no punching of big guys. Rich added one clause: "no ninja-boy shit" (kicks, back flips, levitation, etc.). The contest would begin on his call and end when he grabbed me or quit.

I wish I could describe this encounter in detail. But they don't call me "Two Brew" for nothing—and I won. The alcohol erased the fine points, which had not been etched deeply into my scarred brain tissue by a sense of peril. While he was complaining about my expensive taste in beer, I admitted to cheating. Asphalt is a winner for me. On grass it would have been a pure gamble. On sand or gravel, I would have been meat inside of 10 seconds.

I got to field-test my improved footwork, make a great friend, get drunk for nothing—and was hit with nothing harder than a breast implant! People normally disinclined to train are often willing to engage in such drills.

Consider the following points as you develop mobility.

- Subtlety and economy of motion are the prime virtues.
- Keep it simple.
- Feel the ground; don't just stand on it.
- Planting both feet flat on the ground reduces mobility.
- Rising on the balls of both feet reduces stability.
- When doing forms, never break into a fixed position to punctuate a technique. In this respect, kung fu is superior to karate, because the forms are more fluid.
- Maintain ground contact with both feet whenever possible. Kicking is always risky; though in combat risks are sometimes necessary.

- To deal with an opponent who leads with the opposite hand, a southpaw, you need to keep your lead foot to the outside of his lead foot. Old-timers call that putting him in "the angle," or bringing him into your "wheelhouse."
- Practice from the right and left stances, as well as shifting stances. You cannot count on a chance to "get set." This ability is rarely developed among competitive fighters—and is suicidal for most boxers—since they are always permitted to get set. Some notable exceptions, such as Marvin Hagler, developed the ability to shift stances to maintain momentum and "make knockouts happen." However, most boxers only learn to switch and shift to cover injured body parts.

SPINS AND JUMPS

Spins and jumps look nice and are impressive in a purely athletic sense. However, they offer only the illusion of mobility. Spinning actually fixes your torso position for the duration of the technique, begging for the takedown. It also involves turning your back on the enemy. It is almost never a viable tactic against a skilled or aggressive enemy.

Jumping does have two practical combat applications. It is the preferred method for evading the shin-cut of a swordsman. I also recommend jumping on the back of an armed criminal's head when he is sprawled face-first in the gutter.

RHYTHM

Rhythm is to a fight what the heartbeat is to the body. Even a one-sided beating will, if allowed to continue, develop a rhythm. A sequence of action and reaction results in the opponents synchronizing on some level. In reality this often amounts to a drum solo on someone's skull. But in a stand-up fight a true rhythm does develop.

Boxing has been called "the broken dance" with good reason. Your first objective is to lead, thus establishing a rhythm that your opponent will be inclined to follow. (This is the least coercive aspect of fighting; it requires consent—however misinformed.) Your second objective is to break the rhythm, gaining a beat on your opponent. The fighter setting the rhythm is naturally better positioned to break it, though this is not always the case.

Some fighters specialize in countering, stealing a beat from the opponent. This is the kind of thing that is so much fun about sparring, but it can become a problem. Sparring, especially between practitioners of the same art, becomes a chess match. This is why sparring must be done with skilled fighters of many styles and untrained fighters of various dispositions. Just sparring with members of your school will limit your ability to adapt to the abbreviated chaos of combat.

Sparring with a practitioner of your art is like playing a song that you co-wrote and rehearsed. Fighting some thug in an alley is like being thrown a sheet of new music in the middle of a concert. You have to be able to read the music. Just move without slipping and you're halfway there.

CHAPTER 10

Durability

"No, this isn't a tumor. It's a rib. It's not where it's supposed to be, but at least it's something you're supposed to have. Really, you ought to take up sex. It's just as much fun and isn't so dangerous."

—DOCTOR WAYNE

Durability is the first attribute tested when the action begins with your head bouncing off a bar. The will to train and struggle will keep you alive. The ability to maintain your physical presence in the face of defeat is invaluable. It has brought me to this desk instead of a support group. But dependence on this attribute is the ugly way to fly. There is some ape out there with a bigger heart or harder head. Tenacity is the last-ditch resort, not your first option.

In a fight the knowledge that you can take so much or last so long is the only guarantee you will have. You can't know for sure what you will face until you face it. But if you have developed and tested your body and mind sufficiently, you won't be facing an enemy from within. This is the true advantage of the trained and tested fighter. The typical bully knows what he can and cannot do. What he doesn't know is how durable he is. The question mark is on him.

The trained fighter is like a coach who knows each of his players. The untrained fighter is like a coach who brings the same key player to every game but has a poorly prepared team. He is a gambler who needs to stack the odds. I have a great shovel hook, but if I'm attacked from a certain angle I won't be able to deploy it. But whatever the nature or angle of attack, I know what I can take and how long I can give. Knowing this alone about yourself will relax you, enhancing your durability.

PAIN TOLERANCE

Pain tolerance is not such a big deal. The first blow may hurt, and you will certainly become well acquainted with pain during the days following a serious fight. But your internal pharmacy will supply the necessary painkillers on the spot. The only exception is joint manipulations, which always hurt. I would rather be knifed than have Steven Segal making a wish with my elbow.

A RELAXED STATE OF MIND AND BODY

A relaxed state of mind and body is the core asset of the durable fighter. This is dependent on your mind-set. The relaxed fighter is like a drunk in a car wreck. The rare natural athlete has this going for him. We mortals need to develop it through training. This is an ability with a high achievement ceiling and explains why older—supposedly worn-out—fighters often outlast younger fighters. One mechanical challenge is the ability to tense one body part, such as the fist, while relaxing another, such as the shoulder. Another is beating the sphincter reflex at the urinal.

CONDITIONING

Conditioning is there for the taking. If you have not been in a real fight and would like to rate your effective limit, determine your maximum effective gym performance. How long can you hit the bag continuously? How long can you wrestle without shelling up or going to the guard? Next, determine how upset you would be in a given situation. Rate your state of mind from 1 (whistling while you work) to 10 (paralyzing anxiety attack). Divide your gym performance by your anxiety level. This will give you an idea how long you could fight all out, with blood sugar, cholesterol, lactic acid, adrenalin, and other substances crowding your constricted blood vessels.

Contrast the following pair I have trained.

Paul is lean and fit with a perfect heart rate, blood pressure, etc. He is good for three minutes of unbroken heavy-bag work. However, in a real fight situation his anxiety level will shoot right to 9. Paul would be worth 20 seconds of sustained effort before he hits his first stamina wall, which calls for a major gut check.

Mike is overweight, drinks, smokes, doesn't train, and could go for about 30 seconds on the bag before he started coughing up brown gunk. However, our biker friend here delights in brawling. His father made him and his brothers fight before they were allowed to eat. In a real situation against the smaller Paul, his anxiety level would peak at 1, and the sheer joy of pounding some "pretty boy" might even enhance his stamina, as he relaxed under familiar circumstances. The result is that at 30 seconds of sustained effective aggression, Mike's got 50 percent more gas in his tank than Paul.

Now, Paul's chance is to work on contact conditioning to the point were he automatically relaxes when subjected to aggression. If he were half as cool as Mike, he would have the stamina to delay decisive contact until the big man tired.

TECHNIQUE

Technique, or the proper use of leverage as opposed to muscling or forcing an action, is the immediate objective of the trained fighter. Most techniques—especially punching and throwing—rely almost exclusively on leverage. The muscle simply adds weight and provides stability for proper execution. Though the speed and impact of techniques might be great, they are not intense on a muscular level. If you are straining or pushing, you are doing it wrong. Good techniques burn low levels of abundant fatty acids, while direct intense demands on muscle burn the limited supply of sugar (glycogen) stored in the muscle. This results in muscle failure. It also explains why boxers tire more quickly in the clinch than while moving and punching, which would appear to be more tiring.

BREATHING

Effective breathing will maximize your performance. When you are anxious, you may hyperventilate (overloading the blood with oxygen) or simply hold your breath. When you are tired, you may be inclined to breath through an open mouth, inviting a broken jaw. Teachers argue about the correct method. All you need to do is grit your teeth and suck in air without swallowing bloody chunks of snot. When exhaling with a stroke, blow the air out through the side of your mouth or through the nose if it's bleeding.

THE SIGHT OF BLOOD

Effective bleeding is very useful. When blood flows, behavior tends to alter on both sides. Among wimps, this signals the beginning of the end. Among maniacs, the sight of blood feeds a need for more. To the trained and tested fighter, it's just spray paint. A timid reaction to first blood will hearten your opponent. An angry reaction or intensified effort may demoralize him. However, this is a predictable reaction that will not shock him.

The best reaction to bloodshed (especially yours) is no reaction. I have fought tough men—in and out of the gym—who quit after cutting me. Nothing freaks the civilized mind like a cold indifference to the very stuff of life.[1]

When I was 16 I picked a fight with two big country boys. (I suppose a Rhodes scholarship was never really in the cards for me.) Mike was 17, 6 feet tall, and 180 pounds. John was 18, 5 feet 10 inches, and 165 pounds. They were decent guys, so we actually scheduled the fights.

Mike was first. I cut him under the eye with a rising jab—a

sucker punch. He charged in with an uppercut, which I partially blocked with my right hand. That shot sprained my thumb, knocked the wind out of me, and bruised my sternum. I broke contact, desperately trying to push out my diaphragm and make a fist. When he touched his face and saw the blood on his hand, he quit.

John and I met at the same spot the next day. He was afraid after what Mike had told him, but channeled his fear into anger. While I was forcing my right fist closed with my left hand and turning to face him, he sucker punched me with an overhand right. It landed over the eye, and the impact knocked my knees together, bruising the right quad attachment. His face was lost in a shower of white sparks: concussion number one.

I lunged in for a left hook and ran into a right, which made my feet rattle on the asphalt. The sparks were whiter this time: concussion number two.

I tried to jab, but he stepped back and landed another right. That's when I realized how long his arms were. His big bony fist bounced off my brow in another shower of sparks: concussion number three.

I backed him up a low grassy bank, walking into two plunging right hands that landed over my eye with a dull wooden thud, as opposed to the serious crack of the three previous punches. The familiar thudding sound relaxed me.

When we got to level ground I began to work the jab with some success. On the grass we couldn't get much traction for hard punching. It would have been to his advantage to wrestle, but he kept backing up. He tried to land a punch but let it fall off before contact.

He began to wave me off, telling me to stop. I shoved him and growled, "Wimp!"

He ate a jab when he said, "Look at yourself."

"I can't."

"Touch your face and look at your hand."

My hand was covered with bright blood. As I flung the blood at his feet and put up my fists, he said, "Look man, I'm 18. I could go to jail for this!"

"I don't care!"

"I'm not fighting back."

I relented.

This was a courageous guy with plenty of justification. A gutless criminal has far less resolve.

How you handle bloodshed in the context of a fight puts you on one side of a sharp divide. If your nose bleeds, clear it in his direction. When sizing up punks and thugs at work, I note their response to accidental cuts and rat kills. Once I was approached by the new refuse conveyance engineer. He had just threatened the boss with the fact that "he wa' a boxa."

The boss pointed to me and said, "He's a boxer. Box him."

He leaned on my freight and said, "I hea you is a boxa?"

"Used to be."

"Any good?"

"No."

"Wanna box me?"

"Sure."

"When?"

"After work on the dock."

"But I's goood."

"How good?"

"Real goood!"

"Well, if you're that good you better wear an apron."

"Why?"

"That's a nice sweater, and I tend to cut."

He went slack-jawed and bug-eyed and walked away. We pass on the street occasionally. He never gets close enough to spit.

The most important aspect of durability is a durable ego. The night before I wrote the last paragraph of this book, three coked-up drunks in an oversized working pickup were circling me as I walked through the inner city. They were screaming that I was a gay whore, attempting to goad me into a fight. I didn't get mad. I didn't even stop to consider the fact that they would be heavily armed with bricks and 2 x 4s and that I would be the one arrested.

This is learned behavior. I didn't even give them the finger.

In the past I would have thrown a rock. However, I can't say that my calm prevailed. A young lady driving behind them pulled over and offered me a ride as they circled the hotel for another pass. There are some good people in this town.

NOTES

1. Reay Tannahill, *Flesh and Blood: A History of the Cannibal Complex* (New York: Dorset, 1988) pp. 1–2, 56–74, 75–91.

CHAPTER 11

Defense

"Every matter requires prior knowledge."

—Du Mu

Defense is the aspect of fighting most dependent on other attributes. If you can't move, endure, or retaliate, your defense will be undone or overwhelmed. Effective defense is the province of the advanced fighter. Novice and untrained fighters rarely demonstrate a sound or effective defense. It is probably the last thing you will get really good at. You must be an able attacker to truly appreciate the defender's dilemma. Learning how to defend against a punch from someone who doesn't know punching is not wise. The ability to do something is integral to countering that something.

The ability to defend without the need to attack is a relative luxury in combat. However, in our litigious, mothering society, developing a good passive defense is wise. Your defense isn't the last thing between you and defeat, but it is the last thing between you and the fighter's unhappy bedfellows: pain, injury, and a cellmate.

This brings us back to durability—my old specialty. An important side effect of superior defensive ability is relaxation, which translates into more durability. An absence of anxiety frees the fighter to concentrate on offense. This phenomenon is best illustrated by ultimate fighting matches.

Inside the padded cage grappling is the threat. This results in master hitters not being able to score a single effective blow because they are anxious about the grapple, against which they have no defense. Ironically, it is master wrestlers with marginal punching ability who throw the majority of effective blows because they are operating from a stable physical and psychological base. Since they are confident in their grappling defense, they successfully attack pro kick-boxers with amateur-level punches.

A sound defense against an open-ended attack is best developed through cross training. This chapter examines the range of defensive measures available to the fighter. It is not a study of techniques (specific moves) but of basic concepts. Understanding the principles and theories that form the core of contemporary martial arts doctrine is important. Your teacher will be working from reference points that you must understand to extract the martial from the art he is teaching.

Another reason for a comprehensive study of martial arts methods is to enhance your ability to identify and defend against trained fighters. I have pointed out—and will continue to point out—that your attackers and challengers are likely to be untrained fighters with experience. However, do not discount the possibility of facing a trained fighter, especially if you are a young man.

The type of trained fighter you face in the United States depends primarily on your location. Rural areas produce a high ratio of wrestlers, who typically have two to ten years of experience. Wrestlers inclined to initiate violence double as binge-drinking football players.

Urban areas produce most of the boxers in our happy nation. Boxers inclined to initiate violence have little competition experience or are psychopaths, like millionaire celebrity criminal Mike Tyson. Most boxers have more than a passing acquaintance with ordinary violence and are more likely to carry a handgun than other types of trained fighters. Suburban areas produce most of the United States' Asian-style martial artists. They typically have six months to three years of training, with little full-impact, continuous-contact sparring or competition experience. They rarely have any real fighting experience, except in urban areas, where they are more likely to carry a blade.

Although these are practitioners of "self-defense" arts, most worship the deity known as Bruce Lee, who promoted the now widely held belief that prevailing in combat against a skilled opponent is the martial artist's loftiest goal. Consequently, many fantasize about administering justifiable beatings to practitioners of other arts or in winning challenge bouts. The ads and trailers for home training courses often play to the criminal, punk mentality, and some teachers—cut from the tough-guy mold—encourage students to promote their style through challenge matches.

Recently a Baltimore-based instructor was directed by his California-based master to beat up the master's New York-based rival. On a more mundane level, teachers rarely cover avoidance in the course of promoting their fighting styles. This results in students who are unprepared to avoid conflict, reverse escalations, or even separate threats from insults.

DEFENSIVE FIGHTING METHODS

"Ninety-five percent of everything is crap."

—THEODORE STURGEON

Each of the methods discussed below is followed by a key attribute. Every attribute is important to every fighting method. The listed attribute is the one I consider to be most important to the performance of that skill. There is some overlap. For example, under Punching in Chapter 12 I list poise—as in a relaxed state of confidence—as the key attribute. But I list timing as the essential element of lead-hand striking. There is no contradiction. They all apply, and singling out one is only intended as a training aid for the beginner.

Break-Falling or Tumbling

Break-falling or tumbling is the basic defensive skill of grapplers, contact ball players, and paratroopers who wish to avoid broken bones. It doesn't come into play often in survival fights, but is absolutely necessary for practicing takedowns and throws. If you have no experience in any of the three pursuits listed at the beginning of this subsection, you must learn how to fall. Although an attack on you will not likely result in a fall, hitting the concrete is the leading cause of serious injury and death in unarmed brawls.

Relaxation is the key attribute.

Holding

Holding is the simplest defense against any attack—and it's effective. Pro boxers don't spend half their career holding for nothing. Having said that, it's generally a terrible idea in a self-defense situation. Holding can aptly be described as the best self-defense for the attacker.

To hold effectively, you must be strong and any third parties must be on your side. How many lone runts are going to jump you while you are with friends? Practical applications for holding include the following:

1. Holding a drunk or criminal until the other bouncers or cops are on the scene
2. Holding some bone-rack who is beating the snot out of you
3. Keeping your wife from throwing the rest of the dishes
4. Seducing amazons

Even powerfully built women have weak wrists. I once worked on a rape scenario with a woman who was stronger than I and had previously knocked out full-grown men. I overpowered her with a simple wrist grab and squeeze—as I guarded my groin with my knee.

Strength is the key attribute.

Splaying

Splaying is the basic defensive tactic of wrestlers. Properly done, a two-handed splay against a double-leg takedown can dislocate your attacker's shoulders. I call it goon surfing.

You can splay with one or two hands. At least one hand must be pressed against the opponent's head or trunk. (Splaying off the arm will get you sucked into the grapple.) I prefer to keep the rear hand back for slapping down his grab while I push off his head or lead shoulder. The key is to stay on your toes and make him carry your weight. This is pure defense. He is the only thing keeping you from falling on your face. Effective striking is not an option from this position. The splay is a stalling maneuver. Push-ups of all kinds are good preparation for splaying. It doesn't take much wind but will burn out your muscles. If you drop your knees inside for support any good wrestler will put you on your back.

Timing is the key attribute.

(**NOTE**: The best demonstration of the following two methods was given by Roberto Duran in his 1983 "mugging" of the heroic Davvy Moore. With the assistance of a partisan crowd and referee, Duran gave a clinic on these tactics, as well as thumbing, butting, lacing, and taunting his way to a brutal career-ruining stoppage of the younger Moore. This fight is available on tape.)

Spinning

Spinning is a semi-foul in boxing. It can be learned on the dance floor as easily as in the ring. It is not deliberately taught by many trainers; rather, it is something you pick up. (I am no expert, having been spun more often than I have spun.) When your opponent crowds you against a wall or into a corner, you duck a committed blow, palm his hip, and pivot out, placing him in the corner. It is easier said than done and is probably the most delicate defensive maneuver.

Balance is the key attribute.

Rolling

Rolling with the punches has become a metaphor for handling adversity, and reasonably so. Few situations are more adverse than receiving head blows. This is a simple skill that may be developed through light-contact training, though it must be tested under full-contact conditions. It is a boxing skill, but is understood by all good teachers of the Asian arts.

With the chin tucked, jaw stabilized, knees bent, and body relaxed, you simply give along the line of attack. As the blow reaches maximum extension, you either roll to an advantageous angle or follow the blow back and counter along the same line of attack.

Relaxation is the key attribute.

(**NOTE**: The following methods are described in reference to attacking and defending with the hands but are also applicable to attacks and defenses with the legs.)

Guarding

Guarding is the primary means of defense in boxing. The concept originated with the use of the shield, a small version of which was in common use in the British Isles when modern Western boxing was in its infancy. You simply hang a relaxed limb in front of a critical target. The advantage of the passive guard is that the guarding hand remains cocked or chambered to strike a blow. Much of a boxer's training is devoted to developing a habitual guard. Speed bag work and one-arm bag work with a glove tucked under the guarding arm are two common conditioning methods.

Muscle conditioning is the key attribute.

Blocking

Active blocking, as opposed to passive guarding, is the standard defense in karate. Most styles teach upward, inward, outward, and downward blocks. Karate blocks are probably based on staff fighting. Effective blocks should use the hard outside of the arm to damage the tender inside of the attacker's arm. Properly done, it is devastating to the arm—and ego—of the attacker.

(**NOTE**: My preliminary study of 19th-century bare-knuckle boxing suggests that prizefighters used arm blocks. Many fights resulted in broken arms and hands even though the fighters aimed for soft tissue and light facial bones. I have a photograph of heavyweight Joe Jeannette demonstrating a rising block in 1908. With the adoption of heavy gloves, boxers abandoned aggressive blocking in favor of the parry. Blocking with a bare fist is not an option.)

Here are the pros and cons of blocking.

Pros
1. Injures attacker
2. Discourages attacker

Cons
1. Is reactive, requiring you to be faster than the attacker
2. Exposes targets covered by your guard
3. Sets you up for the feint
4. Telegraphs your counter (when you have that block out there only one of your guns is cocked)
5. Sets you up for the grapple
6. Does not arrest your opponent's momentum unless he is a wimp

These drawbacks can all be minimized by years of training. The basic problem with active blocking is that it is reactive and therefore slower than the action it is intended to counter. This requires you to be more skilled than your opponent.

Active blocks are highly effective against unskilled fighters who prefer to punch. Conversely, they are suicidal against a skilled versatile fighter—especially one who can feint or throw. All karatekas who take up kick-boxing abandon the traditional blocks as obsolete. Perhaps the traditional masters only intended blocking as an intermediate step in the lifelong pursuit of their art or as a mediation on or preparation for weapon fighting.

The key attribute is timing.

Parrying

Parrying is usually done with the rear hand. It consists of a slap or brush that deflects the blow down or out, maintaining the passive guard on your inside line. It is based on European fencing and is an integral facet of the boxer's defense. Parrying is easy to learn, tactically conservative, and expends little energy. The drawback to parrying with the bare hand is the risk of injury to the thumb—a most important part of the fighter's anatomy.

The key attribute is timing.

Trapping

Trapping is like parrying with Velcro. It is a Chinese method known as "sticky hands" or "sticky feet," which is perfected on a "wooden dummy." It is a mainstay of Cantonese gung fu and is probably based on knife versus sword combat. Trapping styles appear to be countermeasures to neutralize hard styles of fighting. Trapping is very effective against lineal striking attacks and in a crowded or darkened setting. The advantage of trapping is that it is something you can continue to do into old age—I call it infighting for the frail.

There are two drawbacks to trapping.

1. Trapping is grabbing without grasping; therefore, all trapping techniques take place within grappling range. In cage combat gung fu people really get "bitch-slapped" by the wrestlers.
2. When trapping is your primary method of defense, it inevitably becomes the reference point for your strikes. Hitting exclusively off the trap is doctrine for some. Many wing chun people practice blindfolded. This results in very poor eye-hand coordination at long range. Put one of these guys in front of a double-ended ball and you won't have to turn the fan on. If you are a gung fu artist you should work on the speed bag.

The key attribute is sensitivity.

Slipping or Dodging

"I'll take a guy off the street and he'll throw punches, but he won't avoid many."
—Tony Atlas

Slipping or dodging is pure defense against the straight punch to the head that gives your offense an edge. Your weapons are not employed for defense. They remain cocked. The objective is to make the puncher miss—at or near full extension—by as little as possible. This sets him up for the counter. Slipping is a high-maintenance skill that ironically slips away with age.

The key attribute is timing.

Bobbing or Ducking

Bobbing or ducking against the hook, swing, or cut to the head, takes less skill than slipping and sets your man up for an even bigger counter—but there are two major drawbacks.

1. Weaving (bending at the waist) under two consecutive swings will usually bring you into the clinch. Of course, if he's knocking pieces of meat off your face, that's not necessarily a bad thing.
2. Just a few good bobs will take the spring out of a pair of unconditioned legs. At that point you become a stationary target.

The key attribute is muscular conditioning.

Intercepting or Stop-Hitting

Intercepting or stop-hitting is the claymore mine of unarmed fighting. This is the art of hitting the hitter, representing that point where the lines between defense and offense blur. This is technically an offensive weapon deployed from within an integrated defensive framework. In other words, you really have to know how to fight to pull this off with any consistency. This is the only way a runt like me is going to knock out a coked-up linebacker. A good stop-hit derives at least half its impact from the forward momentum of the target. Aikido throws are actually the manipulative equivalent of this percussive method. (It beats me how throwing a guy on the sidewalk is more civilized than hitting him yourself.)

Throwing

Throwing—or at least the methods that rely on the passive redirection of an attacker's force, such as in aikido[1]—is regarded as purely defensive.[2] Throwing, more so than any other unarmed fighting method, was an ancient battlefield tactic. (Having fought in competitive Medieval-style battles with wooden swords, I assure you that if you have lost your weapon you'd better run, grab something, or grab somebody. And once you have grabbed him, there is no sense in being nice about it. Kicking and punching are pure suicide.)

Technically, helping your attacker's back find the pavement at velocity is weapon use. So, in my opinion, throwing is at least half-offensive in nature. That's a recommendation.

The key attribute is balance.

NOTES

1. A. Westbrook and O. Ratti, *Aikido and the Dynamic Sphere: An Illustrated Introduction* (Tokyo: Tuttle, 1970).
2. Koichi Tohei, *Ki in Daily Life* (Tokyo: Japan Publications, 1978).

12

Offense

"It is a correct maxim that a good offense is the best defense."

—BRUCE LEE

The prospect of retaliation is the primary concern of the sane attacker. Developed sufficiently, your ability to injure, maim, or kill will render his concerns irrelevant. More important, the ability to deliver a crippling preemptive strike or counterattack is necessary for dealing with the majority of attackers who are deranged, drunk, or drugged.

The concepts and methods discussed under mobility, durability, and defense reflect a general consensus among fighters. Thus far I haven't trod on much sacred ground—excepting the slaughter of the sacred cow, blocking. Discussing methods of offense can be, well, offensive. This is where the martial arts differ most. It is also the seat of the ego.

If you doubt that a good offense is your best defense, note the dizzying array of attacks. Despite the claims to being total mind-body disciplines, most martial arts stress offense. This is where you must begin to pick and choose.

(**NOTE**: If my statements about the primacy of the offense seem to contradict my earlier advice that is because they do. Defense sucks, and avoidance is degrading. I'd much rather rub out every punk who threatens me, but until all those bleeding-heart baby boomers are on life support or playing euthanasia bingo, I'll have to put up with laws that sanction the actions of my criminal enemies and penalize my efforts to walk safely among scum. I study defense of legal necessity. When it comes to small brains, big balls, and bare knuckles, aggression is king.)

I am not suggesting you develop your own art. Bastardizing another's art will do. You will probably find one or two arts particularly appealing. My intent is to supply the beginner with a basis for understanding his options and to present the veteran with information on methods he is yet to explore.

I'm pointing out the shortcuts not to demean the artist, but to serve those disinclined to devote their life or livelihood to esoterica.

THE NUTS AND BOLTS OF AGGRESSION

"The toughest fighter to fight is a stupid fighter. When you feint him, he doesn't even know you're doing it."

—BENNY LEONARD

Punching

Punching is a mainstay of many styles. The fist imitates the handheld rock. How you make a fist is as important as how you use it. Chinese styles feature bizarre and dangerous fist configurations. The most effective fist sits on a locked wrist and is tightly closed with the thumb folded beneath the first two fingers. A properly made fist places a dense weight at the end of the arm.

There are two competing theories as to how the fist should be used. Most arts promote the two-knuckle landing. Wing chun and jeet kune do stress the three-knuckle landing. Both methods are intended to avoid placing all the stress of impact on the middle knuckle. If you break this one, your power-punching days are over. I have used both methods and have injured my hands with each.

Three-Knuckle Punch

The three-knuckle punch is intended to spread the force of impact out over three knuckles instead of two.[1] This method feels right if you don't hit too hard. (Most wing chun and jeet kune do stylists do not hit hard.) The shoulder is not deployed, because the punch is not corkscrewed. The three-knuckle landing is also intended to avoid striking with the fingers when a punch is delivered above the thrower's shoulder.

The fallacy of this method is threefold.[2]

1. The ring and small finger are not anchored to the wrist and are smaller. When you attempt to strike with three knuckles there is no guarantee of success. There is a chance that only the large knuckle will strike. Most likely you will hit with the two small knuckles—*crunch.*
2. The force of a three-knuckle blow is angular, across the grain of the bones, and more likely to cause stress fractures.
3. The thumb and large fingers are the precision side of the hand, with the large metacarpal joints being anchored to the stable portion of the wrist. Striking with the other side of the hand will naturally be less accurate and transfer less force to the target.

Two-Knuckle Punch

The two-knuckle punch, although superior, is not perfect. Trauma to the middle knuckle and thumb is common. Also, there is no guarantee that you will even strike with those knuckles. If your target moves 2 inches at the last instant you could sustain a nasty break.

I once lost a shoving match with a short weight lifter. When he went for a double-leg takedown I panicked (this guy could lift cars) and hit him on the point of the skull—not the crown, but right at the hairline—with a cross. We heard a loud crack, like the sound of a breaking ball bat.

He stepped back and said, "God, are we done?"

I couldn't talk. I was in extreme pain—afraid to look at my hand. I held it against my hip and tried to say, "Yeah, okay," but it came out "yrrrgh."

He quit. The two small knuckles were a half inch from my wrist, piled up in a mass of broken bone and swelling tissue. At church, two days after the cast came off, a tiny, 90-year-old nun turned to shake my hand. I casually extended my atrophied right hand to accept the modern excuse for a handshake. She gave me a good old-fashioned coal-miner's greeting that brought me to my knees with a groan. She was as horrified as I was embarrassed. So much for heroics.

Aside from this little problem, the biggest problem with the two-knuckle landing—which requires you to depress the wrist if you do not turn over the punch—concerns hitting with the fingers. If you try to punch a flat surface, such as a forehead, that is higher than your shoulder, you will strike with the fingers. This really hurts. The solution is to hit the chin with the two big knuckles, which leaves your fingers hanging safely beneath the bone. Other head-hunting tactics include getting up on your toes to punch down and rolling the fist back to the outside (like an upper cut) when striking to the nose and eyes. Perhaps this explains the knuckles-out posture of bare-knuckle-era fighters.

Two other disadvantages are that (1) the wrist below the thumb is liable to be sprained when you dig a hook to the body so hard that it sinks in and (2) locking out the arm when you explode into the target risks hyperextension if you miss. It also begs for an arm lock if you miss against a trained grappler.

The real advantage to bare-knuckle punching is the ability to tear open your opponent's face. Strictly speaking such wounds are not cuts. If you suffer a skin tear to the hand it will be between your knuckles or as the result of hitting teeth. Do not do upper cuts to the mouth. Low-end criminals are incubators for hepatitis and AIDS.

I once watched a co-worker clean his knuckles after relieving two would-be muggers of their front teeth. His knuckles were decorated with jagged punctures, furrows, and flaps of lifted skin. He was lucky not to contract an infection or damage a tendon.

If your opponent's mouth is open, hit the jaw. If his mouth is closed, turn the punch over on his upper lip—just aim for the nose. His lips will protect your knuckles and be torn by his teeth. Most punks don't like the taste of their own blood. Hitting with the fingers isn't so bad if the punch lands on the mouth. I have done this with some success.

Poise is the key attribute.

Open-Hand Strikes

Open-hand strikes, including the slap, have less range than punches, except for the finger jab. The Asian arts feature a wide variety of effective target strikes.

Focus is the key attribute.

Lead-Hand Striking

Lead-hand striking ability is a must for effective adaptable fighting. Untrained fighters *never* possess this quality. It takes work to develop and maintain. However, it is one of the few effective tools for avoiding the clinch and requires little strength.

Steve, a big barfighter, stopped at a bar for a six-pack. On the way in he bumped shoulders with a small guy. When he tried to leave, this little guy wouldn't let him past. Steve didn't want a fight, but what the hell. He took a swing and got cracked. Every time he made a move the guy stuck him. A mutual friend broke it up before he got hurt. His opponent was a boxer.

The untrained fighter rarely understands the mechanics of lead-hand striking. In a real fight it offers big dividends at little risk with minimal energy expenditure. Steve didn't realize he had been getting jabbed until I explained it to him, based on the account he had given me.

Timing is the key attribute.

Rear-Hand Striking

Rear-hand striking offers bone-breaking power and is necessary for combinations. The downside is that the bones broken may be in your hand. It also fixes your position. This is an effective antigrappling tactic only if you are substantially faster than your enemy.

Timing is the key attribute.

Inside Striking

Inside striking (that is, using blows that begin from inside the opponent's guard or below his line of sight) is an excellent finishing tool. The elbow is the most effective weapon from this range and is your most durable striking tool. The brush and drag of boxing (both fouls), muay Thai slashes, and the various strikes of karate are all devastating. The most accurate blows are the rising fist of karate and the uppercut of boxing.

The danger of inside striking is that it places you within wrestling range and tends to fix your position. Inside strikes must confirm or establish your momentum to minimize grappling. If you are stronger or more aggressive than the opponent, these blows may serve as your entry to grappling range. An exception is the shovel hook of boxing, which is deployed at the outside margin of this range from a pivot that permits an outside shift.

Aggressiveness is the key attribute.

Outside Strikes

Outside strikes are swinging or chopping attacks that, ideally, begin from outside the target's field of vision. These are common to Chinese and Western arts and are rare among Japanese, Okinawan, and Korean arts. A chopping pivot is the skilled fighter's version of the untrained fighter's reaching swing.

Strikes that arc around the opponent's line of sight are especially effective in real fights, when stress-induced tunnel vision is the norm. It is also easier to put leverage on an arcing blow. Straight punches require more timing and coordination. The hook is the dominant knockout blow of boxing, and the ridgehand is considered one of the deadliest karate strikes.

The drawbacks of outside strikes are these:

1. Causes high energy expenditure
2. Requires a longer path to target
3. Exposes the thrower's target zones
4. Encourages grappling

Point four explains why so many fights between untrained punchers go to the floor, particularly when women fight women. Aggressiveness is the key attribute.

Circular Striking
Circular striking is a Chinese method by which blows circle vertically along a linear path. These "rolling" punches are done in combination from close range. This fluid attack is an effective tool for establishing and maintaining momentum. Rolling punches lack power but are effective after shoulder fatigue has taken the steam out of your straight punches. This is an excellent method for chaining inside strikes.

Timing is the key attribute.

Combination Striking
Combination striking, or chaining, uses momentum to increase the effect of successive blows. It is the most reliable method for ending a fight through striking.

Aggressiveness is the key attribute.

One-Punch Knockout
The one-punch knockout usually requires the cooperation of your opponent. It is important to train with and talk to knock-out artists and their victims.

Timing is the key attribute.

Kicking
Kicking and the martial arts are firmly linked in the popular mind. If I could kick I would; back and hip injuries have deprived me of the option. Self-defense teachers are divided over

the value of kicks. Most of those on both sides of this debate miss some important points. Before pointing out the pros and cons let's look at the objective evidence.

Of the 320 violent incidents I have studied, 14 featured effective kicks, all of which were decisive. Six involved kick-boxers. Seven involved self-defense students or teachers. One involved an untrained mugging victim. Twelve were single techniques, which break down as follows:

- 5 side kicks, one causing death
- 3 back-leg round kicks by smaller opponents
- 2 front kicks by larger opponents
- 1 back kick
- 1 knee to forehead

One incident involved a kick-boxer using the whole arsenal on some hapless punks. Another saw a woman lying on her back and kicking at a mugger until he ran off. Overall, half of the kicks resulted in knockouts.

Pros of Kicking

1. Begins below an opponent's visual field
2. Adds two more weapons to your arsenal
3. Uses the shoe or boot as a weapon
4. Permits you to attack the leg and hip
5. Provides a marginal increase in striking range

Cons of Kicking

1. Compromises balance
2. Exposes the groin
3. Expends a lot of energy
4. Fixes your position
5. Represents an inefficient energy transfer to targets above the kicker's hip. (Most teachers discourage kicking above the opponent's waist. This is backward. If he's short enough, kick him in the throat. In fact, the real-life mountain man,

Jeremiah Johnson, who stood over 6 feet, was fond of kicking his shorter Crow Indian enemies in the chest. He also ate their hearts.)

6. Increases your legal liability, since current case law is based on the stomping of fallen defenders.[3]

A real survival situation will rarely permit you to get set for a kick. Self-defense experts discourage kicking because they rely on kick-boxing as a combat model. Look, if the guy is a skilled fighter who understands the mechanics of kicking—especially above the waist—kicking is probably suicidal. The front thrust-kick and back-leg round kick are the only kicks that are safe to use against a kick-boxer. Nine of ten kicks in kick-boxing matches are back-leg round kicks. The side kick is virtually extinct in the ring, but remains the most effective self-defense kick. The reason is simple. To kick effectively, there must be a broad skill disparity between you and your target. When you compete against skilled opposition, fast low-commitment kicks are at a premium.

Balance is the key attribute.

Sweeping, Tripping, and Heeling

Sweeping, tripping, and heeling are tactics as old as combat. Many teachers blow this off, but it is the best way to attack with the legs. Sweeping was almost certainly the aspect of weapon combat on which kicking is based. Pick up at least one application.

The key attribute is balance.

Counterpunching

Counterpunching, or the ability to make an opponent pay for hitting or missing, is the cornerstone of any practical, strike-based self-defense doctrine. The very nature of an unprovoked attack deprives you of the initiative. Countering transfers the momentum to you. It is the best example of offense being a better survival tactic than defense. Unfortunately, most Asian martial arts discourage countering through sparring restrictions that arrest the attacker's momentum, giving the defender no opportunity to counter a successful attack.

Poise is the key attribute.

Feints

Feints, or fakes, are deceptive moves intended to open an opponent's guard or draw him into an interception or counter. Feints are an important tool for dealing with trained fighters. They are less useful in brawls, where a drunk or deranged enemy may not even notice their use.

Poise is the key attribute.

Simultaneous Strikes

Simultaneous strikes are exclusive to the Asian arts. Do you remember how Batman would knock out two bad guys at the same time? Well, teachers of wing chun and kenpo seriously advocate such tactics. True masters require only one leg to stand on while they kick and hit three attackers, advancing from different directions at exactly the same time! I know this to be true because I have seen demonstrations and photos of these men in action, and not once did a bad guy have a POW! sign held over his head.

The key attribute is delusion.

Vital-Point Striking

Vital-point striking can be divided into practical and esoteric knockout methods. The drawback of both is that they require striking a specific portion of an evasive target.

The practical approach is to attack the organs—such as the brain, kidneys, lungs, liver, and testes—to debilitate the enemy.

The esoteric approach is called dim-mak, which appears to be related to acupuncture or acupressure in that the body's ki (life force) is affected. Ki supposedly flows through the body along unseen meridians. I don't know whether dim-mak is effective, but I do have some information on acupuncture.

According to the three latest studies, the positive effects of acupuncture appear to be a combination of the placebo effect (the patient's belief in its efficacy) and the release of endorphins caused by the pinprick.[4] Apparently no two practitioners located the same meridian at the same location on the same patient. There is no scientific evidence that the meridians actually exist.

The key attribute is focus.

Pushing and Shoving

Pushing and shoving are underrated tactics. To my knowledge only t'ai chi and sumo prescribe pushing methods. Nevertheless, boxers gain great advantage from the push, and many brawls begin with a shove. There are few tools better suited for gaining the momentum.

Size is the key attribute, though aggression and balance are of almost equal value.

Slamming and Stomping

Slamming and stomping technically constitute weapon use. Whether you are kicking a car door shut on your opponent's face or mashing him between the heel of your boot and the bar floor, you are filling your evolutionary role as a tool-using predator. None of this passes for art but is about as martial as it gets. More important, this will be your fate if your art fails you against an experienced untrained fighter.

The key attribute is aggression.

Butting

Butting with the point of the skull against the light structures of the face is the most brutal strike. Butting with the shoulder—another tactic that is used a lot but never taught—is a great momentum tool and clinch breaker. These skills are easily learned and are among the few shared by trained and untrained fighters. That fact alone begs for the study of their application.

Aggression is the key attribute.

Upright Grappling

Upright grappling ability is probably the most important self-defense tool there is. Breaking a clinch—or arm—can keep you off the ground. Reversing a hold without going to the ground, or putting the enemy there without going there yourself, could end things quickly without much mess and with minimal legal hassles. Instruction should be scenario-based. This is not something to do half-assed. In my opinion military sambo, judo, and Greco-Roman wrestling are the best options.

The key attribute is balance.

Floor or Ground Fighting

Floor or ground fighting is fine if you don't mind rolling around on cracked pavement, crumbling asphalt, bottle caps, broken glass, wrought iron, concrete curbs, and hypodermic needles. It doesn't matter how good you are on the mat when his buddies start to kick and pile on. Most fights that go to the ground result in onlookers or accomplices lending a shoe, a hand, or—ouch—a boot.

As a child I was often attacked by a single person, only to be ganged up on after hitting the ground. If five people threaten you, assume that one will fight you, another will jump you from behind, and the remaining three will only act if you are put down or immobilized.

The pack mentality that is sparked when a combatant goes to the ground is amplified if you are the wrong color. A huge friend of mine was sitting alone in a biker bar, when a large black guy showed up and picked a fight with him. (I think we are looking at a nominee for the Darwin Award for artfully removing one's self from the gene pool.) My redneck pal went out back with the guy and beat him into the ground. When he turned to go inside, he noticed that five to ten bikers had lined up behind him. They took turns kicking and stomping the prone idiot. The last thing he saw when he looked over his shoulder was a 200-pound biker, wearing biker boots of course, jump-stomping on the man's stomach, causing a bloody stream of vomit to erupt from his mouth. He finished his beer and left in disgust.

Take your lady to the ground. Let him go there alone.

Strength is the key attribute.

Small-Joint Manipulation

Small-joint manipulation is sports medicine jargon for breaking fingers and is one of only two ways to deal with a large trained wrestler who grabs you.

The key attribute is poise. (Fine motor skills are hard to perform under stress.)

NOTE: To avoid gouges and small-joint manipulations a wrestler must pin both arms or pin one and control his opponent from that side. Remember, he can rip pieces off you too.

Biting and Gouging

Biting and gouging, which include thumbing the eye and fishhooking the mouth, are maiming tactics. Most people lack the will to actually tear into their fellowman, even if he is bent on killing them.

Thumbing is the simplest method. It is so natural you can do it accidentally more often than you can land a right to the chin on purpose. Keep your hands high when you get grabbed. Whenever your opponent's head is below or inside your guard your hands will naturally go to the side of his head. If you push away, the thumbs will naturally press against his forehead or face as your shoulders deploy. They tend to slide into the eye socket. A little bad intent and you've got a good gouge going.

If you expect your opponent to clinch, jab for the eyes from a distance. This is very hard to score with. But if he figures out what you're up to he will think twice about sticking his neck out for the takedown.

The key attribute is aggression.

NOTES

1. Ned Beaumont, *Championship Streetfighting: Boxing as a Martial Art*, (Boulder: Paladin Press, 1997), pp. 35–41.
2. Joseph Estwanik, M.D., *Sports Medicine for the Combat Arts* (Charlotte, N.C.: Boxergenics Press, 1996), pp. 54–56
3. Carl Brown, *The Law and Martial Arts* (Santa Clarita, Calif.: Ohara Publications, 1998), pp. 34–36.
4. "The Dr. Dean Edell Show."

13

Training Forms, Ranges, and Drills

"You fight the way you train."

—SIFU JIM

Boys have an instinctive attraction to weapons. My brother and I were among the few boys in the small town we lived in when I was 16 who did not own a firearm, so we each improvised some type of hand weapon. Though not rational, perhaps, this was certainly predictable.

Since I spent every possible moment alone in the woods, I decided to make myself a real weapon. Four feet of 1/4-inch-thick steel, a hacksaw, a sledge, gloves, an open coal fire, and a file—and I had a crude broadsword. I based my training on a video of a Japanese master performing a draw and diagonal neck cut. I eventually wore out my wood and sheet-metal dummy and put the weapon away, having discovered the greater joy of sex.

Two years later—as I was arranging some sex over the phone—I heard the crash and groan of my 80-pound brother being bounced repeatedly off our bathroom door by Hug, my 230-pound friend, thus ending an argument over my brother's choice of music. I stepped into the game room and told Hug to stop. He was flushed purple, eyes bulging, mouth drooling expanding bubbles of saliva. He looked at me with a dazed expression and continued to pound my brother. I knew I couldn't hit hard enough on tile to end things quickly, and I wasn't about to wrestle with 230 pounds of pissed-off redneck in front of a picture window. I decided that brandishing a weapon was the solution. I went to my room and grabbed the thing that felt most natural in my hands—the old 7-pound sword.

When I returned to the game room armed, Hug's left hand held my brother by the throat, dangling him a foot off the ground, as Hug pounded right hooks to my brother's body. I told Hug to leave. He ignored me until he noticed the sword. Then he laughed and dropped my brother. He advanced confidently and told me to put down the sword. That's when I realized I had made a mistake.

I didn't want to use the thing, and I couldn't let this nutcase have it. What to do? Hug made that decision for me. We were three steps apart. My back was to a wall. When he took the first step I hefted the sword to guard, otherwise I would have lost the option to use it. When he took the second step I had to strike or wrestle him for it.

This guy was my friend. I really liked him, but he had gone crazy. Ideally, I would have cut the thigh or used the flat of the blade. I was under the kind of pressure that demands action and denies contemplation. If you think, you freeze. When you freeze, it's over. What you're left with is instinct and training (self-encrypted instinct).

I was trained to cut diagonally to the opponent's neck, and that's what I did. Luckily Hug managed an outward block. (That had to hurt.) Hitting his arm felt like hitting a car tire with a stick. The blade seemed to bounce off his forearm, but it got stuck. I depressed my wrist and it popped out with a little drag and a lot of surprisingly dark blood that made a sickening *krrplapp* sound as it hit the paneled wall.

Hug grabbed his forearm and growled, "I'll be back," and walked out. (Hug was a man ahead of his time; this was before Arnold Schwarzenegger uttered these famous lines in *The Terminator*.) I thought Hug wasn't really hurt and figured he'd be back with his deer rifle, so I headed for the woods. My father, on his way home from work, found Hug bleeding to death on the side of the road and took him to the hospital. The sword had cut through the ulna and crushed the radius, bounced off the radius, and got caught on the ulna on the way out. Hug's forearm was almost as thick as his neck. If he hadn't blocked that cut he would have died.

After that, and the legal ordeal that followed, I never again tried to bullshit myself into thinking I would select the most appropriate action when confronted with real violence. What my boxing and wrestling coaches had said about "fighting the way you train" was more true than I could have imagined. I had practiced a sequence of techniques intended to deal with a medieval ambush by a fatalistic swordsman intent on bringing an enemy head back to his *daimyo* for a "viewing," not to deal with a heavy-metal-hating Pentecostal committed to turning my brother into tomato sauce.

Your skills are your tools for countering violence that is imminent or in progress. Preselecting appropriate tools and having them at the ready are what training is all about.

If you don't train yourself to react instinctively with a technique, don't think that you will ever use it in a real fight.

Training to deal for survival requires developing instinctive reactions that have the widest possible range of practical applications. If you only train to do five things you will do those five things better than if you also had to devote training time to doing five other things. Keeping your arsenal uncluttered is a sound principle. Selecting versatile weapons is another good policy. Finally, an examination of your own inherent tendencies, mind-set, and body type, as well as of relevant risk factors and likely antagonists, should determine your choice of tools.

FORMS, KATA, OR *HYUNGS*

"Kata can get you in a lot of trouble. I've seen it."

—KICK-BOXER

Forms, kata, or *hyungs* are prearranged sequences of techniques that form the basic curriculum of most Asian fighting arts. A shorin-ryu teacher described the 21 kata of his art as "the encyclopedia of shorin-ryu." Precise performance of forms are a requisite for belt advancement. A specific form may be required for each belt rank. A few arts feature a basic, an intermediate, and an advanced form that focuses on preparation rather than performance. Many modern martial artists see forms as simple litmus tests or dance formats. They are that and more.

Forms are the most apparent legacy of the secret knowledge ethos of the Asian arts. The memorization of sequential techniques points to a tradition of oral transmission of knowledge common to secret societies and religious orders. The original masters were not illiterate peasant boys, but men of intellect and standing. They could have committed their knowledge to writing had they wished.

Forms are intricate to the Asian practice of withholding crucial knowledge and applications from the beginner to ensure a stable hierarchy. If you know the techniques and sequences of the fourth form, you hold a qualitative and quantitative advantage over a classmate who has only advanced to the third form. Ironically, traditional karate training techniques are reminiscent of 19th-century European military drills.

Teaching students to fight according to identical patterns ensures technical symmetry, encouraging the pursuit of technical mastery and the emergence of intricate sparring strategies. This elevates the art to the status of a pastime worthy of a warrior, just as chess was a game worthy of kings. Forms do for the traditionalist what rules do for the athlete: they intensify the test of skill by channeling effort along a predetermined path. Like sporting restrictions, this encourages habits that are dangerous in regard to survival fighting.

The advancement of students according to forms mastery naturally develops a pool of teaching assistants. In some cases, the student who has recently mastered an intermediate form is better qualified to teach that form than the master, who tends to practice advanced forms and spend most of his teaching time on novice forms.

Although practicing prearranged fighting sequences inhibits the ability to deal with violence, mastering such fighting forms helps bridge the gap between action and meditation. In terms of artistic development this is a plus. Properly executed forms are often beautiful. Fighting is usually quite ugly.

Let me be clear: in regard to your preparation for real violence, forms are not only useless, they are also dangerous. You are wiring up for inappropriate actions, laying the groundwork for failure. Using forms as the basis for survival fighting or simply allowing forms practice to monopolize your training time is the surest way to clutter your arsenal. Being obsessed about your forms mastery in preparation for real fighting is akin to a general fussing over the parade ground etiquette on the eve of war.

On the other hand, I know successful pro fighters and real fighters who still practice their forms out of a nostalgic longing for the 1970s. They have relegated kata to the meditative status it deserves and have managed to keep their arsenal uncluttered. Prioritize.

FIGHTING RANGES

"In a fight, if you lose your wind you lose everything, and the main times in which a person loses [his] wind is when [he goes] from one range to another."

—Paul Vunak

Many fighting arts, especially combat-oriented arts, attempt to express range relationships according to a system. In my mind there are only two ranges: where I want to be and where I don't want to be.

All range systems have their merits and fall into two general categories: relative systems and zone systems.

Relative systems are expressed in general terms like the "inside" and "outside" of boxing, or the long, intermediate, and close ranges of blade arts; or in relation to the contact postures (such as up and down) in wrestling. Such relative range categories usually represent a consensus of opinion or simply training shorthand rather than a systematic effort to establish a fighting doctrine. The idea is to develop a feel for your relative position in a fluid situation, supported by an abbreviated reference.

Zone systems tend to be the basis for fighting doctrine. These systems usually separate the field of action into four decreasing ranges, based on the types of weapons effective at those ranges. These range categories generally reflect an egocentric mind-set concerned with the potential for offensive action.

The popular art of kenpo and the French art of savate each recognize four distinct ranges. Jeet kune do, the premier U.S. combat art, is heavily dependent on its four-point range system. Each range is named for the type of unarmed combat dominant at that range: kicking, punching, trapping, and grappling. Current doctrine stresses the importance of trapping range.

Zone range systems can serve as very useful blueprints for competition and combat, so long as the "ranges" are recognized as the blurred, overlapping abstractions that they are.

Why four ranges? Adopt the following training aid and you will find the answer at your feet. If you have a heavy bag or punching ball suspended over the concrete floor of your garage or basement, get a tape measure and some sidewalk chalk. (Being big on decor, I used permanent black marker.) Draw a 1-foot circle beneath the bag. Trace a second circle 1 foot beyond this, then a third and a fourth and a fifth. Number the circles 0 through 4 from the inside out. Use these to check your range before and after various techniques. Eventually you won't have to look. You will know how far you are from the target.

You might be shocked by the proximity of your lead foot to the target. Notice the overlap when the bag swings. Work the target with various blunt weapons. Notice how much 12 inches means and how easily the range is closed, how naked you feel unarmed at 4 feet, how tough timing is at 3 feet, how quickly things change at 2 feet, and how crowded they get at 1. Above all, don't forget that everything you launch brings some portion of your anatomy to ground zero: precisely where the fat, beer-swilling slobs of your macho martial art fantasies want you to be.

SELF-DEFENSE DRILLS

"That tradition just doesn't cut it any more."

—SIFU GABRIEL

A training partner and focus mitts will help put your hitting techniques into context. I suggest designing your own self-defense scenarios based on the information on untrained fighters contained in Chapter 15. Whether you are working on grappling or striking I suggest you do the following:

1. Start only 25 percent of your sequences from an on-guard position. Few real encounters begin with the defender in a fighting stance.
2. Begin 25 percent of your scenarios defending from a setup stance. Your setup stance is the transitional point between your fighting stance and simply standing there. To find your setup stance start in a natural standing position, step back with one foot, and place your open hands in a half-ready position. You may appear to be shrugging, calming your antagonist, warning him back, fidgeting, or even brushing off your sleeves. What is important is that he see that you are not armed with a weapon or fist. This points to the value of open-hand techniques and closing the fist on impact.

   I prefer, and recommend, starting a fight from a setup stance. If an attacker thinks you are a trained fighter, he might immediately escalate to weapons or group tactics.
3. Another 25 percent of your drills should begin with the defender in an off-guard position: alert but off balance or unprepared.
4. The remaining 25 percent of your drills should begin on impact, with the defender being grabbed, tapped, pushed, or smacked from a blind angle.

Think about all of your potential attackers—stereotypical or real people—whom you could actually imagine attacking you. How many would attack you while you were waiting in your cat stance? Not many. How many would attack you while you were warning them off? Maybe a couple. How many would blast you as you edged by them in a doorway? A couple more. Now, how many would jump you while you were reading the paper? Most of them, right? Every one but the ones with the balls to fight you outright.

An effective non- to light-contact training method is the sensible use of focus mitts. The mitt holder is the "feeder" and, therefore, the more important player. Below are a series of exercises, that, if done in progression, can be used to train your own coach. The coach should be at least half your body weight and no fewer than 6 inches shorter than you. Grab your lady, find a good surface, and tell her she's in charge for a half hour.

Mitt Drills

1. Focusing means working single skills from many angles. The mitt holder alternately displays one, two, or no targets while moving. Movement is key. Work slowly, developing a feel for holding the mitts at proper striking angles. Do not hit for power. When power is generated it should be due to timing.
2. Targeting combinations can be done as soon as the holder gets a feel for your angles of attack. Spend one round working on basic one-two combinations. A second round should focus on a single three- or four-punch combination.
3. Countering is the most important boxing skill in relation to true self-preservation. Spend one round slipping, ducking, and parrying tapping blows thrown by the holder. Do not block or trap aggressively against a partner who is not a fighter. She must be fearless to help you improve. She need not strike properly—a typical opponent certainly will not. Being tapped with the edge of the mitt means you have been punched. Being slapped with the flat of the mitt means you have been slapped or—oh no!—grabbed.
4. Leading effectively is the apogee of survival fighting. Spend

a round using your lead hand to stop, cut off, and control the holder as she attempts to counter you. Take it easy, macho men. These are focus mitts, not heavy bags. Control her with your footwork.

5. Free-style mitt work is the goal, the ultimate training tool. Mix it up. Stay cool.
6. Finishing an opponent without getting tied up is beyond the ability of most fighters. The last round has no time limit. It ends when you are "grabbed" or clinched or when you land a three-punch combination. (Be careful, this is an advanced drill.) The holder alternately evades—with footwork, not by jerking the mitts—and attempts to clinch.

The ability to hit effectively against the grab can be developed by having the holder wear only one mitt, while leading off and countering with shirt and belt grabs, preferably with well-manicured fingernails.

The holder should wear a mouth guard, head gear, and possibly a chest protector. Holding the mitts close to the head and body can get you knocked out and can also ease you into contact. The mitts are good for barehanded work, even if you have some hand trouble. Be careful: a training partner nearly knocked me out last night when he missed a mitt. A heavyweight would have broken my jaw with that punch.

Be certain to establish the parameters of the drill. The mitts are for developing timing, accuracy, rhythm, and counters. Do not "load up" for power. Advanced mitt drills will demonstrate the uselessness of power alone. A good holder will not move the mitts quickly without signaling. This puts the hitter at risk of hyperextending the elbow. The holder must break the rhythm of the hitter's attack with foot and body movement. His hands move much faster than any human target. The holder simulates; he does not compete. Boxers call them focus mitts for a reason.

14

Training Partners and Equipment

"You continually put yourself in a vulnerable position, and from there is where you grow."

—PAUL VUNAK

My training philosophy is based on two principles: avoiding injuries and avoiding rip-offs. Having protected what's left of my physical and financial assets, I settled down to learn the endless lessons I've managed to miss over the years. I'm getting too old to learn much more the hard way.

The most difficult aspect of continuing martial arts study as an adult is maintaining your physical condition. Work saps your energy and monopolizes your time. Injuries take longer to heal and reoccur more often. Loved ones grow jealous of your time. Lesson and membership fees compete with the mortgage and car payments. . . .

Often you're left with whatever training space and gear you have at home. When you do match time with space and a partner, the tendency will be to work on your skills. For this reason I recommend incidental conditioning and training. Incidental training must be specific to your lifestyle.

INCIDENTAL TRAINING

Incidental training allows you to use down time, daily activities, and your everyday environment to maintain fitness and improvise subtle methods of skills maintenance. Doing little things to maintain skills and fitness in a real-life setting develops poise, awareness, and a feel for fighting surfaces. If you train on a mat, canvas, or hardwood floor yet you work on asphalt—where you would likely be attacked—will your gliding step feel right on the asphalt? Incorporate the following into your training schedule.

- Maintain your legs by walking and stretching daily.
- Improve your balance by standing on one foot while waiting. Remain discreet and vary this exercise by using the raised foot to scratch the other leg by tapping the heel and toe, and rolling the foot.
- Instead of reaching for an object, step or shift.
- Try arm presses and leg extensions from the office chair.
- Don't grab a closing door when you can trap it with a forearm or foot.
- Use dumbbells, hand grips, and exercise bands while watching TV, etc.
- Find a basic aspect of your art that is compatible with an everyday activity and make it part of your day.

Basic habits—such as how you walk—can underpin or undermine your fighting ability. I was training with a kenpo stylist who was having a hard time generating power. A boxing trainer would have said he wasn't "sitting down on his punches." He rose above the target instead of sinking into it. He was getting frustrated. I took a good look at the way he walked and noted that he had a very springy step. I suggested that if he modified his step to a glide the power would come, especially in situations that wouldn't permit him to get set.

OVERTRAINING

Overtraining accounts for most injuries among athletes, especially fighters. Boxers are the worst; most boxing trainers are 50 years behind sports medicine. There may be a method to this apparent idiocy. Gyms offer a Darwinian context for improvement. Training the same muscles for three hours, six days a week, ensures that only exceptional physical specimens will remain free of injury long enough to acquire advanced skills. Two days of stressful training is plenty for a part-time fighter, and even the top-ranked pros are beginning to cross-train.

TRAINING ATTIRE

Training for self-defense should be done in everyday clothing at least half the time. Training after work in your work clothes is a convenient way to condition yourself to fighting in the gear you're likely to be wearing if you are attacked. It also cuts down on laundry. Footwear, or lack of it, is very important. Once you have developed effective footwork in training shoes or bare feet, ease into training in your work and leisure shoes. Once you try this adaptation you will understand how important it is. Be sure and warm up those ankles.

WORKING AND SPARRING WITH PARTNERS

"You don't find out what a guy is all about until he loses a fight."

—"DOC" STANELY on greatness

"You're only as good as your training partners." That sounds like a cliché, but it's true. Getting the most out of training with people who aren't necessarily going your way is the essence of cross-training. Finding, scheduling with, and maintaining a network of training partners is a personal endeavor. A recent training session exemplifies much of the benefits and liabilities of cross training.

A friend who holds teaching ranks in multiple arts and has participated in many real fights invited me over for a personal training session. I expected a lesson, but it was actually a test. I later discovered that he wanted me as a teaching assistant. These guys need to know you're tough before they promote you. I also failed to consider that he needed to blow off steam about a personal matter. What I got out of the workout was a compliment on my boxing ability and some nasty injuries.

I neglected to size up the situation and paid the price. I would have been safer fighting the guy in an alley. Giving control of your training to a careless or preoccupied coach can be more dangerous than fighting. Abide by the following guidelines and you will avoid such training disasters.

- Develop a network of serious training partners.
- Decide when you can train and schedule with someone who can make that workout.
- Train with people from different styles.
- Do not submit to pain-tolerance conditioning.
- Defend yourself during drills.
- Do not lend equipment.
- Watch a new partner during drills for signs of machismo, egomania, poor self-control, and excessive emotion.
- Do not spar with someone until you have worked with him a few times.
- Be wary of training with teachers. Teachers often teach because they need to be in control and are incapable of working in a peer relationship. They must be mastered or be the master. This ethos is encouraged by most Asian art forms. A person taught along these lines will be inclined to intimidate or injure those who do not rate as his master. Such a person is confused and threatened by those who are not dominant or subservient.
- Don't spar with a teacher in front of his class.
- Set parameters and agree on guidelines.
- Be wary of those who won't divulge their methods or discuss counters to their own techniques.

- Always wear a mouthpiece, even during drills.
- Never spar without protective gear.
- Heavy bags are for developing power; sparring partners are not.
- Do not spar with someone who can't (or won't) control his power.
- Do not pull strikes short of contact. The best way to limit contact is called "going easy." Boxers routinely spar at half power. Fighters working out of small gyms have to spar with partners outside their weight class, and this demands controlled power. No trainer wants a promising lightweight to get sidelined by a deadbeat middleweight. Pulling punches short of contact is detrimental because it degrades timing, power, and range-finding. It also limits slipping and countering. The closer the miss, the more effective the slip or counter. Pulling punches muddles things.

A good sparring analogy would be playing with toy guns. Pulling punches is like yelling "bang!" Full contact is like using real weapons loaded with rubber bullets—ouch! Controlled contact is analogous to paint ball: not the real thing, but better than arguing over who got shot or going to the emergency room.

Since the lead hand is so important and its use involves such intricate skill yet doesn't break many bones, consider letting the lead fly without cranking the hook/ridge-hand/elbow angle. The lunge, jab, and back fist wouldn't be compromised.

The following recommendations will make training with partners more effective.

- Whatever you decide on, agree to it, and make it clear.
- If you're working with a responsible person, do it without an audience to keep the ego under wraps.
- If you're sparring with an animal, do it on neutral ground with a referee or seconds, unless you're sure he can't take you.
- At some point you should train with someone who has more skill, experience, heart, or strength than you.

- What motivates your partner to train with you? You need to know this before you go far with anybody.
- Avoid the guys who just want "one workout" that has to include sparring. Some of the most dangerous martial artists are what I call duelists, who are not the least bit interested in enhancing their self-defense ability. They're just looking to feed their ego at your expense.
- If you train with a guy who can't resist teaching, just let him roll with it and soak up what you can. However, if he does not permit you to teach him anything, beware. He is attempting to dominate you and may resort to less subtle means.
- Sparring with proven pro fighters is safer than sparring with most others, because they have nothing to prove.

(**WARNING**: Extensive cross training may result in an identity crisis. If you ask the boxers I train with about my style they will say, "Oh yeah, the martial arts guy." Ask my karate friends the same question and they'll say, "Sure, the boxer." It's not a big deal to me, but if you are a social animal, being excluded from every fraternity you associate with might not be too cool.)

You will probably end up sparring under different rules systems designed for competition. Having pushed the idea that combat sports are martial arts I must make it clear that no combat sport portrays real fighting in a comprehensive manner. Sport combat supplies the intensity without the variables. This makes it tolerable. You must be able to recognize the artificial limitations under which you spar and compete, so that you do not use them as crutches, ultimately compromising your real-fighting ability. Many of the limitations will enhance a narrow band of skills that are necessary for successful real fighting, such as lead-hand striking.

The fact that boxers (especially kick-boxers) are not penalized for slipping, results in the adoption of dangerous habits. Recently, while watching a Thai boxing card I saw one fighter fly through the ropes or onto his back five times attempting the very kicks that eventually earned him the decision on power kicking. The judges rewarded tactics that would have gotten him killed in an alley.

An hour later I watched a full-contact karate tournament in which the winner of the second round could not continue because of a concussion. The "loser" was still fresh. Half the heavyweight competitors slipped repeatedly, and none was able to avoid the clinch.

Don't "game" your sparring rules to win. Keep the real thing in mind.

A partner is a must for contact conditioning. Every art limits contact in some way. Remaining injury free is key to maintaining the ability to train, perform, compete, and defend yourself. Unlimited contact will result in injuries. Consider easing into full-contact training one aspect at a time and then backing up to continuous light-contact sparring. Do enough full contact work to learn the lessons and then go to low-risk maintenance.

ASPECTS OF CONTACT

1. *Pressure* (spatial invasion). Practice crowding your partner and angling for an advantage using only footwork. No contact or flinching allowed. This is called shadowing.
2. *Presence* (visual harassment). Continue shadowing with your partner throwing punches over your shoulder and measuring hooks to cut across your line of sight just short of contact. Wear your mouth guard and take turns. Avoid blinking, flinching, or turning. Progress to interactive shadowboxing.
3. *Shock* (mechanical disruption). Return to shadowing, with punches to the chest protector and slaps to the headgear. By the time you progress to the interactive shadowboxing you should be getting the hang of rolling with the punches. The shock to the body—even from a head blow—is more disruptive than the simple, *and brief*, matter of enduring pain.
4. *Pain* (sensory assault). Pain is an injury indicator. Pain tolerance conditioning is stupid. There is enough incidental pain waiting out there to preclude your having to look for it. In a fight numbness quickly overcomes pain.

"Don't fill [the heavey bag] with sand. It will settle and cake—hurts the hand. Use sawdust."

—SIFU GOH

What follows is a list of recommended training equipment and an approximate retail price range as of the time of this writing. Those items that can be constructed at home have a second price in parentheses reflecting the cost of the components if you wish to make it yourself.

RECOMMENDED EQUIPMENT LIST

Piece of equipment	Price
Mouth guard	$1–30
Hand wraps	$5–10
Punching mitts	$20–60 pair
Heavy bag	$40–300 ($5–20)
String bag	$15–80 ($5–10)
Boxing or kenpo gloves	$40–180 a pair
Headgear	$30–80
Chest protector	$20–80
Hand targets	$10–20 ($2) each
Bag gloves	$15–80 pair

MAKING A HEAVY BAG

Components
12 bungee cords or 4 truck straps
Large sack or duffel bag
Roll of duct tape
Sawdust
Rags plus plastic pallet wrap
Two 12-inch 2x4s
8 nails
Shoestring

Construction

1. Fill the bottom third of the bag with plastic pallet wrap. You can get 10 to 20 balls of this crinkled stuff from the "night captain" (who works from 10:00 P.M. to 6:00 A.M.) on freight nights at your local supermarket. Compress this stuff. It traps a lot of air.
2. Fill the middle third of the bag with rags.
3. Fill the top third of the bag with sawdust from under the saw at a lumberyard. So what if they think you're nuts?
4. Knot the top of the bag, leaving a 6-inch tail. Fold the tail over and tape just above the knot. Punch a hole through the taped section 1 inch above the knot. Secure the base of the loop with a shoestring. Tape down the shoestring closure under pressure.
5. Unless you have a heavy canvas bag, wrap the bag with strips of duct tape, overlapping from the bottom up.
6. Nail two 2 x 4s between the support beams in your basement or garage.
7. Hang the bag from the mount with bungee cords, truck straps, or clothesline. Bungee cords and truck straps transfer less stress to the floor above and provide some bounce. One bungee cord is good for 10 pounds; a truck strap for 20. Cover the cords or straps with tape at the point of contact with the brace to limit wear. When it is not in use, prop the bag up on a chair. This is a bitch to hang on your own.

MAKING A STRING BAG

Endless variations on the double-ended bag can be constructed from a variety of materials. Once you have a ceiling fastening and floor anchor you may operate a number of bags from this one station.

I do recommend training with a commercial air bladder bag for hand speed. However, speed is the problem with the traditional double-ended bag—it moves at hand speed. Nobody moves his head that fast. You have a heavy bag swaying slower than a fat drunk and a string bag bobbing faster than a flyweight boxer. Homemade, composite string bags swirl, lurch, and bob, offering realistic off-speed targets capable of frustrating your combinations.

My favorite training partner is the "cigar" body bag. It is composed of bubble wrap and plastic pallet wrap wound around a core of commercial pipe insulation. It is light and easy on the hands, but it hits hard. It only costs $2 for the cord and $3 for the tape. The other stuff was trash.

Components

1. Fastening—an eye hook, angle iron, or bracket and bolt screwed or nailed into a wood beam.
2. Anchor—a barbell plate, toolbox, bucket of rocks, sack of cat litter, or even a bag of magazines weighing 15-plus pounds.
3. Core—a roll of paper towels or toilet paper; a 1- to 1 1/2-inch cardboard or PVC tube, a rolled newspaper, or pipe insulation slipped over and securely taped to the hooks of a bungee cord. If you are using cardboard tubing, wrap the cord with an inch of twine or rags before inserting.
4. Body—rags, foam, diapers, bubble wrap, plastic wrap, or pipe insulation is excellent for ribbing to provide angular target surfaces. You might mark your target with electric tape, but this will harden the surface. Try to keep the bag under 12 pounds. The key is to tape the materials directly to the hooks one layer at a time as you wrap them. I build my string bags hanging at the station where they will be used.
5. Cord—you will need two to four bungee cords of varying length to string the target from the floor to ceiling. Gauze, rags, boxing wraps, or pipe insulation should be used to cover the cord hooks and even turn them into joint targets.

MAKING A CHEST PROTECTOR

Convert a Little League catcher's chest protector by simply replacing worn straps and improving the rib area with foam and duct tape.

MAKING IMPROVISED TARGET PADS

Target pads of folded newspaper covered with cloth are easy to make though not very durable.

SELECTING HEAD AND HAND PROTECTION

Selecting head and hand protection is serious business. Buy leather, buy quality, and consider Velcro closures.

The Untrained Fighter

"How many times can ya hit that fat piece a shit before he tackles ya?"

—BIG RICH on grappling

I sat down at a neighborhood bar in a section of Baltimore where most men are alcoholics and experienced fighters. The barmaid and the other patron, a large 50-year-old man with scarred hands, were watching a Jean-Claude van Damme movie. The fight between the star and the villain was driving this guy crazy. He was shaking his head and muttering like a jock bemoaning the performance of a girls' baseball team. If Mr. van Damme were being threatened by young punks in that bar, I have no doubt that this gentleman would be kind enough to allow Jean-Claude to hold his coat as he disposed of the problem.

For the purpose of this discussion we can group untrained combatants into the following categories:

1. Nonfighters without experience
2. Wannabes (deluded punks) with little experience
3. Experienced or "natural" fighters

---

4. Short guys with experience
5. Tall guys with experience
6. Hitters (dangerous men) with significant experience

NONFIGHTERS

Nonfighters constitute the largest self-defense demographic in America. Virtually all women and most men do not possess the physical or mental qualities to ever fight effectively. The modern culture of helpless victimization and a sedentary lifestyle provides the untrained predator with easy prey. Face it: most people, even those who enroll in martial arts programs, will never be able to defend themselves.

The nonfighter responds to violence according to basic instincts:

- He might grab a weapon.
- He might run.
- He will probably freeze on contact.
- He might curl up or cover his head.
- He will either look down or away.
- He may extend his hands to fend off the attacker.
- He may grab the attacker.
- If he hasn't been completely neutered, he may flail away with both fists, wrestle, bite, gouge, butt, or stomp. If he does this once in his life, he is now an experienced fighter who will probably react similarly if he fights again. This person is as dangerous as a typical black belt of equal stature.

That's right, 30 seconds on the sidewalk is worth three years in the dojo. In fact, most trained fighters are no different from—and no better than—the nonfighter when they are taken out of their game. A karate man taken to the ground before he gets set or a jujutsu man who gets cracked with a beer mug before he knows he is in a fight will effectively be a nonfighter unless his attacker screws up and gives away the momentum. This is the danger of being totally dependent on skill.

This last scenario, getting hit from a blind side, is why I prefer boxing as a survival art. Blind-side strikes are common opening attacks, and boxing is really the only art that conditions you to fight on autopilot when you have been hurt with a head blow.

WANNABES

A wannabe is a young man who fancies himself a fighter but lacks the training and experience to be one. Lack of character is the common personality trait. The wannabe will usually pick a fight with those he suspects are nonfighters or possibly with a trained fighter to confirm his own delusional status. He will not knowingly confront an experienced fighter unless he is really drunk.

His first violent encounter will transform him into a nonfighter or experienced fighter, depending on how it goes. This punk is the best reason for concealing your fighting ability. A run-in with you will prevent him from progressing to a more competent predatory state. If he knows you're a fighter, he won't push it. What he definitely doesn't "wannabe" is your punching bag! Wannabes usually lack extensive athletic experience.

Wannabe tactics mimic the techniques of the skilled fighter or the antics of the movie star or pro "wrestler."

Wannabes may also mimic experienced fighters, such as an uncle who was locked up for assaulting his boss, used to play football, was in 'Nam, or bounced at a go-go bar. The fantasy that they have somehow inherited the instincts and abilities of a male relative is common with this type.

For instance, the old barfighter who took pity on Jean-Claude van Damme might be asked by his nephew, "Unk, what would you do in a fight?" In an attempt to please his nephew and not worry his sister, Unk would probably offer a single skill with little said about application—the real meat of the subject. This results in a wannabe dependent on a single skill for which he probably wasn't supplied with training or context. Don't pity the punk, pummel him!

The following account is a graphic illustration of just how dangerous the wannabe is not.

Bar parking lot, Dundalk, Maryland, at night

A sixth-degree black belt with some real fighting experience was challenged repeatedly by a resident of Fantasy Land. The wannabe attempted all manner of action-movie-type punches and kicks, which the karateka avoided easily. The wannabe basically "beat himself up" as he hit the ground after most of his attempted "techniques."

This guy was lucky he picked on a trained fighter. An experienced untrained fighter must play the offensive role to be effective in most situations. The only smart thing this guy did was pick an opponent with highly developed defensive skills.

The above account is a perfect example of a trained fighter using his ability in an appropriate manner and reaping the benefits. What follows are examples of trained but inexperienced fighters exposed to the hard glare of reality by untrained fighters, nonfighters, athletes, and trained fighters.

Sidewalk, Baltimore, Maryland, during the day

A kung fu student accepted the challenge of a large skinhead. While attempting to get set, he was sucker punched and then kicked with steel-toe boots as he hit the pavement. The skinhead enjoyed himself very much.

Alley, Curtis Bay, Maryland, during the day

A karate black belt challenged the local bully, a large football player. He sank into his stance with a deep "kia!" His attempted rising block failed to deflect his opponent's first overhand right, which broke his nose, ending the fight.

Construction site, Harford County, Maryland, during the day

A black belt in kempo threatened a co-worker (a 160-pound former high school wrestler) who tackled him and made him say uncle.

Nightclub, New York City

Jean-Claude van Damme was knocked out by his former bodyguard with a single punch to the chin.

Health spa, Atlantic City, New Jersey, during the day

A 270-pound bodybuilder (a former Golden Gloves champion) agreed to fight the 180-pound boyfriend of a girl he was seeing; the boyfriend was a former high school wrestler. The "skinny kid" got behind the bodybuilder, took him down, hit him behind the ear, and choked him out.

High school, Baltimore County, Maryland, during the day

The captain of the school wrestling team threatened a former tae kwon do student, also a wrestler and an experienced fighter, who cracked his sternum with a single overhand right, not a reverse punch.

Clubroom, residence, Washington, Pennsylvania, during the day

An adult tae kwon do black belt challenged a smaller, untrained, teenaged fighter to a "friendly" sparring session. He opened with a crescent kick to the face and sank into a low stance with a Bruce Lee-like purr. Angered, the boy threw off his handgear like a hockey player and charged with a growl. The black belt, paralyzed with fear, was shoved against a wall, where the boy held him by the right sleeve with his left hand while he beat him with right hooks. This continued for about five seconds, until the two were separated by their seconds. The black belt left in tears while his opponent yelled, "Karate this #*and%@¢-$¢*and%°!"

(**NOTE**: The Mr. Feared versus Mr. Hated spectacle in Chapter 8 belongs in this category.)

THE EXPERIENCED OR "NATURAL" FIGHTER

"It's the application not the style."

—Sifu Gabriel

The natural fighter is a rational fighter. The belief that untrained fighters go nuts or lose it is myth. The notion that their effectiveness—which often exceeds that of trained fighters—is based on irrationality is wrong.

These people may be stupid, but the dangerous ones are rarely deluded. Keep in mind that the dangerous experienced fighter is still at large precisely because he is lucid enough to elude the law for most of his unlawful life. There are exceptions, but common sense guides the successful untrained fighter in his selection of opponents and victims, his evasion of the law, and his choice of tactics. If he's worth a damn in a brawl, the fighter is certainly aware of his abilities. And if he has a lot of experience he is also aware of his limitations.

Common traits of the untrained fighter include the inability to do the following:

- Strike effectively with the lead hand
- Strike a moving target
- Grapple decisively

What these three traits produce is a tendency to combine grappling and striking. What the experienced untrained fighter is likely to do is set up his opponent to offset his own lack of long-range fighting skill. What is almost certain is his need to finish with strikes of some kind. Long-range striking and upright grappling are sound strategies for dealing with this opponent.

The untrained fighter's strength is his ability—based on his need—to set up an advantageous encounter. He prefers the come-from-behind grab, blind-side strike, and sucker punch.

Sucker punches are not techniques; they are applications. One could write a book on sucker punching, and some people have. I suggest you talk to people who have been sucker punched, as well as those who have executed such attacks. My own rather primitive method was to look down to the right, make a fist with both hands, and hope they were still looking at my right hand when I popped them with the left uppercut. The most effective sucker punches are done at a walk as you pass your target.

Short Guys with Experience

"I just about shit myself when they went over the Oreo cookie display! But whatta ya do with a little black dude that's bouncing some big redneck's head off the meat case? Grab him? Yeah, right. Fuck that! He had a mean right hand."

—SUPERMARKET MANAGER

Whether you call it attitude, penis envy, or the Napoleon complex, short men (especially the ones who know they're short!) are more trouble than tall men. They tend to use a cluster of commonsense tactics appropriate to their body type.

Primary Tactics

* Right hook to head
* Looping overhand right to head

Secondary Tactics

- Two-handed shove
- Waist tackle
- Left-handed lapel grab
- Swinging left hook to head
- Two-handed lapel or head grab
- Head butt
- Side headlock

Finishing Tactics

- Head smash to curb, railing, bumper, bar top, or doorway
- Improvised weapon

Typical Combinations

- Two-handed shove and waist tackle
- Left-handed lapel grab and overhand right to head
- Two-handed lapel or head grab and head butt

Short guys are more likely to use a weapon. Even though they employ a narrow range of tactics in contrast to taller untrained fighters, they tend to execute these with an excess of bad intent. The key to understanding the short untrained fighter is the realization that he is motivated by fear, envy, and frustration. This finds expression in the need to injure, maim, or kill. The right hook to the head is a literal attempt to decapitate the opposition.

Tall Guys with Experience

"Mostly I use the ground . . . I got in at least one fight every week for two years. I lost one to a fence post—slipped on some ice after I decked this guy. I think that's the only time I ever got hurt. Boxing with my brother was much worse; I was just a punching bag—so I didn't mind fight'n. . . . They mostly deserved it. My friends really were jerks—but the guys they picked fights with were just as bad. Got old after a while. I prefer being married."

—GREG, a vendor I wisely (actually it was an imminent sense of doom) declined to fight on a bet put up by my co-workers

Tall men are rarely the targets of criminal assaults, but they are often sucked into brainless brawls because friends and family look to them for protection, short guys see a win-win situation, and unscrupulous trained fighters see a soft, high-yield target to feed their egos. The few real brawls that could actually be considered competitive involve a big, experienced fighter against a shorter, more aggressive man, who is either experienced or trained or both. Kind of like the classic T-Rex verses triceratops dinosaur battle. Consequently the big man's tactics are geared toward dealing with a small, motivated antagonist. When two big guys meet, size will usually be the deciding factor since they are both conditioned to battle a smaller man.

Large, experienced, untrained fighters rely on three or more of the following tactics.

Primary Tactics

- Looping overhand right to head
- Straight right to head (with elbow winged out)
- Right hook to head

Secondary Tactics

- Lead-hand shove

- Lead-hand lapel, hair, hood, or right-shoulder grab (grabbing the rear shoulder sleeve of a short man's shirt kills his best weapon—the overhand right to the head)
- Lead-hand slap, or slapping hook, to face
- Lazy jab to face, chest, or lead shoulder
- Rear-hand uppercut
- Rear bear hug
- Head "dunk" with lead hand
- Front headlock or choke

(**NOTE**: Tall guys don't have to put leverage on their punches for them to be effective. Don't expect them to commit like a short guy. Of course they might, but plunging or reaching arm punches are the rule. Aikidoists, beware.)

Finishing Tactics

- Drag down (holds on with his lead hand, shifting his weight off his lead leg and onto you, as he pushes you down with the lead hand)
- Pin and pummel (pins you with his lead knee, controls you with his lead hand, and pummels you with straight rights)
- Toe kicking, heel stomping, and jump stomping a prone opponent (big guys have knee trouble to begin with, so don't expect them to stay on the floor long enough to finish you, unless their knee is comfortably lodged in your gut)
- Frontal choke/wall smash, or Darth Vader one-handed elevator choke and right uppercut

Typical Combinations

- Lead-hand shove (to put you at the end of their punch) followed by a looping right to head
- Lead-hand slap under the chin (to lift it) followed by a straight right to the chin
- A hair grab or head dunk followed by as many rear-hand uppercuts as you can eat

The key to understanding the mind-set of the tall, untrained fighter is to realize his need to dominate. Dominating usually over-rides the immediate thirst to injure, maim, or kill. Like the short man, the inner drives of the tall man are appropriate to his body type.

You can get a pretty good feel for this type simply by sparring with local heavyweight boxers. In any given state there is only a handful of heavyweights who have any real boxing skill. In the ring most spend a lot of time pushing, clinching, and lying on you. I sparred with one kid who used to hook my arm in the clinch, lift me off the floor, and feed me right upper cuts while I dangled in the air. A thumb in the eye puts an end to such tactics.

THE HITTER

"Seems like big 'uys is oways fight'n lille guys. Don' it, lille man?"

—BUBBA CRANK

The hitter is a rare version of the short or tall man who has had enough success to formulate a recipe for doing business. He is more dangerous than most trained fighters and often has a background in scholastic sports.

In the case of Bubba Crank we are talking about a part-time hit man or enforcer. Bubba was the youngest of five brothers, the smallest of whom was 6 foot 4 inches, 220 pounds. Since you only do about three years for "breakin', capin', or shankn' a known brutha," these guys always maintained at least two of their number on the outside, to intimidate—to say the least—witnesses. When possible, things were taken care of manually to avoid handgun charges. These guys dished out more injuries on the basketball court than most wife-beaters do on Friday night.

For a good example of this mind-set in action, watch videos of "Tank" Abbot's earlier Ultimate Fighting Championship fights, Mike Tyson's postprison fights, and any Paul Varlens Ultimate Fighting Championship fight. These are all examples of undisci-plined, poorly trained fighters who nevertheless retain the ability to bully most of the world's best fighters. Conversely, Marco Ruas (versus Varlens) and Evander Holyfield (versus Tyson) demonstrate the character and skill required to deal with an experienced brute.

Characteristics of the Hitter

- Physically superior to his peers
- Quiet
- Stands off or withdraws from the group, giving himself space to time an effective attack
- May dress inappropriately to conceal weapons
- Will rarely posture or pose if he's really dangerous

REAL ONE-ON-ONE ENCOUNTERS

"I don't appreciate people attempting to take something that belongs to me."
—A CONVICTED FELON, 7–1 in real fights

I have selected anecdotes involving at least one untrained fighter. Note the relative ages of the antagonists and the intensity and location of their struggle. All accounts are firsthand or eyewitness testimonies from the violent incident survey I initiated in 1996.

Elementary school hallway, Baltimore, during the day

A 10-year-old bully attempted to steal a 9-year-old's lunch. The younger subject successfully defended himself by knocking out the bully with repeated two-handed head blows with his metal lunch box. At the time of this interview, the victor couldn't remember which cartoon superhero was depicted on the lunch box.

Playground, Baltimore housing project, during the day

A 14-year-old boy attempted to rob a 12-year-old. The two pushed, punched, slapped, and wrestled until the 12-year-old subject got a mount and slammed his attacker's head against a concrete sidewalk repeatedly. Just kids, right?

High school gym locker room, Baltimore, during the day

The 15-year-old subject (a heavyweight boxer) was hit in the side of the head with a baseball bat wielded by a smaller classmate. The subject clinched with his attacker, lifted him to chest level, and threw him down on the aisle bench, breaking an unknown number of ribs. The boxer was expelled.

Front yard of house, Northeast Baltimore, during the day

I witnessed a short, muscular 16-year-old overpower a tall 15-year-old, tie him with a short rope hanging from a tree (I believe it was the weathered end of a dog's run), press him over-head, and throw. The rope broke the boy's fall—and some ribs—short of the ground. I assisted the injured boy, who was not grateful. I challenged his attacker to a fight, which he declined. . . . Punks.

High school, Towson, Maryland, during the day

A 17-year-old, 135-pound wrestler subdued a 6-foot 3-inch, 215-pound 17-year-old who was beating a fellow student. Though in excellent condition, the wrestler described it as a tiring struggle.

Living room, South Baltimore, at night

An experienced 35-year-old bar brawler caught her stoned husband on the couch with a younger woman. The brawler and her drinking partner drank beer and watched her spouse and the woman "go at it." Then the irate—and inebriated—wife beat the girl unconscious with right hooks and threw her through a first-floor window onto the sidewalk. No hospital, cops, or divorce. Amazing.

Street corner, South Baltimore, at night

A toe-to-toe brawl between a 5-foot 4-inch, 140-pound female and a 6-foot 5-inch, 250-pound male, both about 25: the fight lasted for more than a minute before the antagonists rolled down a steep sidewalk and out of sight. Tactics included kicking, kneeing, pushing, slapping, punching, wrestling, tripping, and blocking. The man was struck in the groin at least once.

Bar, Washington, Pennsylvania, at night

A 6-foot, 190-pound man grabbed the breast of a 5-foot 8-inch, 180-pound woman, who hit him in the chest with a right jab that knocked him over a table. The woman was ejected by the owner. This woman was not a trained fighter and didn't know what a jab was.

Parking lot, East Baltimore, during the day

A man, 25 to 30 years old, pushed and pinned a woman against a brick wall and robbed her. Typical predatory encounter.

Parking lot, Dundalk, Maryland, at night

Two 20-something gear-heads got in an argument over a racing bet. One pulled a club out of his car as the other drew a gun. Mutual friends, who apparently didn't trust the aim of the gunman, talked them into fighting like men. They fought for five to ten minutes—like girls, grappling and talking on the asphalt and up against the cars as they attempted to hold and hit, knee and smash. The action was indecisive and was eventually broken up.

Bar, East Baltimore, at night

A 5-foot, 10-inch, 220-pound man walked up to a 6-foot, 2-inch, 180-pound man, grabbed his lapel with the left hand, and broke his nose with an overhand right. Another incredibly typical encounter. The men were about 40.

Bus stop, Northeast Baltimore, at night

A 40-year-old man of average stature was approached from behind by two larger, younger men who beat him severely. The victim, who was not robbed, believed the attack was racially motivated. He could not give a clear account of his attackers' tactics.

Street corner, South Baltimore, at night

A large 50-year-old man with more than 20 wins in real fights tried to hit a large younger rival with a straight right. He missed, slipped on the ice, slid downhill, and broke his hand. End of encounter.

Oktoberfest, Baltimore

The 6-foot, 205-pound, 46-year-old chief of a private security detail caught a 6-foot, 1-inch, 200-pound, 35-year-old drunk hassling one of his female officers. The chief was a brown belt in kenpo karate and applied a rear overhead thumb lock, subduing the drunk before walking him out.

This is how it usually goes for security, bouncers, and cops, because they have the initiative and the backup. The professionals generally deal with fools who are stupid, drunk, and not focused. The target of a criminal attack must deal with a predator (or predators) who is mean, hungry, and focused.

And just for fun, there is this account from the *Washington Times*, Wednesday, November 12, 1997:

> PHILADELPHIA—Two airport workers got into a fight and crashed through a plate-glass window yesterday, falling about 30 feet to the tarmac. One man was hospitalized in critical condition, the other in stable condition.
>
> Police said they did not know why the men were fighting. One works for Delta Air Lines, the other for an airport magazine vendor.

I theorize that the Delta guy was pressuring the vendor for some free skin mags—I've seen it happen in supermarkets.

Below are incidents from the 1996 survey pitting amateur or pro boxers against untrained fighters.

Bar, Glen Burnie, Maryland, at night

The subject picked a fight with "some little dweeb" who turned out to be a pro fighter— "Kid Somebody." The boxer knocked him out with a right cross.

Bar, Southern Maryland, at night

A local heavyweight working as a bouncer fought a pro baseball player, resulting in a broken jaw to the ballplayer and a lawsuit against the boxer.

Bar, Baltimore, at night

An amateur welterweight danced with an offensive lineman's date. When the football player attempted to bump chests with the boxer, the boxer knocked him out cold with a right hook. The boxer went to the floor and cradled the limp man's head, chopping into his face with uppercuts. The boxer was ejected and had sustained no hand injury. The opponent had a probable broken jaw.

When I reprimanded this young man—my student—for going to the floor and punching the jock, he said, "I know, Mr. Jim. You always tell me about the hands. I should have stomped him, right?"

"No. You were wrong."

"Oh, yeah. Okay. I didn't think about that."

When we look at this last example, we should look at the mind-set and previous experience of the fighter, not his art. This was the kid who, when he was 8 years old, had knocked out his 300-pound uncle (and I saw it). When you fight this "kid," you are facing 16 years of contact sports competition, experience in a dozen real brawls, a genetic disposition toward aggressive action, and the hard edge of a boy raised amid violence.

Parkway median, Baltimore, during the day

A former amateur welterweight (now an overweight referee) became involved in a traffic dispute with a very large biker. The biker attempted an overhand right and was intercepted with a right uppercut to the jaw, resulting in a KO. No hand injury or legalities for the former amateur.

Apartment, Parkville, Maryland, during the day

A former middleweight contender attempted to retrieve his teenaged daughter from the apartment of a young adult drug dealer about his own size. A wrestling match occurred in the doorway. While clinching with "this maggot," the once 26–0 boxer remembered he was a boxer and hit the punk on the bridge of the nose with a chopping left hook. (The guy wasn't known as a "hooker."), resulting in a knockout and cut. No hand injury.

Bar, Boston, at night

A former light-heavyweight contender now tending bar dealt with an obnoxious patron by reaching over the bar, grabbing the jerk by his shoulder sleeves and pulling him into a face-crushing head butt. Knockout.

Nightclub, Baltimore, at night

A former Marine Corps boxer asked a large redneck to stop hassling a woman. The redneck missed with an overhand right, ate a jab, and had the bridge of his nose broken with a cross. The boxer broke his middle knuckle. He had previously broken that same knuckle in training.

Emergency room, Baltimore, at night

A patient's large relative got physical with a technician, who was a pro fighter. The 150-pound technician knocked out the larger man with a jab. (It's easier to knock out a large aggressor with a straight lead than a smaller one because he shifts more weight into your punch.)

Nightclub, Baltimore, at night

A 250-pound bouncer attempted to evict a 160-pound amateur fighter, who knocked him out with a three-punch combination. (This was the eyewitness account of a fellow bouncer, who let the boxer walk.)

Urinal in rest room of a restaurant, Hollywood, California

A former world champion blind-sided an actor—of whom he was jealous—with a right hook, knocking the actor unconscious.

Parking lot, Dundalk, Maryland, night

A novice heavyweight was sucker punched by a short, stocky man. This irritated an otherwise gentle novice heavyweight. The two clinched and wrestled on their feet for about a minute. When the boxer finally got his right hand free, he bounced a hook off the sucker puncher's head.

The sucker puncher ran to his friend's car, which was pulling away. As he tried to get in the passenger side of the car, the boxer kicked the car door shut on his back repeatedly. Each time the door slammed against his back, his head was driven up against the top of the door frame, foiling his attempt to dive in. Two other passengers eventually pulled him to safety, as they sped off.

A pattern is definitely evident in all of these examples. Most of the above hits were sucker punches, delivered by trained fighters who had plenty of fighting experience prior to boxing. Since I know most of the above subjects or their sparring partners, I suspect that boxing ability had little effect on the outcome of these fights, although it probably accounts for the low incidence of hand injuries. You can't just look at the skill factor. Here we have athlete versus slob, physical versus verbal, experience versus overconfidence, etc.

There is another pattern I noticed when interviewing combat-arts athletes about their run-ins with untrained fighters. Most of these athletes enjoy having the option of using restricted techniques or those that are esthetically pleasing or fun in training but useless in competition.

All the wrestlers want to find out whether a full nelson is really that devastating. Most of the boxers delight in the opportunity to wing away with a right hook, knowing that they aren't going to eat a jab doing so. Kick-boxers, who all know that the side kick is their most powerful weapon but can never score with it in a bout, love cutting some maggot in half with the edge of their shoe or boot. This is something to consider.

PREPARING TO FACE THE UNTRAINED FIGHTER

When you are training alone, select your imaginary attacker. Give him three tactics and one combo selected from the list appropriate to his body type and focus on him for your entire session. As a trained fighter, you should bring to the table the following six assets:

1. Mobility, including splaying
2. Wind
3. A straight lead
4. Accuracy
5. Combination striking
6. Poise to counter strikes, reverse holds, arrest an opponent's momentum, and control the rhythm and pace of the encounter

The strengths of the experienced untrained fighter are these:

- Sizing up
- Setting up
- Finishing up

His weaknesses will be found in the middle ground. He lacks all of the six advantages you should have. If he has any of those six things going for him, you have just bought yourself a bad time. Of those abilities, the one he will most likely acquire through experience is number six, which is the big one.

Be very careful about trying to finish a dangerous fighter. Unless I have a glaring advantage, I prefer going for the draw and letting my attacker walk. Don't use extreme force (GO TO JAIL!) in any encounter that could be described as a fight.

Criminal assaults are a different matter. If he's armed or has help, do what you have to do to stay alive.

Outnumbered!

"Fighting four men may not be as tough as beating one really good fighter."
—LOUIS L'AMOUR, *Education of a Wandering Man*

We would like to believe that Mr. L'Amour was correct (he was a successful pro boxer and experienced fighter) and not just in a broad sense, but about us in particular. I *want* to believe it more than I *do* believe it. In the final analysis we are preparing ourselves to deal with that ultimate test: the fight against the odds, where our personal quality is staked against a potentially overwhelming quantity. We will be taking a hard look at the dynamics of group attack. But, first, let's look at what's possible.

At 30, I had a reputation for being a hard worker, so it was no surprise when DonDon, a 22-year-old ice cream vendor, offered me a job working on his truck. However, I soon realized that he was more interested in my reputation as a fighter. I was the instrument that would repair his "Rodney Dangerfield" image. He imagined my terrorizing the many threatening people of his life: the bread vendors he cut off at the loading dock, the receivers he insulted daily, the homeless people who begged for out-of-date ice cream only to have it hurled into traffic, the managers he screwed on inventory, the boyfriends and husbands of his many lovers, the boyz in West Baltimore, and the semipro football players who collected for his bookie.

After neutralizing these many threats through diplomacy, I asked DonDon why he thought I could have successfully fought my way through the veritable rogues gallery that was his sordid life?

He said, "Because you remind me of this guy."

"What guy?"

"You know, this guy; little like you, quiet like you."

Now DonDon is a complete—and admitted—coward, who is honest to a fault. He is also an excellent source for real-fight anecdotes, since he has no ego and his mouth and love life keep him in constant trouble. I have questioned him in detail once a year since 1994 about the incident involving "this guy." He sticks by this story to the letter even though he recounts it in a matter-of-fact style. Besides, you have to trust a driver who will admit to his boss that he wrecked his truck (three times) because he was rubbernecking at girls while smacking the dashboard and screaming, "Who's your daddy?"

According to DonDon, the incident happened like this. DonDon was leaving a party. "This guy" (Matt) was holding the door for him when they noticed five average-looking guys beating a prone man. As DonDon turned to go inside, Matt said to the attackers, "Get off him."

One of the guys said, "It ain't your fight."

Matt replied, "I'm not watchin' this."

One of the other guys said, "We got nothin' against you."

Matt turned to DonDon and asked, "Would you hold my jacket? I don't wanna get anything on it."

DonDon said, "Sure. That's me."

Matt was not a trained fighter. He just winged away with lefts and rights like his opponents, whom he defeated in detail. He approached them one at a time and hit each guy before each could get off. The fifth guy ran away before he could get to him, but the other four stayed down from the effect of head blows delivered by a smaller—but calm and athletic—man who wore no gloves but did not injure his hands.

The victim turned out to be a scumbag who really deserved what he got. Matt didn't have to buy a beer that evening as DonDon took him to one bar after another, proclaiming to all that he (DonDon) was the second toughest guy there—and they'd never find out how tough that was.

According to DonDon, Matt was not "soft" but was athletic. He also had a clean jacket, thanks to DonDon.

UNDERSTANDING GROUP VIOLENCE

"Get there first with the most men."

—Gen. Nathan Bedford Forrest

Group dynamics (or, more specifically, primary group cohesion) is what you are dealing with when facing more than one potential attacker. University eggheads write vast indecipherable books on this phenomenon. I will communicate the concept using wargaming shorthand. Use this exercise for developing training scenarios and in your constructive visualizations. Practice typing groups you see daily. This is an exercise, *not a tactic*. Unless you are the aggressor, don't use this as an actual tool. It is for simulating and visualizing only.

(**NOTE**: Criminals often demonstrate group cohesion in the form of division of "labor." For example, many of the drug dealers who solicit your author work as a team: dealer, runner, and hitter. Even a simple "hit him high while I hit him low" or a basic "holder and hitter" approach will often be effective—and luckily beyond the organizational capacity of your typical drunken thugs.)

Size up each person in the group and rate him from 1 to 3:
1 = couldn't fight you
2 = could fight you
3 = could beat you

Size up the group and rate its cohesion level from 1 to 3:

1 = crowd/mob
2 = clicque/gang
3 = team/unit

To rate the group's effectiveness, add the members' individual ratings and multiply by their cohesion level.

Example 1: Three wimps = 3
Three drunken wimps hassling you = 3 x 1 (3)
Three vicious wimps who hate you = 3 x 2 (6)
Three vicious wimps with a premeditated plan to do you in = 3 x 3 (9)

Example 2: Two sadistic athletes = 6
Two drunken sadistic athletes looking for fun at your expense = 6 x 1 (6)
Two drunken, racist, sadistic athletes on the prowl for members
 of your ethnic group = 6 x 2 (12)
Two sober, sadistic athletes collecting for your bookie = 6 x 3 (18)

To determine the odds you face, divide their effectiveness rating by your rating of 3 because you are a cohesive, motivated fighting unit. (Macho men, remember that you have already rated them individually against yourself.)

In other words, fighting three drunken wimps at the bar is a 1–1 proposition. Dealing with them when they come looking for revenge is a 2–1 deal. And, finally, having them jump you from behind while you're at the urinal makes it a 3–1. Through team effort they have the potential of multiplying their collective ability by three. This gets really scary when you consider facing the two goons in example two. Being ambushed by a minor league football player and a former heavyweight boxer—who have a system—is a kiss-your-ass-good-bye, 6–1 stomping.

In military terms a 3–1 effectiveness is considered necessary for a credible attack, 6–1 odds ensure success, and 7–1 or higher is a clean kill, provided there are no negative terrain, weather, or supply modifiers. (Stay up-curb on a hot day and hope they're asthmatic.)

Military analogies are entirely appropriate when considering violent groups. A mob, gang, sports team, or military squad is organized for aggression.

Using this system, I will list the odds for encounters documented in this chapter.

Let's look back at DonDon's story. . . .

The five guys versus the scumbag was a 30–3, or 10–1 deal. The same five versus Matt was a 5–3, or 1–1 situation. Matt turned this potential struggle into four consecutive 3–1 battles in his favor by vigorously applying the most aggressive strategy: dissection (see below).

STRATEGIES FOR THE INDIVIDUAL AGAINST THE GROUP

"Kill them all; God will recognize his own."

—ARNALD AMALRIC, Cistercian General, Papal legate to Languedoc, at Béziers, 1208, Albigensian Crusade

---

There are four strategies for dealing with groups: discouragement, delay, decapitation, and dissection. No strategy is superior or exclusive. They are all appropriate for certain circumstances and inappropriate for others. Most martial arts instructors adhere exclusively to one strategy. This is unfortunate.

Discouragement

Discouragement, or avoidance, is certainly the preferable method for dealing with aggressive groups. In military terms this is the bluff perfected by such military geniuses as Alexander the Great and Frederick the Great. The success of this strategy has as much to do with your image and personality projection as your actual fighting ability.

Sidewalk, Baltimore, at night, 10–3 or 3–1

A man was approached by three older boys who yelled, "Give us money!" as they surrounded him. He began yelling loudly, "I know what you want!" They backed off.

Sidewalk, Baltimore, at night, 20–3 or 6–1

Two men were approached by five men. One of the five hit the lead man in the face, knocking off his glasses and disabling him. The second defender pointed out that the fight between the two groups really wasn't much of one and that it had been effectively decided by the disabling of his partner. The five left, apparently satisfied with his declaration of defeat.

Restaurant, Northeast Baltimore, during the day, 12–18 or 1–2

A boxer and his wife (an experienced fighter) were dining, as three construction workers sat in an adjacent booth bragging—in gory detail—about the previous night's stomping of a helpless wimp.

The woman said, "What assholes."

The construction workers became silent.

The woman's husband asked her to be quiet. She insisted loudly, "Not for those assholes!"

The construction workers remained quiet.

Her husband responded in hushed tones, "I'm tired and don't need to deal with three men."

She countered, "What men? Those aren't men! Besides, I wouldn't let anything happen to you."

At this point husband and wife became embroiled in a heated argument. He was mad at being dragged into a brawl, and she was upset that her husband didn't want her fighting by his side. The argument ended abruptly as she noticed the three leaving without finishing half their meal. Obviously, she pointed out, they were afraid that she would get her way.

Street, Northeast Baltimore, during the day, 9–12 or 1–2

Nine teens, armed with sticks, were faced down and driven off by two unarmed 20-year-old men. A small cohesive team is far more effective than a mob.

School yard, Baltimore, during the day, 3–3 or 1–1, plus the weapon factor

Three teens approached and threatened a man who was walking with his young son. He looked at the punks while talking to his son. After deploying his blade he explained to his son—with clinical precision—what the weapon's purpose was, how it was to be used, the effects to be expected, and that he and his son were to walk away calmly after the enemy had been neutralized. The punks backed off.

Bus stop, East Baltimore, 6–3 or 2–1

A martial artist was approached by four punks who demanded his radio. As he was successfully frightening the three to his front with vicious threats, the rat behind him bricked him in the back of his head. He gave up the radio.

Sidewalk, Baltimore

An elderly man exchanged threats with a group of punks. The verbal confrontation escalated into a brief exchange of punches. Shortly, thereafter the man died of heart failure.

Sticking to the hitter is how I personally discourage threatening groups. It may be hard to select the leader. It's much easier to pick the most dangerous member of a group and then treat him respectfully, as your equal. I prefer to form a bond with such an individual as I diss, step on, or shoulder aside the lesser members of his group. This enhances our status—it also gets me close enough to the hitter to take him out.

Leering is an effective way to bond, superficially, with groups of punks. Sexual predation is a big part of their ethos. The "one-eyed dog in a meat market" posture won't score points with the ladies, but it does establish you as a predator. It is not recommended when dealing with Hispanics.

"Don't care" is the preferred attitude to project among (or around) punks. Their perceived advantage over adult males is that they have nothing to lose. Dressing down, not noticing things that concern ordinary folks, standing where people sit, sitting where they stand, eating where they don't, and relaxing where they wouldn't all contribute to the "lethal loser" image. Adopting this image will make you an unsavory proposition.

Delay

Delay is a defensive strategy for dealing with a force that has momentum and is too powerful to meet. The military analogy would be the classic delaying action or cavalry screen. The defender does not commit himself to any action that will fix his position or place him between two attackers. When his position is fixed, or he is sandwiched, the delaying action has failed, and the slaughter begins.

Note that all of the following attempts to delay an imminent assault go right to the slaughter segment, with the defenders covering or fighting blindly. None of the subjects had trained to delay any type of attack, let alone a group attack.

High school bathroom, Washington, Pennsylvania, 15–3 or 5–1

Two sisters launched a racially motivated attack against a girl with beautiful long hair. The objective was her hair. The target and her attackers pushed, grabbed, wrestled, slapped, and attempted chokes on each other. The attackers pulled out some of the girl's hair before she broke up the assault by beating off one with a stall door.

Parking lot, Washington, Pennsylvania, 30–3 or 10–1

A large athlete was surrounded, beaten, and kicked by 10 boys of various sizes in a racially motivated assault.

Parking lot, Northeast Baltimore, at night

A large, muscular wrestler was finishing off a drunk who had jumped him when a crowd of the drunk's friends began kicking and punching him. He managed to run to safety.

Stadium parking lot, Baltimore, during the day, 48–12 or 4–1

A small boxer recovering from knee surgery and a large wrestler recovering from a serious auto accident were approached by four men at the top of a flight of stairs. Two of the men attacked the injured men with sawed-off baseball bats. The boxer suffered a broken nose while covering for the wrestler. Both avoided serious injury by rolling down the stairs.

High school, Fort Meade, Maryland, during the day, 12–2 or 6–1

Four older boys attacked two younger boys and threw them down a staircase. The younger boys were hospitalized with serious injuries. One of the older boys got jail time.

Sidewalk, Laurel, Maryland, during the day, 21–3 or 7–1

A 35-year-old Salvadoran laborer was attacked and kicked to death by seven "really nice" young men. I got this one from news reports. I figured the odds based on the fact that the raw punkmeat produced by our high schools averages 5 feet, 10 inches, 150 pounds. I work with a lot of these Central Americans. You're talking 5 feet 4 inches, 120 pounds, tops. These are the peasants, not the aristocrats that we see kissing our president's big white ass on CNN.

The poor laborer was walking home from work and got stomped by a pack of rich brats who will be living off their parents for longer than his entire life expectancy—which they cut short. The punks won't do serious time. This stuff burns me up.

Street corner, Northeast Baltimore, during the day, 15–3 or 5–1

A large man was robbed at gunpoint by a large punk. Not satisfied with the $7 in the victim's wallet, the punk pocketed his gun and attempted a body search (what an idiot). The victim wrestled the punk to the ground but was rolled when a second assailant began hitting him from behind. The punks fled when a passing car honked its horn. The victim was not injured.

NOTE: The ambush victim was not even aware that he was the subject of a group effort, and simply tried to delay what he believed would be the primary attacker's attempt to shoot him for only having $7. This one is really hard to categorize. I listed it as a delayed attempt based on the victim's perception of his own actions.

"Decapitation"

Removing the functioning head is the classic primal tactic for taking out a group. Such ruthless conquerors as Alexander the Great and the Spanish conquistadors used this strategy to win control of well-established and extensive civilizations. Theoretically, this is the strategy preferred and promoted by most teaching martial artists, and—theoretically—it is ideal. However, people who have successfully fought off attacker groups rarely report the employment of this method. Of the hundreds of people I have interviewed, none has reported using or even witnessing this ultimate method.

The idea of decapitation, of course, is to physically take out the leader. I used this strategy to a limited degree when torturing the leader of the punks in Chapter 4, in preparation for what I expected to be a brawl. Perhaps the best method of depriving a group of its leadership is discouragement. Could it be that the above examples of this tactic were effective because they discouraged the leader? Who knows? You see, the central problem with decapitation is that the defender is rarely able to pick out the "leader" if, in fact, there is one.

In my opinion, decapitation is the best strategy to employ if you are the aggressor, targeting a group. Before launching a premeditated assault you have the opportunity to observe the group and then select and target the leader. If you go back and examine the punks-on-the-bus incident in Chapter 4 you will see that I used a combined dissection/decapitation strategy.

I did witness a lone bouncer outside a go-go bar attempt to demoralize a group by literal decapitation. He kicked the largest member and obvious leader of the group in the eye.

The leader blinked and told him not to do it again. The bouncer complied. The group then left, as was their original intention, before their leader was accosted by Mr. Karate Man.

Although the following example is not a self-defense situation, it does point to the effect a successful decapitation can have on group cohesion.

No Neck, a 5-foot 10-inch, 220-pound boilermaker, went into a bar to accept an arm-wrestling challenge issued by the leader of a group of three average-sized construction workers in their late 20s, who had not yet seen this guy, No Neck. Upon seeing him, the construction workers withdrew their challenge. An argument ensued. No Neck threw the leader against a wall, leaving him stunned on the floor. No Neck then stomped on the leader's head four or five times, picked him up, and threw him out the door. This generated an attack by No Neck's friends against the two remaining construction workers, who were too dazed to offer a coherent defense.

The barmaid described being overcome by nausea as she saw the prone man's head bow with each stomp.

Dissection

Dissection, or defeating the enemy in detail, has been the dominant strategy employed by successful military commanders in the modern age. It is also the preferred tactic of experienced fighters. The basic premise is that the group is a carcass and you're going to tear off one piece of meat at a time. Going after a weaker member first is preferred because he is less likely to impede your all-important momentum than would a tougher member of the group. Also, effectively injuring supporting members often discourages a leader.

Do not count on the demoralizing effects of this strategy when dealing with highly cohesive small groups. In such cases, such as fighting siblings, you will increase the enemy's will to resist.

Visualize the following accounts and you will realize how brief most of them were.

Bar parking lot, Washington, Pennsylvania, at night, 2–3 or 1–2

Two young ladies were being hassled by a pair of rednecks on the way to their car. The larger man attempted to force the smaller woman into the cab of his pickup. The larger lady turned on her would-be date and pushed him to the ground. She then advanced on the larger man, turned his left shoulder with her left hand, and punched him in the side of the face with an overhand right. The men backed off.

Street corner, West Baltimore, during the day, 18–3 or 6–1

A 16-year-old boy was waiting for the bus, listening to his boom box when five boys approached and asked him for a cigarette. When he reached into his pocket, four of the boys ran forward to grab his radio. When he began punching the lead boy, the largest boy came up and knocked him down with a punch to the nose. When he dropped to his knees, he lost hold of his radio, which was taken by the attackers as they fled the scene.

Nightclub, Towson, Maryland, at night, 24–5 or 4–1

A young black belt came to the aid of a friend under attack by six men. He was punched on the lip and was grappled by a man who grabbed his genitals. He responded with a poke to the throat, which caused the man to retreat. The altercation was then broken up by the club's bouncers.

Field, Marion, Illinois, during the day, 6–3 or 2–1

A large athlete was threatened by a group of country boys who agreed to line up and fight him one at a time. He disposed of them one at a time, mostly with big right hands. No hard feelings were reported—this would never have happened in Baltimore.

Bar parking lot, Washington, Pennsylvania, at night, 4–3 or 1–1

A large 55-year-old biker was approached by two athletic, medium-to-large college boys, demanding his money. He grabbed the nearest punk's right shoulder sleeve with the left hand and broke the punk's jaw with a right uppercut. He then grabbed the second punk's open brown-leather jacket with both hands and threw him against a brick wall repeatedly, breaking some ribs and tearing the jacket in half. The biker was jailed for six months and had to pay for the ribs, jaw, and leather jacket.

Strip mall parking lot, Essex, Maryland, 2:15 A.M., 6–3 or 2–1

A small man driving a car was driven off the road by two large, drunken—you guessed it—rednecks, in a—you guessed it again— pickup. He pulled over in the parking lot of a supermarket in which your author worked on the night crew. He bailed out as they bailed out. He hit the first drunk with a cracking overhand right to the jaw, knocking him out. He hit the second drunk with the same punch and the same results. He was arrested by a cop who had just pulled into the parking lot. (Cops get a lot of blow-jobs on supermarket parking lots.)

Disco, Chicago, at night, 4–3 or 1–1

A Mexican boxer "destroyed" four "rich Arabian guys" in a completely brainless brawl. He talked with, taunted, and encouraged his hapless opponents as he broke their ribs and jaws, while carrying on a conversation with his drinking buddy, who is my sparring partner.

Store front, East Baltimore, during the day, 2–3 or 1–2

A martial artist was threatened by two "geniuses" with their backs to a bike rack. He shoved them over the rack and then beat them separately as they tried to rise. He used no technique at all.

Street, West Baltimore, at night

A martial artist was held up by two men, one of whom had a sawed-off shotgun. After taking his money, the unarmed robber slapped the subject, who responded with a side kick to the ribs, knocking the robber down. He was then shot in the hips by a blast of buckshot. The robbers fled. The subject recovered, with a pellet lodged in his left lung.

Street, West Germany, at night

A drunk U.S. serviceman was threatened by five larger local drunks. The American responded with an attack on the nearest one. After the others surrounded him he threw short, chopping straight punches continuously as he "bounced off them like a pinball." He was later amazed that he had run off all five with such a brainless approach. Some elderly Germans backed up his story when military policemen showed up.

(I learned about this incident when this guy picked me up at the side of the road and dropped me off downtown, because he respected me for walking instead of "thumbing." He turned the conversation to his one significant physical accomplishment: the above fight. He was a nut and almost wrecked his truck while demonstrating his punching method while speeding through city traffic.)

We are thankful that multiple group situations are rare. All I can offer in the way of advice is two personal anecdotes. The method employed in both is to divide and depart. There is also one surreal incident from the survey.

Street corner, East Baltimore, during the day

I unwisely accompanied a co-worker who was a hard-core crack addict to the ugliest patch of asphalt and concrete I had ever seen. For some reason two rival dealers were operating on opposite corners without resorting to firepower. Maybe it was because they were all Jamaicans. I was overdosing on fear as my co-worker stepped into traffic with a fistful of bills—his whole paycheck—and began the bidding process. He was a one-time auctioneer and former barker at a whorehouse, so he put his paycheck up for auction. I got the hell out of there and never bothered to find out which "Rastamon got the crazy-mon pay." The co-worker did make it to work that night unscathed.

Sidewalk, Northeast Baltimore, during the day

I was walking past a vocational-technical high school when my path was blocked by a solid throng of students, divided into two distinct groups: eight large, athletic, loud girls and 30 to 50 small-to-medium "gangsta" wannabes in reversed baseball caps, gray hoodies, beltless triple-X designer shorts, and $120 sneakers. To avoid the girls I would have to figuratively castrate myself by stepping off the sidewalk into the gutter or diss the boyz by shouldering my way through their silent rap session. Not wanting to die or be humiliated, I dissed the boyz.

I made a deliberately wide semicircle around

the amazons as the boys pouted and gave in reluctantly. Any thought they might have had about swarming me gave way under an avalanche of mockery as alpha amazon glared at me and snorted, "Cracka wanna keep 'is pretty long hair!" She said this for her crew to hear—who must have been the girls' track team.

This caused all eyes to fix on me. When one of the lead boys attempted to puff out his chest, she turned her attention to all the little gangstas, "Y'all ain't shit! Ya'll weak!! Ya'll lame!!! Bye-bye, cracka-man."

I actually felt sorry for these guys. But, hell, if I hadn't been married at the time, I would have asked her out. She looked to be at least 20 and would have made a great bodyguard.

Alley, West Baltimore, during the day

Two small men spotted two big men abducting their pit bull. They gave chase as the two big guys ran down the alley, with the dog being held by its legs, swaying between them. As the dog thieves passed the back of a crack house two huge "bruthas" blind-sided them and made off with the dog.

The small men elected not to chase the mutant-dog thief-muggers. They did, however, enjoy kicking and stomping the downed dog thieves.

And just for comic relief, feminine escalations . . .

Residence, Northeast Baltimore, at night, 2–3 or 1–2

A large, muscular, wrestler/boxer arrived to pick up his date. Noticing that his date's kids were still underfoot, he asked about the baby-sitter. His date asked him for $20 to pay the baby-sitter. He gave her the money and followed her into the living room. She introduced him to a tall, thin man and identified him as the "babies' fatha." When she gave the $20 to the father, her date declared, "I'm not paying any man to watch his own kids."

The father stepped over a low marble coffee table and pushed the mother's date—to no effect. The date (wrestler/boxer) hit the dad in the chest with a right forearm-smash, launching dad over the coffee table, stepped over the table, grabbed the dad by his long hair, and began "feeding him the right hand." Mom then jumped on her date's back and began hitting his shoulders. This made the date mad, so he reversed his grip on the dad's long hair and bounced dad's face off the table five to ten times, shook off his date, and walked out the front door pumping his arms and grunting, "Yes!"

The boxer/wrestler guy never got his $20 back, but he felt that he'd gotten his money's worth. (He couldn't keep his hands out of my hair while telling his story.)

Nightclub, Glen Burnie, Maryland, at night, 3–3 or 1–1

DonDon asked a large man who was dancing with DonDon's girl if he could cut in. The man grabbed DonDon's jacket with his left hand and began beating him with his right. DonDon's girl then jumped on the guy's back and began hitting him. Angered, the large man began beating DonDon's head against a brick wall. That's all DonDon remembers.

"Sure was [worth it]. Winning a fight at my age—great."

—MARK

Police officers are usually smart enough to determine what went down, but don't bet your freedom on it. Say "sir" a lot, get the officer's name, and make sure he files the report.

Judges can be really lame, but are far more competent in court than the state's attorneys (i.e., the district attorneys) and public defenders. Generally, the only sharp operator in the courtroom will be the private criminal attorney defending the scumbag who tried to shank you. If you didn't get the cop on your side at the scene, expect a circus or worse.

THE BOTTOM TINE

I heard a radio news report of a group attack that occurred in a section of town I have to pass through to get to my day job. The report was sketchy, so I picked up the morning paper and pieced the mess together with the aid of two eyewitness reports. (I have friends in low places.)

> **Pier, Baltimore Waterfront, 1:00 to 1:15 A.M.**
> A 41-year-old preppy guy who had recently beaten up a punk or broken up a fight (there are conflicting accounts) was fishing with two friends when two of the punk's friends came looking for revenge. After a brief argument the punks left.
>
> They returned 15 minutes later with five males in their early 20s. After a brief struggle the man's two friends dove into the harbor as he was knocked to the ground, where he was kicked in the head.

Witnesses disagree over whether he was then kicked or thrown into the water. The harbor police unit pulled him from the water, dead, shortly after.

One of the attackers was arrested and charged, having been turned in by his accomplices.

LESSON 1

In such a case the accomplices—I'm sorry, "witnesses"—are going to describe the affair as a one-on-one fight. If the guy in the above example had lived, he would probably be charged with assaulting a minor. Cops like it clean. So what if three guys held you while one kicked you? Only the kicker gets charged. The guys who made the attack possible will step back and become witnesses: for him if you live or for the state if you die.

LESSON 2

The more the punk deserves the beating you administer, the more likely he is to engineer an effective payback.

LESSON 3

No matter how tough your friends talk or how much they care about you, they will probably leave you to die rather than risk a hangnail or bloody nose.

LESSON 4

Your attackers will almost always be cast as innocent witnesses or wayward youths in need of love. The guilt-ridden, self-hating ex-hippies who make up the judiciary and social services department devote their considerable influence and abilities to protecting these punks from you and me. Although your ultimate jeopardy is mortal, the more likely danger is legal.

If you are aware and appear fit to defend yourself—but do not appear to be armed—a group attack is your most likely survival scenario. In such a case luck is important. If you're not lucky, I hope you take one of the bastards with you.

C H A P T E R

17

Unarmed?

"It went right in, and I can remember thinking, in the back of my mind, 'Jesus, it's just like cutting cheese.'"

—Lewis Millet[1]

I've only used a gun once, and I didn't have to fire it. I didn't like the way it felt leveling that thing and certainly hope I'll never have to do so again. Guns are beyond the scope of this book. Blades, sticks, and stones, however, have been with us from the beginning and will likely never go away. They area covered here.

Defense against armed attack is the area in which martial arts students are least well served. Many "experts" promote suicidal methods for dealing with the knife-armed attacker because they have little knowledge of the subject.

Since quitting high school on my 16th birthday, I have been involved in twice as many blade encounters as bare-knuckle fights. Since I moved to Baltimore at 18, virtually all of my experience with violence has revolved around the use of a weapon. These situations feel much different than a naked brawl.

I've faced a knife, used a knife, cut meat, cut a man, and been cut. But I'm no expert. Where the knife is concerned, I offer only real-life examples and tips based on my own study. I was involved in some of the following incidents, and the balance comes from a survey I conducted. All the subjects regarded a "stabbing" as far more dreadful than being cut.

EXAMPLES OF VIOLENT ATTACKS

"Put it 'way, whiteboy. I gotta .38 in da car, and I'll bus' a cap in yo crazy white ass."

—ANONYMOUS

Department store, Baltimore, at night
The subject threatened a smaller man, who then drew a razor. The subject drew a large sheath knife. The smaller man grew angry and stomped away, swearing under his breath.

Restaurant, Baltimore, during the day
The subject was blindsided by a larger man, and then shoved about four times. He drew a razor and stood his ground until his assailant backed away.

Sidewalk, Baltimore, at night
The subject was surprised by a large attack dog poised for a final leap. As the man drew his blade, the dog made eye contact, looked down at the blade, made eye contact again, and then silently walked away.

Warehouse, Baltimore, during the day
The subject was threatened by a larger

man who had a balisong knife sheathed later-
ally to his belt. As the larger man attempted
to draw his knife, the smaller man stepped on
the other's right foot with his left, while covering the drawing hand with his left, and placing his right fist against the man's mouth.
The knifeman unsuccessfully attempted to
step back . He then raised his left hand in surrender, later giving the blade to the subject as
a gift.

House, West Baltimore, at night
The subject was threatened by a bayonet-
wielding jerk who was tackled and held by
friends.

Bank, Mount Vernon, New York, during the day
A criminal holding a woman at knifepoint
was tackled by a passer-by, who held the criminal down until the police arrived.

Bar entrance, East Baltimore, during the day
A bar patron was confronted by a heroin
addict who drew a switchblade and demanded
money. The subject sent the addict to the
pavement with a front kick, applied a wrist
lock, kicked the blade into a storm drain, and
continued on his way.

Parking lots, Northeast Baltimore, during the day
On three different occasions in northeast
Baltimore, unarmed criminals threatened a
snack-food vendor and backed off when he
drew his razor knife.

Warehouse, Baltimore, during the day

Two men agreed to fight with razors until "first blood." When the younger man extended his hand to shake on the deal, the older man slashed open one of his fingers.

Alley, Baltimore, at night

The subject saw three large men dragging and beating a smaller man. As the small man was being held and hit by all three, he drew a knife from his rear right pocket and began stabbing the man to his right and the one to his front below their left arms. The men, apparently oblivious to the knife, continued to beat him and dunked him into a trash can.

As the small man tumbled from the trash can with a bloody knife in his hand, his attackers looked down at their blood-soaked clothes, panicked, and ran off, as the small man staggered away.

The witness believed that since the man drove his knife to the fist his attackers assumed they were being punched if they even knew they were being struck. All the men were drunk, and the attackers may have been on crank, crack, or coke. He estimated about three stabs on the center man and five on the leftmost man.

Park, Baltimore County, at dusk

The subject was walking his dog when an apparent jogger stabbed him in the forearm—using an ice-pick grip—without breaking stride.

Bar, East Baltimore, during the day

The subject was sitting next to two arguing men. The larger man drew a knife and began stabbing the small man in the back and shoulders—using an ice-pick grip—as they ran around the table and eventually outside and up the street, screaming all the way.

Bar entrance, Baltimore, at night

The subject was confronted by a larger man holding a switchblade high to the right and demanding money. The subject drew his knife from his rear right pocket and plunged it into the robber's left breast. The robber stood still, so the subject stabbed him again. The robber's coat began to darken as he swayed, and the subject stabbed him again. The robber began to fall forward, so the subject ducked right as the man fell and continued on his way.

Restaurant kitchen, Baltimore, at night

Two of the subject's co-workers were arguing, when the older man grabbed a butcher knife in an ice-pick grip and plunged it into the younger man's chest, killing him.

Sidewalk, Northeast Baltimore, at night

The subject was approached by four heroin addicts who mistook him for your author—whom they had been paid to kill. The punks each produced a knife and attacked in a disoriented manner—they were stoned, having been paid with heroin. The subject fought off the punks, suffering many cuts. Two of the punks were arrested, and the other two were worked over by related parties. Their employer fled the state.

Prison, Baltimore, during the day

The subject and three of his cellmates were sitting at a table playing a fantasy role-playing game. One of the players had a favorite character killed in battle. He grew angry and stabbed the game judge in the eye with a sharpened, full-length, number-2 pencil, killing him and thus ruining the subject's game and contributing to the boredom of incarceration.

(I included this under knives, because in prison anything you can stick into somebody is a knife.)

Nightclub, Houston, Texas, at night

A Mexican boxer was putting the finishing touches on a beating that he was administering to two "cowboys" when one of his opponents drew a folder and slashed upward from the floor at him. The slash cut across the boxer's left guard before ripping into his throat. The encounter was interrupted by the cops. The boxer received prompt care and survived.

Prison, Baltimore, at night

The subject, a murderer, was grabbed from behind by two larger men, who held him face-first against a wall. One of the men slashed open his rectum with a razor before sodomizing him.

Side street, South Baltimore, at night

A retail clerk pursuing a shoplifter was cut on the forearm when the criminal went for him with a small penknife. The clerk decided to retaliate with his boots but backed off when the criminal threatened him with a hypodermic needle.

And my favorite newspaper account of a knife fight . . .

Motel room, East Baltimore
Two men were reported to be fighting with knives. When the police arrived on the scene both men had died from their wounds.

Must have been a blast while it lasted!

Before gangs became big business knife fighting was an appreciated art. I have interviewed three former gang members who were active in different cities in the 1950s, 1960s, and 1970s. They each spoke of their gangs having a knife fighter who fielded challenges from members of rival gangs. In each case the knife fighter's success was attributed to his use of a coat or leather jacket as a shield. (Incidentally, Hannibal's African light cavalry used leopard skins in a similar fashion.)

I hope your appreciation of violence with a blade has been enhanced. Available knife fighting and knife defense literature and doctrine are vast and contradictory. My best advice concerning the knife is to become proficient in its use. Even if you hate the weapon, learn its mechanics. Having done so you will be able to rate available teachings from an educated perspective. Let's hope you never acquire any actual experience.

If you defend yourself successfully against an unarmed opponent, expect him to be armed when next you meet.

LEARNING TO USE A BLADE

"The dumb bastard just stood there and stared at me—so I stuck'm again."
—A CONVICTED FELON

To appreciate the knife—or any hand weapon—you must understand two basic facts:

1. Weapon fighting is easier to learn than unarmed fighting. It is more natural, requiring little gross body leverage, because . . .

2. . . . every portion of the human anatomy is "vital" when hit by a stick, stone, or blade.

In other words, a 120-pound scrub, shucking oysters at the local seafood market, can do more to damage a human body with a flick of the wrist than any 250-pound karateka can with a reverse punch.

About the only people who seem to appreciate this simple fact are students of the Filipino blade arts, perhaps because they rarely weigh more than our hypothetical seafood clerk.

The worst situation you're likely to encounter is a knife attack (except if you are attacked by someone with a firearm, of course). Also—since you were designed to fight with a hand weapon—knife fighting will be easier to pick up than, let's say, Thai boxing. Additionally, training with hand weapons develops basic abilities that are readily generalized to empty-hand fighting. Developing a keen sense of spatial relationships is, perhaps, the most important basic fighting ability, and it is best learned with weapons. This is especially true of women, who tend to be weak in this area.

Learning a weapon will help you do the following:

1. Develop basic fighting abilities
2. Enhance your ability to use improvised weapons
3. Become a lethal customer in your own home, where you are legally permitted to keep such weapons
4. Attain the first prerequisite for defending against an armed attacker—that is, the ability to conduct an armed attack

The following is an incomplete guide to understanding available training options based on my limited study and experience. (I'm in deep water here. Knife people are really fanatical about their art and know more about their blades than most fighters know about their bodies.) In my mind there are only two important points to practical weapon study: drawing and sparring. The rest might look nice, but it's all crap when the punk clears leather.

I have carried and used a large sheath knife, a folder with a 7-inch blade, and two types of razor knives for self-defense. I prefer the razors because they are easy to carry and are related to my employment—I draw them about 500 times per shift. I don't carry them when I'm not working.

I used to carry the big blades in a sheath on the belt behind the right hip, concealed by a flannel shirt tied around my waist. I had previously draped a spare bandanna over the hilt, until I figured out that all those good-looking older guys driving BMWs and wearing leather pants were not offering me rides out of kindness. Apparently the colors I usually wore translated to "be my sugar daddy" in gay sign language. These days I keep the big blades at home.

The Knife versus Sword

Blade traditions can basically be defined as knife or sword. The knife was to the sword what the pistol is to the assault rifle. On the battlefield the knife was strictly a weapon of desperation. A knife can be defined as a blade that, if used as a stabbing weapon, will commit you to grappling range. In this view, bowies, kukris, bolos, toothpicks, and other such choppers and pigstickers are short swords.

The sword was the weapon of the establishment warrior. The knife was the weapon of the conquered underclass because warriors didn't think much of it as a weapon. Consequently, strong sword traditions have been preserved by peoples—for example, the French and the Japanese—who, in their day, kicked a lot of ass on the battlefield. Such cultures generally disdain the knife, the traditional weapon of the guerrilla warrior who was driven from the open field to fight on in the hills or woods.

In the Middle Ages, Wales was the home of the knifer. The English king even raised units of Welsh knifemen. The modern counterpart would be the Filipino escrimador with his balisong or the Native American concealing a knife in an urban setting. (In Baltimore there are at least three bars frequented by Native Americans who carry knives.) Carrying a knife is a natural reaction to conquest. Political or geographical fragmentation—such as in the United States, the Philippines, or Indonesia—also contributes to strong knife traditions.

The sword is an instrument that demands deft footwork to achieve success in competition. Remember, footwork guarantees you a practical edge over the untrained fighter. For this reason, I recommend the study of fencing or kendo—these being sports—as opposed to traditional forms. Swordplay is just that; it's fun! I also recommend the sword for home defense. (A good case for this is made by Marc "Animal" MacYoung in *Cheap Shots, Ambushes, and Other Lessons,* also available from Paladin.) An elderly co-worker of mine, who happened to be a sword-bearing member of the Knights of Columbus, once foiled a home invasion with a saber.

Preparing for Different Types of Knife Fighters

Not only must you learn how to select and handle a blade properly, you must also learn how to recognize different types of knife fighters and how to defend yourself against each type.

The Untrained Knifer

The untrained knifer depends on his weapon to keep you at a safe distance. This type will tend to rely on the threat and the flicking slash from an extended knife-hand posture. You can expect to get cut against this guy, but you can also bet on making him pay. He is subject to demoralization.

Fling blood in his face, spit, or, better yet, put something in your hand and he will likely go away.

The Untrained Killer

The untrained killer hides the knife. He will stick or rip you from short range. His biggest concern is that you might get away! Expect to be grabbed. His relationship to the knife makes him psychologically "bigger" than you. For him the blade is a "bridge" to your guts, as opposed to the untrained knifer, who regards the knife as his "suit of armor." This guy isn't your opponent—he is your executioner! Encountering this kind of opponent is where traditional martial arts training will get you killed.

The Experienced Knifer

The experienced knifer is a convicted felon or gang member. The ex-con will be inclined to grab and stab (prison-made knives usually aren't edged). The gangster can be expected to have had knife training or to have settled on a method for doing business suited to his style of dress and choice of a blade. This guy might be able to take you without the blade—the blade is just an insurance policy. A scenario involving such an attacker will likely see you sustaining multiple cuts or stab wounds. Let's just hope you don't make the evening news.

Choosing the Proper Training for You

Traditional Asian Knife Training

Traditional Asian knife training is usually reserved for advanced study and, for this reason alone, should be avoided. Learn the knife from someone who will teach it to a beginner. Most knife defense doctrine is based on traditional techniques—like the overhand ice-pick attack—which use armor-piercing grips. Remember, these preserve medieval methods.

The Filipino Arts

The Filipino arts are based on the very practical premise that everything is a stick. I do not like the stylized training drills. However, these styles are easily learned and generalized, and the promoters have left behind almost all of their cultural baggage. The Filipino stick/knife arts—such as arnis, kali, escrima—are often integrated into eclectic arts and also taught alongside traditional arts. I highly recommend learning one or more of the Filipino arts.

Military Knife Systems

Military knife systems can hardly be called defensive in nature. The focus on the quick kill, and minimal technique results in methods akin to those employed behind the bars of our wonderful prison system. They are a blind alley for defensive application and definitely fall into the know-your-enemy category of study.

Traditional American Knife Fighting

Traditional American knife fighting, with the bowie or Arkansas toothpick, is fun, easy to learn with a book and sparring partner, and pretty useless beyond home defense. It's basically sword work.

Modern American Knife Systems

Modern American knife systems, if practically conceived and competently taught, offer the best of the above traditions without the political and cultural baggage that come with most arts. To rate the promoter of such a system, do the following:

1. Study the root arts he has applied to his synthesis and test his knowledge.
2. Learn the laws concerning the weapons and applications of his curriculum, and test his knowledge of them.

If he is the originator, he must have real experience, be highly intelligent, and be willing to alter his doctrine.

PERSONAL OBSERVATIONS ON
BLADE FIGHTING

1. When I draw in a real situation I become afraid that I will use the blade. This causes my palms to sweat, which brings on the fear that I will lose the blade. This causes me to grip so hard that I am unable to perform some of the subtle techniques that I depend on in sparring. I become a different, less versatile, and more ruthless fighter. I've given up on the blade for defense. I might be thinking defense when I go for it, but after the draw I've got that pest-control mentality.
2. Live bone is much harder to cut through than butchered meat bones of comparable size.
3. The blade is a very personal weapon that will tell you plenty about yourself and your enemy.

PRACTICAL IMPROVISED WEAPONS

"The black belt is nice, but I have a truck full of tools."

—SENSEI ERIC

When considering a weapon for defense there are three considerations, listed below in order of importance.

1. Can it be carried in your hand, at the ready, without putting you at odds with the law?
2. Can it be used on the streets of your community without putting you at odds with the law?
3. Can you deploy and use this weapon effectively?

The least important consideration is the inherent deadliness of the weapon: sharpness, size, caliber, etc. You need a weapon that you can (1) carry past a cop without becoming part of his job, (2) use without the judge suspecting you of criminal intent or premeditation, and (3) count on to do the job.

What follows is a list of weapons, all of which fit these criteria and have been used by me or people I have interviewed. In all cases, your training and visualizations should focus on your ability to clear the weapon for action in a situation where your attacker has the initiative.

The most important aspect of carrying a nonweapon is the deterrent effect. Any item carried in the hand, which is not a valuable or a burden, will deter most men and virtually all dogs and punks from attacking.

- Change in the hand is better than a knife in your pocket. Keep a handful of loose pennies in your front pockets for hand-strengthening exercises to while away idle moments. Do not use rolled change (this would indicate premeditation) or larger coins that might cut into your hand. Determine how many pennies fit your hand and casually arm yourself whenever you smell a rat. A handful of copper lends weight and stability to your fist and when hurled into an attacker's face or tossed beneath his feet further enhances your edge.
- A jacket or shirt in the hand makes a fair blinder or blade catcher. I always carry a spare insulated flannel shirt. I have successfully used it as a blinder, though I wouldn't want to test it against a sheath knife—that's a job for a leather jacket.
- A handbag, if nearly empty, can be used like a shirt. If it's loaded, either push-throw it into an attacker's chest with the lead hand or drop it at arm's length between you and him. To make contact he will have to step on, over, or around it, or kick it away. That's a lot of time when things are going down.
- An umbrella is the perfect improvised weapon.
- A cane is the most obvious and effective choice. If you are an arnis or jo-stick student, bring the cane to class. If you aren't old or handicapped, tell the cop you carry it to keep dogs at bay.
- A rolled newspaper is a fair substitute for the stick if you

are strong on the thrust. Use the tall papers like the *New York Post* or the citywide free weekly, wrapped tightly with four rubber bands: one at each end and two (a hand's width apart) in the middle. Large magazines, such as *Life*, are even better.

- A can of food is a deadly—and edible—weapon. Soup is ideal. ("I beat him with my lunch, officer.") If you're going for effect, use a can of sweetened condensed milk, tomato paste, or corned beef. Place your canned good in the bottom of two of those cheap plastic supermarket shopping bags that tear on the way to the car and knot them just above the can. Strike with the rim. And you thought those nunchuka lessons were a waste of time!

- A long-necked bottle is good in a pinch and best when full. Be warned, though, they aren't as common as they used to be, especially where you need them. A few years back I was being followed by some boyz as I strolled through a decidedly low-scale neighborhood. The first thing I looked for was a chunk of loose road tar. No potholes—amazing—no luck. Of course, all the bottles on the sidewalk had been shattered, so I ducked into a Korean liquor store to grab a quart. The cooler was packed with 40-ounce malt liquor with no handle—I mean neck—and $5 bottles of fortified wine. I only had $2. Sensing that my plight was one of taste rather than survival, the proprietor unearthed an ancient 22-ounce long-necked Heineken he had been saving for a pretzel vendor—and waved the container tax. What a deal. What a weapon.

- A soup stone is an "edged" missile-weapon. For decades, heartless supermarket clerks have been taking down homeless shoplifters, thieving heroin addicts, and greedy food-stampers with well-aimed volleys of canned cat food and tuna fish, favored for their space-age aerodynamics. For serious business I prefer the 12-ounce soup can thrown at the head. Extend your lead hand while cocking the throwing hand. The index finger is placed on the rim so that the thrown can will tumble, cutting with the rim on impact. You do not throw until your target advances to within two arms' length. I developed this method after seeing a customer knocked out by a can that tumbled only 2 feet before impact. My only actual application was against a teenager who drew an air gun on me. I measured the punk and cocked for the throw. He got the shakes after about 30 seconds and backed off.

- A pencil or pen is an effective weapon. But it's only good for one shot, because it breaks or shatters when hitting bone. It works particularly well on fat guys if you put it in the arm pit. I once used a pencil on a big guy and snapped off the point between his ribs. Lucky for me he was a wimp. Stabbing with such a short object commits you to grappling range.

- A choke chain for an 80-plus pound dog makes a wicked flail, although it is only effective against such light, sensitive structures as the face and hands. It is suitable for strangulation, but that's not something easily passed off as "self-defense."

- Items unique to your trade such as a tool belt, rolled change, briefcase, or stethoscope are your best bet. My standard in-hand weapon is a pair of hard leather kneepads buckled together over a bundle of rubber-coated gloves, secured with a bungee cord. This weapon offers hand protection and pairs well with the flannel shirt for defense against the blade.

- Body armor is advisable if you have some forewarning concerning a knife attack—like if you just beat up a meat cutter who caught you with his wife. Go to a hardware store or supermarket and get a roll of wide tape and two stapled magazines. Take your shirt off and tape the magazines to your body. (Put your shirt back on.) The fold should be over your nipples. This will overlap in the front and wrap around to cover the kidneys from the front angle. Tape the left one three inches above the nipple to cover the heart and the right one at the nipple to cover the liver—hell, you have two lungs. If you're going to go to all of this trouble you might as well buy a screwdriver or claw hammer. If you're hairy, shedding the armor will be lots of fun.

Pick-Up Weapons

Pick-up weapons can be reliable assets and require little explanation in court. I recommend walking a known route that you have scouted for loose items that may be picked up on the run.

In low-class neighborhoods hard trash items, such as boards and pipes, are common in alleys. On the street you have the ruined furnishings of evicted tenants on every fifth block and broken curbs and lifted road tar.

Up-scale environs offer slim pickings, with the exception of garden bricks and those flimsy aluminum security signposts.

Working-class areas offer the best of both worlds—road tar and garden bricks—and have plenty of pickups loaded with rusty tools, boards, and bricks.

In any area trash days are like a gun show for the improvised weapons connoisseur. My survey was chock full of examples of pick-up weapons being used. Welcome to the real-world of do-it-yourself armed mayhem. . . .

"I had to fight at least once every time I took over a new crew—you know, they never wanna work. There was this one big boy, he really kicked my ass. He was gone the next day though . . . was a shame 'bout his leg. Beats me what happened—you know, freak accident. Hell, I was working on the scaffold right above him, and I didn't see that cinder block fall. Poor guy."

—RAMROD RICK

Apartment, Wheeling West Virginia, at night

A man came home drunk and was attacked by his wife. She struck him in the eye with his favorite bowling trophy. Blood squirted out with every beat of his heart as he "tried to get the bitch." He was arrested and hospitalized.

House, Baltimore, during the day

A man was pole-axed with a commercial push broom, resulting in a disabling brain injury.

Porch, South Baltimore, at night

A bodybuilder was asked to break up a fight between too larger brothers. He tried to pry them apart with an umbrella. The men turned on him—one holding the umbrella, as the other punched him out.

Street, South Baltimore, at night

A small, middle-aged man came to the aid of a woman being beaten by her boyfriend. The boyfriend retrieved a baseball bat from his car and beat the older man severely. The good Samaritan suffered a disabling brain injury. The boyfriend did a little time.

Street, West Baltimore, at night

A man high on "super pot" fought two men, one of whom produced a bat. He sustained a broken forearm and multiple bruises.

Bar, Glen Burnie, Maryland, during the day

A pool shark began to hassle his opponent, who was leaning with his back to a wall, chalking his cue. The pool shark pretended to turn away, but wheeled and hit the man over the head with his cue. A large patron grabbed his cue as he cocked for another swing at the downed man and pushed him across the room, ending the confrontation. The victim had his scalp split from the back of his ear to his eye. The pool shark was not charged with a crime.

High school, East Baltimore, during the day

A jealous girl brought a 2x4 to school and split open her rival's skull with one swing.

Parking lot, East Baltimore, at night

An old woman was attacked and robbed by three punks, one of whom was armed with a pipe. She suffered crippling injuries.

Sidewalk, Baltimore, at night

Three men kicked a man into the gutter. One wrapped a chain around his neck and held his head to the curb as another kicked him in the teeth.

Backyard, Northeast Baltimore, at night

When a woman took the last rib off the grill, her sister-in-law split her head open with a beer bottle.

Street, South Baltimore, at night

A "diesel dyke" tackled a smaller heterosexual woman from behind, took off one of her shoes, and beat her in the head. A man intervened.

Stairway, West Baltimore, at night

A man came home from work and was

attacked by his "bitch," who took a swing at his head with a crutch. He blocked the blow with a raised shoulder and disarmed her. She called the cops and had him arrested.

Garage, East Baltimore, during the day

A gunman was apprehended by a mechanic who held a nailgun to his chest.

Lunch room in a supermarket, Northeast Baltimore, at night

A manager closing for the night was attacked by two men. One held him, while the other hit him over the head with an electric frying pan. He was knocked out and suffered a severe scalp laceration.

Bar, South Baltimore, during the day

Following an argument, a man returned with a sickle and struck another man from behind, taking off the top of his head. A bar patron helped hold his scalp on until help arrived. The psycho did three years.

You get the idea, right? Among the remaining weapons reported in the survey were pencils, hatchets, stones, bricks, bottles, purses, and hammers. The most surprising finding was that such a high percentage of women used weapons, though none used knives. (The knife must be a phallic symbol.)

I suppose tools are our thing.

NOTES

1. Rudy Tomedi, *No Bugles, No Drums: An Oral History of the Korean War.* (New York: Wiley, 1993), pp. 109–116.

CHAPTER 18

Survival

"The fact that most people act predictably is literally what holds human societies together."

—Gavin De Becker, *The Gift of Fear*

This was not intended as a book on street survival. I do have a great deal of experience in a few specific areas, but handling barroom situations is *not one of them*. That's not my element. No loss there; doormen and bouncers such as Geoff Thompson *(Watch My Back: A Bouncer's Story* and *Dead or Alive*, both available from Paladin Press) and other authors present a wealth of information on this unique environment.

Bar fighting is similar to domestic violence, being alcohol related, one-sided, and generally tolerated by the law. The only real difference is that barfight victims have reliable backup.

Now, let's take a tour of the nasty subculture of the mass-transit-dependent city dweller. . . .

"They be offerin' me three, but be talkin' seven—suspended. Yo crazy nigga took a offer for ten—suspended. And yo dumb nigga be doin' two. I thinkn' seven good. That way I stay in bidness."

—Spin

"Shit, there's more dope in prison than there is on the street. If you got enough cigarettes you can get all you need to get well."

—Little John

Two million American adults are doing time. For every one of them, two more just like them are on parole or probation. For every criminal caught in the gossamer judicial web, three slip through the cracks. This means that about one in ten American adults are involved in crime.[1] In some areas that I frequent only one in ten adult males are *not* involved in crime.

The urban criminal is a guerrilla fighter who uses various means to wage war on civil society. Like any insurgent, the career criminal is organized. If you are a law-abiding citizen your contact with career criminals should be with the least sophisticated thugs, such as muggers. Unfortunately, it is not always so. On four occasions I have been compelled to deal with organized criminals who posed a threat to me or family members. Without putting myself in legal jeopardy, I will discuss the habits of low-level organized criminals and how to deal with them.

Basically, you have two options:

1. Make a credible threat of retaliation. This requires that you be willing to proceed with the next option.
2. Kill or cripple the criminals making the threats.

Option one worked for me on all four occasions. Be fore-warned though: without a gun, knife, or reputation, no thug is going to take you seriously. Also, you must be able to hunt the criminals down to lodge or carry out a credible threat. Where do you find them?

TRACKING CRIMINALS

If you have to become the hunter, know your prey. The time to hit is usually morning or afternoon; a criminal usually stays up till daybreak. Criminals and bad guys are dependent on one or more sanctuaries. The more experienced criminal has access to a variety of safe houses.

Follow the Women

"Mama's place" is home base for juvenile delinquents and is known to the cops; for the "mature criminal" it usually serves only as a communications relay point.

The wife's or main girlfriend's crib is the basic safe house. Our boy knocks up a girl so that she can get a subsidized apartment. He is a phantom resident and supplies her with cash and weed.

The side girlfriend's place is often a forward base of operations. Our boy is now a man. He finds a lonely, gainfully employed young lady who is estranged from her abusive common-law husband and treats her like a human being. In turn she supplies him with sex, food, possibly a vehicle, and access to her apartment, which, ideally, is situated in the midst of a middle-class or working-class community. Retaining a side girlfriend affords him transportation, a safe forward base, and access to relatively affluent drug markets and burglary targets.

Criminals are also commonly found at another "crib": an establishment operated by a woman they know, who is usually a whore. In any case, she is shared by a number of men who may be close, loosely associated, or a complete strangers. She may supply sex to a married man for money. She may provide sanctuary for a hitter in return for protection. She is probably trading drugs for sex with a dealer and may even be selling some of those drugs to one of her other men.

This is where our man is most vulnerable. I once overhead a conversation between two men on the back of a bus the day after a triple stabbing. Apparently it was one of their mutual friends who did the deed on his own. He "cleaned out that crib" in a brutal fashion.

Gang Places

The "ranch"—a house occupied by a gang, deep in a lower-class or ethnic area—is where you *don't* go looking for your man unless you have a tactical squad or a terminal case of cancer. The owner may be a sister or mother but is probably a landlord who likes cash and has an aversion to lead.

Fast-Food Joints

"You go first. You eat here? My black ass is sittin' right here. If they wann me they gonna have some hippie first."

—SAND MAN

Fast food is the staple of the criminal diet. If you can only narrow your prey down to a project or apartment complex, stake out the local saturated-fat emporium. Pick the one closest to a corner (where cabs can be hailed) or at a bus stop.

Bars

Bars that open at 6:00 A.M. are populated with hard-core alcoholics who often work at night, but these establishments also offer a lifeline to the career criminal. Many who work midnight are addicted to some kind of drug and don't have credit, so they carry cash.

Hair Salons

In the city, hair salons are often money-laundering fronts. Your local dealer can set his sister up in business and wash a lot of money. More stolen goods are sold in salons than in bars or on buses. The dealer won't show up, but the guy who stops by to sell hot videos probably knows him.

"Preventiveness—avoiding trouble—is infinitely superior to using physical self-defense."

—Jerry Samuelson

As a Pedestrian

Walking more than two city blocks once he has accessed the main road is degrading; walking any distance in the city is conspicuous. If any man walks in the same direction as you for more than one block at night or two blocks during the day, go to Condition Red, a state of extreme alertness. Don't look at any suspicious follower unless he is changing directions to approach you.

If he is behind you, listen for his steps and turn your head to look across the street. His partner may be over there, waiting to cut you off. More important, this puts him in your peripheral vision, without letting him know you are spooked. At night I get to the curbside and use the shadows cast by the street lights to watch my back.

To determine if he is following you, slow down to let him pass or turn a corner. Definitely abandon whatever regular route you may be following—unless you remember where that loose chunk of curb is. If he persists on a main street, go to the median and walk the centerline. He will probably quit right there, and if he doesn't, being up on the median gives you leverage to shove him into traffic.

If he follows you up a side street, turn on him. If he has a weapon, he will probably pull it after your second turn. I once turned on some guy who had followed me for 10 blocks. It turned out that he was just going my way, but I'd rather be safe than sorry.

As a Bus Passenger

At the Bus Stop

Relative to your general level of risk, waiting for the bus or any ride can be the equivalent of conducting a long-range reconnaissance patrol in a hot landing zone. Many muggings happen at bus stops, especially where suburban-to-downtown lines intersect with the crosstown lines that link rehab centers, courthouses, and housing projects with the white-trash drug dens that proliferate in old ethnic neighborhoods. Rate the risk factors of bus stops based on the number of intersecting bus lines and the amount and composition of the ground litter. Other contributing factors include proximity to automatic teller machines, liquor stores, check-cashing shops, public schools, prisons, bars, and beauty salons.

Bus stops are worked by winos, bums, and career panhandlers. The winos and bums are easily shrugged off and respond well to modest handouts, but the panhandlers are far more sinister than the media would have you believe. Your panhandler may be your brother's shoplifter, your son's mugger, your wife's rapist, or your mother's murderer. Treat him like the garbage he is. Do not encourage or validate his activity.

Two local panhandlers once fought to the death barehanded over a $300-a-day white-guilt bus stop location. One of my slimy co-workers seriously considered quitting work and knocking off the winner so he could get his spot! Panhandlers tend to be addicts, and thus their blood is as deadly as gunfire. Their operational handbook for panhandlers suggests the following tactics:

1. Establish a bond based on race, drug use, or bus use.
2. Appeal to the subject's sense of social guilt or human compassion. Use this as a lever to extract a small quantity of cash for "food" or "bus fare."
3. If the subject is nervous or otherwise vulnerable, escalate to outright begging.
4. If the subject is alone and shows weakness, escalate to threat.
5. If the subject is alone and incapable of defense, use force.

Not too long ago I was approached by an inexperienced panhandler who conducted a disastrous interview. His chief error was in applying the common white-guilt/white-fear tactic on an honorary African-American. It went like this. . . .

The panhandler approached me at a bus stop at 9:15 P.M., no doubt assuming I was leaving the bar across the street (drunks are generous). He was slightly smaller than I and pretended to wait for the bus for only five seconds (the standard is two minutes) before asking, "Could you spare . . ."

"No!" I interrupted him.

He hesitated and then began again, "Could you spare some change for bus fare?"

"No!" I yelled again.

He backed away, hesitated, and asked, "How long before the bus comes?"

I answered politely, "Ten, maybe fifteen." (I lied, it was five minutes.)

He mistook my politeness for guilt and tried to salvage the situation by asking, "What's with the attitude?"

I don't remember exactly what I said, but I definitely violated the nuclear test ban treaty. I had only enough change for my bus ride, was nursing various injuries, and wasn't looking forward to 16 hours of humping freight. The result was a vicious torrent of threats and obscenities as I pinned the panhandler against the wall, stabbing my index finger into his face to punctuate every four-letter word. His arms gone limp, eyes bulging, and mouth open, he simply stood in a daze. However, I eventually took a breath and stepped back.

Obviously not fluent in postindustrial white male angst, the panhandler repeated his question, "What's with the attitude?"

I stepped in with the intention of throwing him into traffic but hesitated at the lack of comprehension in his eyes. I gave the answer, in his face, in his language because, as I explained, "I'd rather spend the night in jail than go do what I have to do."

He said, "I understand," and backed away.

He stood around for a few seconds as I tried to pace off the adrenalin shakes before mumbling, "I better go," and walking away.

The whole deal was a shock to me. I usually have impeccable self-control. The week before I'd calmly read the newspaper as two attractive young ladies screamed obscenities in my face for a full 15 minutes. In any case, I hope my behavior pushed the panhandler into early retirement.

Here are some safety tips that have worked for me over the years.

1. Stay mobile. Pace as if your ride is overdue or walk the bus line, pausing only briefly at suspect stops.
2. Vary your arrival times and, if you drive, your parking locations.
3. Do not stand in the open or against a wall. Put your back to a trash bin, mailbox, or light pole. This protects your back against a rear attacker and can be used as a "post" to frustrate a frontal attacker.
4. Stay near the curb. This is the most reliable terrain feature in the city. Stepping off—or onto—a curb will require the enemy to alter his approach tactics, either backing off or tipping his hand.
5. When approached, take a single step to the left of your antagonist, look straight ahead past him, shift any burden into your left hand, drop your right to a concealed position, and speak briefly with authority, as you scan for a possible secondary attacker with your peripheral vision.
6. Smiling and nodding positively to yourself, while avoiding eye contact, deters all but the most confident or deranged pests.

On the Bus

"Yo, I hate whitemuthafucas. I paticuly hate that long-haired white muthafuca. Yo, if I had my shit I'd bus' a cap in 'is Crocodile Dundee-ass, yo."
—ONE NORTH AVENUE BOY TO ANOTHER ON THE #19 BUS LINE

I was two seats from these fine young men, pretending to be asleep. The scary part was that they were talking in hushed tones. This wasn't a case of harassment—they were discussing options for eliminating one more of "The Man's soldiers."

The night before I had overheard a similar conversation on the back of the same bus. Three gangstas were arguing over how many times to shoot their target—a dealer they were scheduled to meet—in the head. They decided on three, because one "had shot a brutha in a head who live," and another "know a female who eat two 'n live."

Where you sit is very important on a bus. A bus seats about 45, but not comfortably. Where you sit pretty much determines your options and flags you for the predators, who may number as high as 10 percent of the passengers on some lines.

I always avoid confrontational eye contact with armed or intoxicated punks. But sometimes things get even more entertaining in this strange alternate reality. . . .

"I'd been laid low by life, by 'Nam. But was brought up through the Pit of Redemption by Jesus, who is the liv'n organism of The Word of The Lord—and I'll kick yer ass too, boy, right off this bus!"

—Prophet, #19 bus line

The following are some tips to help you choose a seat on a bus to avoid trouble.

1. Window seats are dangerous because they expose you to incoming fire. I have been stoned, bricked, egged, and shot at by boyz as I presented the only white target on buses cruising through their 'hood. I didn't get hurt, but three windows did. Also, the forward-facing window seats permit you no leverage or footing in case of attack. I once had to bite my way out of such a spot.
2. The 10 or 12 handicapped aisle-facing bench seats are "safe," being close to the driver and his security phone. However, sitting there flags you as vulnerable and may set you up for some bus-stop action.
3. The first four rows of forward-facing aisle seats are pretty safe, and sitting there doesn't make a statement either way.

The psychology of bus seating is identical to classroom-seating patterns in high school.

4. Sitting in the back of the bus is a challenge to the punk ethos. I do it all the time. This almost guarantees some level of discomfort or harassment while on the bus, because all of the scum sit back there. Over 50 percent of those who choose to sit at the back of the bus have criminal records. However, since you have flagged yourself as a criminal or nutcase, you have saved yourself from a lot of bus-stop harassment. I sit in the back and then get off the front. This is a clear challenge. (The convenience of sitting in the back is in getting off through the back door. That way you don't have to squeeze past the mass of unwashed humanity that is crowding onto the front of the bus.)

5. Your prime tactical seats are the middle back bench seat and the seat across the aisle from the rear door well. Both are good bailout spots and good attack bases. Any of the seats next to one of the 10 upright rails is superior. These are all aisle seats. The left side of the bus (when facing forward) is better than the right side, because it allows you to hold onto a rail with your left hand while you take care of business with your right. It also makes it easier to apply banking and dumping tactics, since the bus is always banking right to load and off-load.

Bus Fighting Tactics

Bus fighting tactics are based on seating, gouging, biting, and rail swinging. These are all subject to the accelerating, decelerating, and banking of the bus. Striking, tripping, and butting are dependent on rail swinging, which, in turn, is subject to the movement of the bus. Strike to your rear when the bus accelerates, to the front when it decelerates, to the right when it banks to a stop, and to the left as it reenters traffic. The most effective techniques, listed in order, from my most to least favorite, are as follows:

- Eye gouge
- Trip and shoulder-butt dump into the stairwell

- Skull grind on the square aluminum rail
- Shoulder-butt into the windshield
- Swinging heel kick to the face of a cretin in an aisle-facing seat
- Elbow
- Hand bite
- Knee to groin
- Leg trample
- Back fist

I have used all but three of the above tactics.

Safety Tips

- Be nice to the driver. One driver saved me from gang members who tried to board the bus to get me because the only other passenger was a black girl they thought was with me.
- Pick out the people who use the bus to commute to work and befriend—or at least nod to—them.
- Back the driver against punks and drunks.
- Take a rolled newspaper or magazine on board a bad line. Free publications are often available at major stops.
- Pick out a likely victim from up front and adopt her. Don't say a thing. Just be polite and be her Secret Service agent. The predators pick up on the big-brother syndrome and go look for greener pastures. They don't want competition or opposition. Give them either and they walk.
- Don't overdo the last point. I once saw two boyz hassling a white woman in a most obnoxious manner as I waited for a bus. I wanted to step in, but she was shrugging it off, so I just kept an eye on the situation. They were yelling, "Give us money!" She kept smiling and walking. She was a big babe, and I figured she felt like she could handle these punks. I personally know two martial artists who would have wiped these guys out by this time.

As they came next to me the lead punk demanded once more, "Give me money!" with his hand out.

She smiled and said, "Not until you cut the grass."

He said, "Come on, Mamma? Please?"

She would have worked me over with that 20-pound purse!

Protecting Yourself against Dogs

The urban dog problem is related to pet neglect and the dog-fighting industry. Here are three profiles of canine antagonists. These are all groups; an individual dog of any size or temperament does not pose a significant threat to a healthy man, armed or not.

Roving Male Pairs

Roving male pairs are the most common—and weakest—canine threat. It basically comes down to whacking the leader of the pair. I usually chase the dogs into traffic or offer them a handout and then attempt to break their lead shoulder joint with a stomp kick. Roving dogs are dangerous to kids, pets, and old ladies, so don't get your teddy bears in an uproar. Cops in big cities sometimes shoot them at night.

Stray Canine Gangs

Stray gangs rarely have much cohesion, are unhealthy, and do most of their damage against decent pets. However, I do remember one pretty impressive canine gang that lived in a rathole called Pig Town, behind the Orioles' stadium in Baltimore.

I figure no place is bad at 6:00 A.M. on a Sunday in January. So I walked through a deserted industrial park and rail yard and bumped into two well-dressed black dudes arguing over the contents of the open trunk of a Mercedes—oops! I hobbled over to the residential area in a hurry, only to be confronted by a gang of seven dogs sleeping in a circle in the middle of an intersection. The alpha male rolled over, looked at me, and barked to the others, once. The two smallest mutts trailed me while beta shadowed me from behind the parked cars and omega loped across my path as if to cut me off. Just as I was cursing all the derelicts and heroin addicts in Pig Town for not buying dog food, these dogs peeled off and let me turn left. Whew!

Packs

Packs in the city are primarily composed of escaped or retired fighting dogs. They are smart, have a lot of cohesion, and avoid people. There is a pack in Northeast Baltimore made up of two mangy pit pulls, a black Staffordshire, and a white Staffordshire. They slipped right by me one night, headed down a major street toward a park. They stayed in the shadows and moved fast. Alpha checked the side streets with his bitch. The other female scanned the road, while her male guarded the rear, looking over his shoulder every four steps. It was like watching a commando team.

Dog-Fighting Tactics

Any dog-fighting tactics you adopt should be based on three factors: (1) dogs must attack with their face because they have no other weapons, which presents the eyes and tender snout as targets for you, (2) their tendency to circle, and (3) the fact that they usually have to rear up as well. This makes gouging, sweeping, and stomping prime. Dogs usually attack as a group and go for the throat. My favorite tactic is to grab an attacking dog by the scruff of the neck and use it as a missile. For you big guys this should be a one-handed deal. Put a little spin on it and aim for the curb. Dogs are basically all ribs and legs. For some reason, they almost always take a good shot to the head. I hit an 80-pound mutt with punches that have stopped tough middleweights, just to have the thing growl—of course, the last middleweight I fought had growled too.

REVENGE

"When Percy was told that they had been felled by a single assailant he laughed loudly and implied that if they were killed by one man they were hardly worth avenging."

—JAMES MACKAY, *William Wallace: Brave Heart*

Many people study fighting in hopes of developing the ability to avenge past beatings or insults. But what happens when you finally get that chance? I've gotten the answer to that question on four occasions, and each time the answer came as a surprise.

1. At age 12 I had finally emerged from my wimpy shell, with a resolve to never again suffer another insult. Having been insulted by a classmate, I sentenced him to an after-school beating every day for the rest of the school year. Our friends were horrified; one pointed out that there were 32 remaining school days! After a couple of beatings, he stopped fighting back. The business got pretty grim after that as I dutifully carried out the sentence day after day. One day he looked up at me and asked, "Aren't you getting sick of this?"

   I replied, "Yeah, but I can't let them know."

   He suggested that I "chase" him behind the trees and pretend to tackle him. I would then follow him home where we would play with his model collection. He promised to tell everyone that I did indeed beat him up. By the close of that school year Charlie's accounts of my ruthless beatings had convinced the entire student body that I was a bloodthirsty fiend, with the result that Charlie became my only friend. The reputation was worth the ostracism. I didn't have to fight again until our family moved to Pennsylvania.

2. When "Unk" moved out of town, "Cuz" got to stay with us to finish his senior year in high school. We had had little contact since his brutal swimming lesson four years earlier. (See Chapter 2 for this and other stories about "Unk" and "Cuz.") At 15, I was lean and savagely mean, always itching to fight. I lived in the woods, returning to the house long enough to work out, shower, and hoard food for my cache. Cuz was now 6 foot and 230 pounds—the varsity wrestler at school. He regarded me with the same love, respect, and understanding that ranchers have for coyotes.

   I was shadowboxing on the back patio of my father's hillside ranch when Cuz began poking me with a broom handle. I turned and tore the stick from his hands and then broke it over his head. He growled, got red in the face, and charged me like he was coming off the line of scrimmage. (He was an offensive lineman too.)

I ran like hell up around the hillside as he closed in, puffing like a trained sprinter. I ran in the front door, with him so close behind that he caught the storm door before I got through the doorway. As he was chasing me down the basement stairs I decided to go to my room for a knife. I was four steps below him when I hit the smooth tile floor of the basement. I stepped right toward my room, and then—without thought—pivoted back around a 180-degree with a right uppercut. The punch caught him in the solar plexus as he came down off the second stair with both feet. He hurled enough air to blow back my hair. I ripped a left hook to his jaw and followed up with a right elbow to the temple.

As I stepped back to survey the damage—the most common weakness of the young trained fighter—I couldn't hate him. He was weaving in a daze. He put his hands on his knees, looked at me, snarled silently, and sucked in air. I panicked and ran for the woods, picked up my spear and club, and headed for my campsite to set an ambush. Adolescent fantasies of hanging him by his toes and extracting fingernails filled my mind as I waited till nightfall. He never came. The next morning we observed an unspoken truce, which has endured to this day. We had both been scared, and we both admired the other's effort.

We settled our differences with an eating contest that saw him consume 13 steak sandwiches to my 11. He won the heavyweight crown, and I was pound-per-pound champ.

Sixteen years later we discussed the incident at a family reunion. When I mentioned the time he almost drowned me at the ocean he couldn't recall the episode. When I explained, he got a sad look on his face and said, "I'm glad I didn't follow you into the woods." He still thinks I'm a freak of nature, but we get along just fine.

3. I was headed home drunk. I don't usually drink much, but some older co-workers were so impressed with my walking

10 miles to work—after my cokehead driver decided to snort his gas money—that they bought me tequila and beer for six hours. Needless to say, I was pretty pickled when I ran into the skinhead who had put out a contract on me five years earlier. They had knifed the wrong guy, and he had skipped town. But I was still a little miffed. He was bigger than me, and I had offered to fight him as a way of satisfying our mutual hatred—then he put out the contract!

When I saw him with his hair grown in, looking dejected as his new wife nagged and their little baby cried, I saw no need to relieve him of his suffering. I walked up to him—as he had a cow—and forgave him. He said something agreeable, and we shook hands and parted.

4. Because I picked up jobs in pursuit of better wages, and Geno (you'll remember him as one of the two people who ambushed me at work in Chapter 1) was fired from supermarkets regularly, it was inevitable that we would meet again as co-workers. (Between the two of us we have worked in more than 60 area supermarkets.) The odd thing was I had gotten to know some of his drinking buddies. One told me that Geno once confessed to "fucking up some young guy" and that he appeared to be haunted by it. However, I wanted revenge. I had found out that he and the super had already lined up work before they jumped me on the job years ago. They had wanted to cripple me and get me fired.

In addition, I now had four part-time jobs and two full-time job offers on the table. When I heard that Geno was being transferred to my store—as a demotion—I prepared for satisfaction! Losing the job was going to be his problem this time.

For two nights I refused to look at him. I was that sure that I'd go for him. I had promised my supervisor that I wouldn't waste him until after the shift. That became frustrating. I could smell the bastard! He smelled the same as he had 10 years earlier—cheap cigars and cheap cologne.

He was getting away each morning. He would count my freight (280 to 340 cases) and then get his buddy—the super—to assign him 80 to 120 cases. I was being set up again.

Geno had once been the best clerk in Baltimore. He was the first guy to freight 300 pieces per shift, back in the 1970s (the benchmark in the grocery business is 200 cases per eight-hour shift). On the third night I stared at him, and he knew that this would be the morning. For four hours we raced through our freight. The years of drinking had taken their toll. He gave up and paced himself, so he could leave late with his friends. Outworking this macho-man by three to one had brought a measure of satisfaction, but he was still going to get his beating. (You can make a boring job like freighting a supermarket interesting by turning it into a sport.)

I waited in the parking lot as he gathered his escorts: two guys who were terrified of their own shadow and who promptly split when I approached him. Geno begged me not to beat him, right in front of the wimps he had once bullied. He really couldn't afford to lose this job, he begged. This was the end of the road for him.

I gave him an out: he could fight me off company property. We'd keep our jobs, and I'd let it go after that. He motioned to his sagging gut and said, "I can't fight ya, Jimmy. I ain't what I used ta be."

"Yeah. Ten years does a lot—ya look like shit."

"I'm really sorry 'bout what happened, Jimmy. I don't even remember how it went down. That other guy got me drunk and smoked-up and said you was gettin' me fired for the shit he stole. I had to talk to the Jamaican the next day to find out how it went down. I always liked ya."

"So you won't fight?"

"It wouldn't be a fight."

"A fight wasn't what I had in mind."

"I know. I deserve it."

"Well, I'm not doin' it. I'm sick a thinkin' about it."

"Thanks, Jimmy."

There went another made-for-video-macho-vengeance-fantasy down the toilet. He treated me like a king for eight months, until he punched out our boss—who actually deserved it—and got fired.

Last year he came to me looking for a job. I tried to help him out, but he left empty-handed. When I watched him walk out the door I could hardly imagine him standing over me in the aisle growling threats that he was capable of fulfilling. I'm hardly pious, but God does appear to do it best.

NOTES

1. "Crime Trends," *Personal Defense Newsletter*, October 1998. I used their figures as the basis for mine. However, the official statistics are always a matter of politics. I factored in active criminals who are not currently under government supervision, as well as the "oppressed" patrons of our wonderful juvenile justice system.

Conclusion

When I began this book three years ago I invisioned a 60-page cross training handbook. The research was only intended to fill in obvious blind spots. I soon found out how much I had to learn. Paradoxically, after learning how to order my thoughts in preparing the manuscript, I discovered that I knew far more than I originally suspected. Balancing the acquisition of new knowledge with a better understanding of previous experiences has made this an enlightening endeavor.

If the reader of this book learns half as much as the author did in its preparation, it will be a lot. However, this project was personally important in other ways.

First, if I get whacked on the bus tonight, the advice I intend to give to my younger son at puberty has been preserved. That would certainly be a comfort as I spat blood into the eyes of the dope fiend who was shanking my guts out.

Second, since recovering from the initial shock induced by

the discovery that I had been an idiot for most of my adult life, I can honestly say that it's nice to be intelligent. I've been living the book for three years—every threat an interview, each punk a case study—and it's been real!

Finally, I hope your decision to read this book has been one of many smart moves you make in preparing to deal with real violence. There are few things more valuable than the ability to fight effectively for survival. Good luck.

APPENDIX 1

Training
Survey

According to a survey of 20 self-defense instructors, the most important piece—or set—of training equipment is . . .

1. Heavy bag   5
2. Grappling mat   3
3. Wooden dummy   3
4. Sparring gear   2
5. Stick   2
6. Focus mitts   2
7. Groin, neck, and eye protection to
   be worn by the aggressor in
   defense scenarios   2
8. "Clapper" hand targets   1

Most of those surveyed described most of the other items on the list as being very important.

One objection to the heavy bag was based on the unsuitability of standard hanging bags for adult and child students without time-consuming hanging adjustments.

One strong objection to the author's recommended use of the chest protector is based on the fact that novice students become dependent on the equipment and do not learn to protect their torso.

APPENDIX 2

Fighter Survey

I have typed more than 200 subjects of a three-year study on personal violence according to the nature of their involvement with violence into the following categories They are listed in order from those enjoying the lowest level of subjective success to those who do best handling or dispensing violence.

- Inexperienced trained fighters (ITFs) almost always had unsatisfactory first experiences with real violence.
- Nonfighters also tended to get negative results though they suffered less emotional distress than ITFs.
- Punks or wannabes achieved their mendacious ends in less than half of their encounters.
- Women who fought did surprisingly well and were satisfied with the results of their efforts in most cases, except for those selected by unintoxicated sexual predators.
- Athletes in all categories fared better than nonathletes.

- Experienced untrained fighters reported the highest ratio of indecisive encounters, the least satisfaction with law enforcement, and the firmest belief in weapon use.
- Experienced trained fighters were successful in almost all of their violent encounters.
- Violent criminals almost always selected vulnerable prey, enjoyed an almost perfect success rate, and rarely faced serious legal penalties.
- Habitual fighters were all exceptional physical specimens, fought almost exclusively under the influence of alcohol against pathetic to light opposition, and averaged 20 brawls a year while drinking.
- Compulsive fighters represented 2 percent of the participants. They were all trained fighters, were either sadists or egomaniacs, and were most likely to maim or kill their opponents. The author uncovered no evidence that an adult in this category ever failed to impose his will on an opponent or victim.

APPENDIX 3

Violence Survey

The following is a breakdown of 460 violent incidents collected by the author from June 1996 through October 1998, via questionnaire and interview.

Indoors	221
Outdoors	240 (1 from inside to outside)
Night	241
Day	219
Attack	279
Mutual combat	181
Drunk attacker/defender	204–223
Attacker/defender on job*	65–61
Female attacker/defender	40–51
Group attacker/defender	105–51
Armed attacker/defender**	129–46
Trained attacker/defender	88–119

Decisive outcome***	325
Knockout	134 (incapacitated by strike)
Grappling	123 (includes upright holds)
Medical attacker/defender	31–118
Legal attacker/defender	48–29
Death attacker	7 (includes 1 attack dog)
Death defender	16 (includes 1 guard dog)

By Decade

1960s	12
1970s	84
1980s	156
1990s	208

* Each year one in 12 high school students are threatened or injured with a weapon, UFCW Action, Vol. 20, #4.

** According to the Bureau of Labor Statistics, of 2 million workers subjected to violence in the workplace between 1992 and 1996, 67 percent were male.

*** Decisive action requires the imposition of one party's will upon the other, including cessation of hostility, surrender of property, or physical incapacitation.

APPENDIX 4

Martial Art Survey

Incidents involving opposing trained fighters break down as follows.

1. Small wrestler humiliates large kempo stylist
2. Large wrestler dominates small wrestler
3. Large wrestler humiliates small wrestler
4. Small wrestler chokes out huge boxer
5. Small kick-boxer maims large wrestler
6. Small boxer fights huge wrestler to draw in extended brawl
7. Small boxer fights large wrestler to draw in brief encounter
8. Small boxer fights large wrestler to draw in brief encounter
9. Small boxer fights small wrestler to draw in brief encounter
10. Small wrestler/tae kwon do stylist knocks out large wrestler
11. & 12.
    Involved pro heavyweight boxers sucker-punching smaller martial artists. These scenarios do not address the question

of art, but merely highlight the grim fact that size and surprise, backed by bad intent, are the competent thug's recipe
for success.
13. Small tae kwon do stylist surprises a large karateka in a doorway, quickly finishing him with a muay Thai style knee.

The results suggest the following:

1. Small fighters are more versatile than large fighters.
2. Strength is very important. Of the "wins" only the kick-
boxer was physically weaker than his opponent.
3. The fist alone is not a decisive weapon against a competent
wrestler. The kick-boxer kicked, gouged, and palmed, in that
order.
4. When a skilled fighter commits to defense, he is not easily
brought to bay, unless it is a "same style" contest.
5. An average hitter who can wrestle hits as effectively in a real
fight as a superior hitter who can't wrestle.
6. In same-style fights the superior technician is just as likely to
lose as his mediocre antagonist—who is more apt to "fight
dirty."

Bibliography

BOOKS

Many of the quotes throughout the book are taken from books that are generally available; and if I think enough of the authors to quote them, consider that a recommendation.

Books—though usually incomplete, flawed, or hopelessly slanted—are good sources of combat-related information. Every self-defense-oriented book I have read has offered unique and valuable insights. If I had the money I would buy them all. The following books are highly recommended.

DePasquale, Peter. *The Boxer's Workout: The Noncontact Program Boxers Use to Get Fighting Fit.* Brooklyn, N.Y.: Fighting Fit Inc., 1988.

The author presents a practical white-collar boxing program. It is available by direct mail order (Fighting Fit, P.O. Box

021334, Brooklyn, NY 11202–0029). My copy came with a free poster featuring real boxers demonstrating basic skills.

Quinn, Peyton. *A Bouncer's Guide to Barroom Brawling: Dealing with the Sucker Puncher, Streetfighter, and Ambusher.* Boulder, Colo.: Paladin Press, 1990.
This is an excellent guide to practical martial arts application.

Lee, Bruce. *Tao of Jeet Kune Do.* Burbank, Calif.: Ohara Publications, 1975.
A philosophical synthesis of practical fighting methods distilled from Asian and Western arts. An excellent study guide.

Steiner, Bradley J. *Close Shaves: The Complete Book of Razor Fighting.* Port Townsend, Wash.: Loompanics Unlimited, 1980.
Combat attitude is what this book is about. I'm sure anything by this author will raise your combat awareness.

Burrese, Alain. *Hard-Won Wisdom from the School of Hard Knocks: How to Avoid a Fight, and Things to Do When You Can't or Don't Want To.* Boulder, Colo.: Paladin Press, 1996.
Alain's book is written in the same vein as mine. I recommend it for balance. Alain and I disagree on most of the broad points of real fighting. He believes in the win; I don't. He believes in the cops; I don't. He likes to grapple; I don't. He's a social fighter; I'm not. . . . His work on conditioning and physical development is excellent.

TRAINING VIDEOS

Videos are a mixed bag. For what you get, they are expensive. Video instruction often includes a lot of replay footage. Don't expect a wealth of information. Of the many tapes I have reviewed I can recommend the following.

Vunak, Paul. *The JKD Streetfighting Series*, Tape 8: "Mass Attack." Oley, Pennsylvania: PFS-Video, Inc.

I have viewed seven Vunak tapes. The tapes in this series are overpriced, slick productions with trailer material that ranges from childish to morbid. However, this guy is a tactical genius. The "Mass Attack" presentation concentrates exclusively on dealing with two to three aggressive attackers according to the DELAY strategy. It is as an excellent teaching aid. Contact PFS-Video at the following address: P.O. Box 112, Oley, PA 19547

Quinn, Peyton. *Self-Defense against the Sucker Puncher*. Boulder, Colo.: Curve Productions,

For less than $20 I don't mind the low production quality of this series. (I don't think they even had a cameraman, and Peyton is obviously uncomfortable talking to the camera.) You get two hours of insight and instruction, with none of the replays that are used to stretch higher-grade productions. It is basically the same stuff covered in Peyton's book, but with plenty of keen observations and cautions thrown in. (Available from Paladin Press.) Another of Peyton Quinn's videos, *Defending against the Blade*, is also good and available form Paladin.

GENERAL REFERENCE BOOKS

Pfouts, Chris. *True Tales of American Violence*. Boulder, Colo.: Paladin Press, 1993.

If you want real, raw, first-hand accounts of violence to work into your world view but don't want to talk to the people who engage in it, Chris has saved you the trouble. Gritty and entertaining.

Estwanik, Joseph, M.D. *Sports Medicine for the Combat Arts*. Charlotte: Boxergenics Press, 1996.

I wish this guy was my doctor. Don't train anybody until you read this.

Corcoran, John, and Farkas, Emil. *The Original Martial Arts Encyclopedia: Tradition—History—Pioneers.* Los Angeles: ProAction Publishing, 1993.

If you are considering traditional Asian martial arts study I recommend this reference for two reasons: (1) Read up on the lineage and history of your art, so that you can rate your teacher's knowledge. This will give you an idea of how watered-down his art is. (2) If you attend a Japanese or Okinawan school you can learn the Japanese terminology that will be used in class, permitting you to focus on actually learning the material, as opposed to trying to remember the difference between a *haishuuke* and a *moroteuke.*

MAGAZINES AND NEWSLETTERS

Periodicals offer insights into training methods, as well as the politics and delusions afflicting the martial arts world. What they generally don't do is present realistic—or even sane—self-defense coverage. However, this does not deter me from buying every one that I can lay my arthritic hands on.

Black Belt, Rainbow Publications, Inc., P.O. Box 918, Santa Clarita, CA 91380-9018.
This magazine usually features one good article. Its strength is in the quality of the contributing editors, who often write sensible columns. The publisher also puts out a slim quality spin-off, *M.A. Training.*

Combat Knives, Peterson Publishing Company, 6420 Wilshire Blvd., Los Angeles, CA 90048-5515.
This is an annual review of knives and related products. The two knife-fighting articles in the 1998 issue and the pointers scattered throughout the product coverage far surpass the quality of blade use and knife defense coverage found in martial arts magazines.

Combat Handguns, Harris Publications, Inc., 1115 Broadway, New York, NY 10010.

I hate handguns. (The pistol is my enemies' weapon of choice, and I am not legally permitted to carry one.) Again, this publication is devoted primarily to product reviews. But it gives quality coverage on "self-defense" and the law, and the dynamics of real-life survival situations. Gun lovers—nuts or not—tend to view violence in a more reasonable light than do martial artists; although the presence of ads for Asian wives and Bulgarian steroids leads one to believe that gun nuts and ninja boys have a lot in common.

Personal Defense Newsletter, Personal Defense Group, Inc., 5160 S. Valley View, Suite 106, Las Vegas, NV 89118.

An annual subscription for this four-page monthly is a steep $36 dollars. I only subscribed because they offered a 50-percent discount. The information is sound, reliable, and keeps you up to date on crime trends. If you live in a large city, it may prove useful. If you are a traditional instructor who would like to teach a pure self-defense course, this material could form the basis for your curriculum.

About the Author

James LaFond has been training in various American, European, Korean, Chinese, and Filipino martial arts since 1974 at a total cost of $160. Since 1981, he has worked as a laborer alongside violent criminals and common degenerates.

As a man of average physical ability, he has fought thugs, wimps, football players, slobs, bodybuilders, drunks, wrestlers, punks, and dogs . . . on grass, carpet, tile, dirt, sheet metal, concrete, and asphalt. James deals daily with the worst elements of society—alone and unarmed.

James currently lives and works in Baltimore. His spare time is devoted to writing, training, physical therapy, and playing with toy soldiers.